MILE-HIGH

MISSIONARY

A JUNGLE PILOT'S MEMOIR

JAMES RUSH MANLEY

COPYRIGHT

DEDICATION

To Regina
You inspire me to be better than I am

CONTENTS

Preface

It started with clouds. At first I suspected their shapes, colors, and vistas merely fired my imagination. But as I spent more time in the air, something deeper, more visceral stirred. Eventually, I realized three things:

First, I'd become an outsider. As a missionary pilot, I bounced between Earth-side places, touching many but never becoming part of any. I dropped out of the sky, walked about as a visitor, then flew away. I shed no lonely tears over that. God wired me as an introvert, ideally crafted for aerial service. I finally found my sweet spot.

Second, the Psalmist speaks more than metaphor when he says: "*Let the skies sing for joy! Let the earth join in the chorus. Let oceans thunder and fields echo this ecstatic praise until every swaying tree of every forest joins in, lifting up their songs of joyous praise to him!*" (Psalm 96:11-12 TPT). Did I see little creatures scurry amongst the clouds? No. But I did see that our Creator has a more complex relationship with His creation than we materialists suspect—something we can neither measure, nor catalog; something we can only glimpse out of the corner of our eye. If we turn to look, it's gone. The eyes in our head see nothing, but the eyes of our heart suspect something.

Third, I felt more at home in the sky than on the ground. The 3D life in that vast unified space seemed more real to me than Earth's little disparate worlds. Air was air. Clouds were clouds. The principle of lift operated uniformly everywhere on the planet. But dirt-side, in the convoluted warren of human dens, life was neither safe nor predictable. And it was 2D, always binding me to the ground.

Fortunately, God showed me his perspective.

So, this book is not about mission policy, politics, or strategy. It does not address doctrine. It is not a tell-all book. Many important people are left unnamed. And, I talk little about family life.

Instead, this book is the story of how I had to become a sort of sky-creature in order to see things His way. To tell that story accurately I put you into the pilot's seat with me. You see what I saw, hear what I heard, feel what I felt. I've softened the technical jargon for non-pilots, but left enough for authentic flavor. But be warned: Flying is an addiction for which there is no cure. So, read on if you dare.

James Rush Manley
Meridian, Idaho
November 2018

Meeting the Beast

We scanned the Amazon Jungle a mile below. The mottled green expanse stretched ahead like an emerald sea fading into the eastern haze. Behind us, hills like frozen waves mounted ever higher assaults against the Andes' snow-covered peaks. The jungle lay there a primordial, liquid creature occupying either a different space and time, or else our world as it truly was. Civilization seemed remote, safety far off, security not a part of that place.

The jungle's mocking similarity to ocean unnerved me. An aircraft like our Cessna C-185 could float on water for a while if ditched properly. And life rafts would grant a chance at survival. But the jungle offered neither place to stand nor opportunity to swim. Instead, its leafy tentacles opened to swallow whatever dropped into it, then closed again, digesting new arrivals beyond recognition or recall. A forced landing here would be bad.

Job Orellana talked fast. Assigned to begin my new-pilot orientation before formal field training began, he deluged my first jungle flight with detail. Could I remember it? I returned to my notebook, scribbling in route data, terrain features, strip conditions and weather patterns. I'd be the pilot in command soon enough, but for the moment, those sweat-smudged scribbles began the framework of my career as a missionary pilot.

He stopped mid-sentence, quiet, the aircraft's roar muted by our helmets. He scanned ahead, glanced at the chart on his knee, turned the plane a few degrees left and searched again. Habit and training had narrowed my focus to the technical business of flying, but while Job navigated, I took a tourist's look outside.

A few breaks in the undulating surface of the dark canopy below emerged and flicked away. Twisting ribbons glinted color like serpents sleeping in tall grass. Rivers. Of course. Once seen, they appeared and disappeared everywhere, snaking off in all directions. Sometimes they flashed silver when catching sun, other times gray or blue, reflecting sky, and still others, the stagnant brown of rain-washed mud. Any trip overland—even a few miles—would cross and re-cross the same river a dozen times. *No wonder we fly here*, I thought. How would anyone ever build a road?

On our right, a larger river glinting silver flowed toward us, down from a distant mountain gorge, through a broad valley then disappeared under the plane. "That's the Rio Upano," Job said, dipping the right wing. "And, here below us, where it joins the Rio Pastaza, we call 'Pastaza 39.'"

I realized only then that we were flying directly over a wide river filled with rocks, rapids, backwater pools and tree-covered islands.

"Pastaza 39. Got it." I wrote in my notebook, not mentioning what I'd missed as one of professional aviation's secret fears rose, unbidden, from a subconscious cave. Tom Wolfe taught in his book *The Right Stuff* that every true aviator contained a certain quantity of unique essence lifting fliers above the rabble, endowing special courage and enabling correct decisions. Those so favored commanded total situational awareness at all times. No matter the circumstance, he or she remained stoic, laconic, almost bored while overcoming impossible odds. Despite knowing it for myth, everyone working the sky felt the dark fear that their supply of magic aeronaut potion might leak out, exposing them as unworthy of the lofty realms.

"This is Copataza," he said, tipping his helmet left. "We'll start our descent here." He lowered the nose slightly, allowing the airspeed to build.

Occasional openings punctuated the tops of the crowded trees. Sporadic glimpses through them revealed lower, shorter trees with spiky branches invading taller neighbors. In other places tree carcasses entombed in choking vines stood in slime-covered bogs—a slow-motion war only the earth had the patience to endure. *So, who could live here?* I wondered. What sort of people would even want to? Then Job announced, "Here we are."

A notch cut from the jungle appeared on the left bank of the river. Lying atop a low cliff jutting above the water, a stripe of bare dirt ran perpendicular from the river toward two small hills. Three thatched structures lined one edge of the strip. Small gardens lay along the opposite side. Near the middle of the strip, more huts clustered around a larger open area.

"Charapacocha, it's called. Atshuar Indians live here," Job said.

Job radioed our dispatcher, Pancho Farez. "Shell, Alas Zero-Six landing Charapacocha."

"Copy Zero-Six landing Charapacocha," Pancho answered.

"Affirmative," Job confirmed.

MAF's (Mission Aviation Fellowship) first invitation to operate in Latin America contained the condition that we not operate under any name containing the word "mission." So, we became Alas de Socorro—Wings of Mercy. In Ecuador, our radio call signs became "Alas" followed by a number indicating the order that specific airplane entered service. The C-185 that Job and I flew was the sixth added, so its call sign became "Alas Zero-Six."

We flew over the center of the strip. A thin smoke trail leaned toward the river, revealing wind direction, so Job turned right into a shallow, descending 270-degree turn. After a minute he rolled level again, timing the turn to line up exactly with the centerline of the small runway.

"Not bad," I muttered admiration. Job smiled with a slight nod this time.

We crossed the river, skimmed over the cliff edge, and Job placed the main wheels firmly onto the dirt. With the tail still high, he pushed hard on the brakes and then allowed the tail to slowly settle to the ground. As we rolled on all three wheels, we each opened our side windows, glad for a blast of outside air.

Even before we stopped, I saw the Indians running. Kids led, pelting sandy dirt with fast, bare feet. Moms trotted behind if unencumbered or waddled with babies in slings across back or breast. The men walked deliberately as befitted their dignity. Clearly, this was a big event.

Attention back on the airplane, I watched as Job stopped two-thirds of the way down the strip. He looked left and right, then with a burst of power swung the tail around and taxied back along the runway to the village center. Charapacocha's residents waited in a tight semicircle about 30 feet from the plane as we eased up to the apparently normal parking area. Job pulled the red mixture control and, as the engine shuddered to a stop, the people surged forward, pressing tight against fuselage and windows. Still in professional mode, I focused inside and followed Job through our shutdown procedure. We removed our helmets, hung them on the windshield cross bracing and unfastened our harnesses. Even with all my officially dictated activity, I could only pretend to ignore the strange mob outside.

Job was already halfway out the left side when I unlatched my door and pushed gently. The crowd gave way just enough to permit my exit to the right. I crouched for a moment on the doorsill then hopped down from the C-185's high perch into another world. Neither broadminded upbringing, nor science-fiction alien tales, nor formal cross-cultural training prepared me for standing toe-to-toe with living, breathing difference. As my feet hit the dirt I remembered everyone back home was "American" regardless of color. Here I faced not one, but an entire village of different.

Smiles hit me first. Neither smirks nor grins, but open, toothy smiles. Their skin, dark like the tan I envied, covered well-proportioned bodies. At home I was short. Here, I was tall. Muscles, distinct but not large, showed on every visible arm, leg, and belly. Adults and older kids sported clothes. Little kids not so much. Ladies wore long bright dresses, the men jeans or shorts with a smattering of T-shirts. The clothes seemed clean, but holes and frayed edges revealed age and hard use. A few feet hid in shoes, but most wiggled bare toes in the dirt. The women's hair was uniformly black, thick, and long. Some pulled it back, while others wore it straight. Most of the men had bowl-guided haircuts, but a few wore it long in one or two braids wrapped in twine net. Then I noticed. Red streaks lined some faces. And, all the men carried long machetes, edges glinting.

Smiling automatically, I nodded, avoided eye contact and moved around the front of the plane, left hand always touching aluminum. I reached Job's side just as he waded into the crowd, shaking hands vigorously with every offered palm.

"Buenos, días [good day]!" he repeated to each one greeted.

"Buenos días, Capitán!" they replied, returning his salute with the traditional title given to all pilots. Little kids bounced up and down, echoing the greeting in a discordant chorus. Teenage boys vied for position. Men, shoulder to shoulder, offered hands in turn. All pressed forward, eager to touch the magic sky men. Women and adolescent girls, however, hung behind the jostling press.

Waving a hand toward me, he added, "This is Capitán Diego, our new pilot."

My "Capitán Diego" identity felt like shoes fresh from the box. A few months earlier, the language school director in Costa Rica told us that failing to use a Spanish version of our name would render our ministry unfruitful, our personal lives a failure, and would doom untold numbers to perdition. I suspected exaggeration but sensed truth as well. Oddly, I had three choices for rendering my name: Jaime (pronounced, *hi'-me*), Santiago or Diego. I didn't like the sound of Jaime. Santiago came across as snooty. That left "Diego" as the new me. There in the hot Amazonian sun I wondered, *Had I already become that person? Was it someone I was turning into? Or was it just an act to learn? And, where was "Jim" in all this?*

Playing the role of experienced, almost bored missionary pilot tempted. After all, I did have some of the "Right Stuff" sloshing around inside. Besides, the Indians' limp grip revealed that they also assumed a role. They copied the foreign practice of shaking hands from the Latinos but didn't understand the firm squeeze and direct eye contact expected with it. On the other hand, the Indians' odor of hard-earned sweat divulged daily contact with honest work. That expelled any thought they'd tolerate pretense. I felt more visible than I intended.

This stop was different, Job explained to the crowd. We understood, he continued, how important it was to send food to family members who were out of the jungle and in the town. And, we knew that it was very important for them to receive it because, of course, they wouldn't be able to find any of their normal food. And, besides, doing anything in the town was very expensive. And...

My fledgling Spanish should have followed a simple explanation, but after a few minutes, I lost the conversation's thread entirely. Finally, Job concluded, "... and so because we're visiting different villages to test the new radio system, we're sorry we can't carry cargo or passengers today. But, if you have letters, we're very pleased to take them now."

I wondered why he hadn't said that in the first place. In the few weeks I'd been in Ecuador, Job proved to be outspoken and occasionally blunt. Such direct speech was unusual for a Latino, but Job's years of study in the US influenced his style. Still, he was Ecuadorian and sometimes displayed his native culture's indirectness. This talking in circles, though, went beyond Spanish custom and seemed vaguely deceptive.

But then it was my turn to work and Job's to watch. Most of our aviators were dual qualified as both professional pilots and mechanics. I was different—a mix of pilot and electronics technician. I came to set up equipment to test a new radio system, run the test, log the readings, repack the gear into the airplane and leave. We planned 15 minutes per village. That, plus flying time between villages, added up to a full day. So no time for socializing. I had important work to do.

Jerry Miel, an electronic engineer from our support center in Southern California, flew via commercial airline to Ecuador just for these tests. At that moment he sat alone on a peak in the foothills of the Andes Mountains 100 miles west of Charapacocha waiting to hear from me. I unloaded a small two-way radio mounted on a tripod. Next, I unloaded a spindly array similar to a six-foot TV antenna, leaned it against the tripod and connected a cable.

I turned to fetch the mast from the airplane and realized I'd acquired an audience. A gaggle of Atshuar kids pressed in, leaving me a six-inch free-space bubble. They looked where I looked, walked where I walked. When I opened the rear cargo door and leaned into the airplane, they ran to the windows or open passenger doors. Their eyes tracked every twist and followed each turn as I untied the cargo straps. When I moved to the front left door, eyes scrutinized my hand-over-hand motions drawing the six-foot telescoping mast from the dark interior. Other eyes locked onto fixed points along the tube and followed its progress out into bright sunlight.

Nothing was lost to their observation or comment. One would point and whisper to a neighbor, then all would laugh. The teenaged girls, bunched in a tight knot, kept to the back and giggled constantly. The boys and little girls were bolder, venturing quick touches on metal tube, box or cable. Some gently stroked the hair on my forearms with one or two fingers. That stopped me for a moment, but then I remembered not seeing a single hairy arm, leg or face. I wondered, *Who's the alien now?*

My entourage and I moved between plane and tripod a couple more times until I assembled everything for the test. Using a compass, I sighted along the direction to Jerry's distant perch. Then I raised the now-extended 18-foot mast to vertical. The antenna, secured at the upper end, jutted out at right angles. I twisted the mast until the antenna pointed toward Jerry and keyed the transmitter. This sent a radio signal to his equipment. That unit, in turn, sent a signal back to me. When the needle moved, I logged the reading.

All done. Just pack up the gear and move on to the next strip.

I checked my watch. Seventeen minutes. Not bad, but I knew I'd have to do better at the other strips. Still, the experience was proving less difficult than feared. After all, the principle of lift kept airplanes aloft regardless of where the air resided, and radio signals still traveled at the speed of light. My anchor in my universe regained some solidity. Strangeness retreated a bit.

Then, as I pulled the last cargo knot tight, an Atshuar man—still with painted face and long machete—walked up and said in Spanish, "Capitán, today is a special day. We're all eating together. We'd be honored if you and Capitán Job would join us for lunch."

Images of strange "things" ran through my mind—dripping, wiggling grubs stuffed into mouths, chanting rituals in dark, smoky lodges, mashed together with sweaty bodies, cutting, piercing. Yes, I'd come to minister truth to strangeness, but I was done with strangeness for the day. Besides, we had hours of clean, mechanical, out-in-the-open, back-in-the-air work to do. We'd be hard-pressed to finish before sunset. Delays were unacceptable. I looked over at Job, to see how he would extricate us from an obviously untenable situation.

He grinned and boomed enthusiastically, "Of course we'll stay! Thank you."

Our host sent a boy running toward a long pole building with a high thatched roof, but no walls. Then he and the crowd escorted us across the sandy runway. We ducked and passed under the narrow palm leaves drooping over the low-hanging eaves. Inside, shade brought some heat relief and the breeze remained free to move. Two tables made of branches and sticks lashed together with vines ran the length of the building. Long benches made the same way ran along either side of each table. At the far end, men stirred something in large, steaming aluminum pots set on smoking fires. Women carried smaller pots. Young girls spread wide, shiny dark green banana leaves over the entire tabletop. More people appeared, moving in, side-stepping, shuffling between bench and table, filing in and filling all the space. A few youngsters and agile teens stepped over the benches to occupy chosen places.

The helper girls raced along behind the benches, hands darting in between each person, dropping large soup spoons. Then the cooks ladled the hot brew into bowls—gaudy plastic, dented aluminum, even some half gourds—and set them at the end of the table. The first person passed the steaming bowl on and it progressed hand to hand toward me. I pictured fish entrails garnished with eyeballs, or maybe mashed monkey brain. It got closer. I could send the first few on by, but eventually one would stop and trap me.

Years of hard work, hours of study, interminable sweaty check-rides, the sacrifices of all our supporters had brought me to this? Suddenly the whole "missionary, go to the lost of Earth's remotest corners" didn't seem like such a good idea after all—even if it did involve flying. Closer and closer—bump, hand, bump, hand—the first smoky bowl approached. What if I wretched? The first reached me and I passed it on without looking in, smiling instead at the striped faces on either side. Bump, hand, bump, hand, the parade continued.

I didn't look down but looked around. Their world was like a different planet. Except for our plane, MAF's battery-powered radio, a few aluminum pots and the still-glinting machetes, the entire village would've fit in the Stone Age. The next village lay a day's walk away, our base in the town of Shell unimaginably far. Job and I flew there in forty minutes; but without the airplane, Charapacocha might as well have been on Mars. Again I wondered, *How can anyone live here? Why do they want to?*

The chattering around me stopped. Everyone was seated—men at my table, women and children at the other. Steam rose from the hot bowls—I still didn't look down—and everyone waited, quiet, expectant. A man stood and, in Spanish for our benefit, asked God to bless our food and our work in spreading the Gospel.

Suddenly, it was gone. The strangeness vanished. The dividing wall shattered.

Different cultures wrapped each of us like costumes, but underneath we all wore skin that bled when cut, shivered when cold, sweated when hot, stank when dirty, yet also longed for touch. We were citizens of the same Kingdom, siblings in the same family, fathered by the same Creator. He equipped them with the culture, language, and desire to communicate the Good News with their neighbors. He equipped me with technical skills and gave me access to financial resources. Apart, the differences remained. Together, we each supplied what the other lacked.

The chattering resumed, and I looked down at my bowl. Grilled chicken covered a mound of steaming rice.

A half hour later we took off, roaring over thatched huts, upturned faces, and waving hands. The open space "island" with its sandy airstrip was swallowed up once again, and we were alone with our marvelous, precise, expensive machine. As my pilot mind resumed its work, I was surprised at how privileged I felt to be their servant.

BACK TO THE BEGINNING

Ten days after I turned 40, I was a student again. In my previous life, I ran an aviation business, flew charter flights with multi-engine aircraft, fought forest fires from the air, and taught people to fly. But when I got up that morning, I was still too new, too unknown, too unproven to be trusted with an airplane all by myself. Professionally, I understood. Personally, it grated.

Jungle flying differs from shirt-and-tie aviation. Throwing 3,000 pounds of aluminum at a mud strip I wouldn't drive my car on—if I could get it there—bore little resemblance to centering instrument needles until the destination airport appeared in the windshield.

The principle of lift remained as valid over the Amazon Jungle as over California. The propeller still needed to turn. Air molecules still had to move over the wing to produce lift. And clouds still looked pretty on the outside but bumped on the inside. The differences lay in finding the airstrip, and what I did in the last hundred feet after I found it, and then what help I could expect if things didn't go as planned.

Developed countries establish high standards for both airports and the airspace between them. Their regulations, while sometimes byzantine, offer thick safety buffers. But not so in the jungle. If a village wanted an airstrip, they built it themselves with machetes, rocks, sticks, and baskets. Heavy equipment, if they could get it, consisted of a shovel and a wheelbarrow.

They cleared thousands of trees and all vegetation to form a rectangle 1,200 to 1,400 feet long and 50 to 100 feet wide. They also cleared all the tall trees 500 feet beyond at least one end of the strip to create an approach and departure path.

To prepare the surface, they flattened hills and filled holes. Then they chose to make either a grass or dirt runway. Jungle rain didn't erode grass strips as quickly and building them required less work—just cut everything down to the same flat level. However, these strips committed the village to fielding a sizable grass-cutting team every week—forever.

Dirt runways, on the other hand, required no cutting. But constructing them demanded all the extra work up front. After clearing the trees, laborers started at one end of the strip, digging out all remaining tree and bush roots. Then with machetes, they cut six inches below ground level. When the cut spanned the strip's width, they jammed poles into the cut and pried up, exposing more roots. They cut those roots, then pried some more. Cut and pry, cut and pry until they created a huge roll. When the roll became too large to turn, they cut off slices and rolled them off to burn.

Building an airstrip required the entire village to buy into a major public works project. All 60 to 100 people (young, old, men, women, kids and babies) spent a year or more completing it. Our flight operations manual specified airstrip dimensions as well as approach and departure space required. However, most villages lay in terrain offering only limited choices, forcing them to select the least bad option—along a river inside a twisting canyon, up a steep slope, or on a narrow spot with one end of the strip terminating hard against a hill.

Every strip concealed its own proclivities—mean, vile, sneaky tricks that would rise up and bite hard if dismissed or ignored. Just like Mark Twain learning Mississippi river bends, we pilots practiced under careful tutelage at each strip until mastering it. And just like him, we kept a book, one page for each strip. Instead of submerged logs and shoals, our book stated geo-location, elevation, length and width, surface slope(s), surface composition, recommended touch-down zones, soft spots, obstacles, and abort points. We divided all the strips into five categories: "A" through "E." Category "A" strips were suitable for the average commercial pilot to use without a check-ride with an instructor. Of the 140 strips in our directory, six qualified.

New guys started their checkouts on "B" strips like Makuma. Built by missionaries in the 1950s, DC-3s once used the strip. When Gene Jordan, my boss and check-pilot, introduced me to Makuma, he said, "A group of villages maintains it now, so no one village wants to keep it up. It looks big and wide from the air, but a lot of it is unusable." He flipped open the directory. "See? The chart says it's 3,300 feet long and maybe 50 feet wide."

I entered a standard traffic pattern 1,000 feet above the ground, checked the wind direction, then made a left turn parallel to the strip. I was on the leg called "left downwind"—"left" because the strip was on my left side, and "downwind" because we were flying the same direction the wind was blowing.

"See where the grass changes color?" he asked.

"Yeah."

"Okay, that's your threshold at this end. It runs down to"—he leaned over, looked and pointed behind us—"there where the dirt changes color and you can see more rocks. The useable length is about 1,000 feet less than the book says."

As we flew exactly abeam of the real runway threshold, he said, "We're not going to touch down this time. Just make a low pass at 80 knots so I can show you the real centerline."

I reduced throttle, set the airplane up for a low approach, and completed the mechanical checklist until the green light came on. Standard MAF practice for surface checkout was to add 20 degrees of flaps and slow the airplane to 80 knots (92 mph) so the pilot could see detail, but also maintain enough airspeed to maneuver, climb quickly, or most importantly, avoid stalling. When my virtual touchdown point was about 45 degrees behind my left shoulder, I turned perpendicular to the runway—base leg. This gave me a good look at the landing area and allowed me to check my descent rate. Then I timed my last left turn so when I leveled the wings, I would be aligned with the runway centerline. I continued the descent and leveled off with the wheels three feet over the runway surface.

"When you touch down, stay in the shorter grass here, with the dirt showing through," he warned. "Only a gear-width swath [8-10 feet] in the center is hard. If you wander into those taller weeds on either side, the mud's soft enough to break a gear leg or cause a nose-over."

A humbling, but wise, message came through loud and clear. Strip taming separated the pros from the students, and no one flew alone until approved. So when I woke up that morning, only 12 of my more than 3,000 flight hours counted—the ones I'd flown in Ecuador.

At the hangar, I checked the day's plan with Mike Ross, another MAF pilot serving as that month's Flight Coordinator. "Too much going on this morning. Let you know in a minute." He strode past, a sheaf of scribbled notes waving between spread fingers.

Working out the flight schedule during new-pilot checkout presented extra challenges. On one hand, the experience had to be as close to normal as possible, so the new guy learned what was going on and how to do it. But all his early flights included an extra passenger—the instructor pilot—taking up space and weight. And the duo could only go certain places if the PUI—Pilot Under Instruction—was going to get any experience at places he'll initially fly to. So, the Flight Coordinator got only half a plane at best to attack the day's requests. That put extra pressure on the other guys—carry a little more weight, make a couple extra landings, or tell some passengers they'd have to wait until the next day.

Mike called back to me over his shoulder as he turned in to the pilot's ready room, "Gene said to preflight the 180."

The 180? Interesting. Gene and I hadn't flown that particular plane yet. Of five aircraft in our fleet, three were Cessna C-185s, one was a C-206, and the other a C-180, a C-185's little sister. The uninitiated eye would see the C-185 and C-180 as the same. But the C-180 was powered by a 230 horsepower, carbureted engine while the C-185 sported a fuel-injected, 300 horsepower motor. That meant that a full C-180 weighed only 2,800 pounds as opposed to the C-185 at 3,350 pounds.

No matter. I completed the inspection, hung my helmet from the front brace and plugged in its radio connectors. Then I pushed the plane out of the hangar onto the ramp by the fuel pump.

"How many gallons?" Pancho asked.

"Don't know. Gene hasn't told me where we're going or what the load is yet."

I waited. Finally, Gene walked up to the airplane, but without his helmet or flight bag.

"Take Jerry to Makuma. Wait for him while he talks with Marco, then bring him back," he said then started to walk away. He stopped, turned back and asked with a suppressed grin, "Think you can do that without getting lost?"

Professional pilots perform a number of first solos: first time flying an airplane alone, first time flying in instrument conditions alone, first time flying a multi-engine airplane alone, or my scariest, the first time I soloed a student I taught how to fly.

So that solo flight over the Amazon Jungle, while neither my first nor my scariest, did carry its own anxiety. What if I couldn't find Makuma? What if the weather changed? What if I did something stupid and sullied MAF's good name? What if? What if? What if? Pilots learn to plan for the million-and-one most likely "what ifs" and then ignore the rest. But on that day Gene was willing to trust me with a multi-thousand-dollar airplane and a passenger. Maybe I was a real missionary jungle pilot after all.

I flew Jerry to Makuma. He spoke with Marco for a half hour about our new radio system and we flew back to Shell. I taxied up to our ramp, shut down the engine and ran through the checklist. Then I noticed my wife, Regina, and the kids inside the hangar. Odd that time of day.

I hopped out of the cockpit and Gene strolled up, studied nonchalance punctuated with a poorly suppressed grin.

"How'd it go?" he asked.

"Fine. Makuma was still where we left it yesterday and Marco was still there to talk with Jerry."

"So, no trouble finding Makuma?"

"No..."

"Airplane ran okay?"

"Yeah..." Something was definitely up. Suddenly many strong hands grabbed me.

"Gimme everything in your pockets," Mike demanded, freeing one arm.

I fished, removed and handed over wallet, pen, knife, papers. Then more hands grasped, lifted me off the ramp and carried me to the far end of the hangar. They set me on my feet again but kept firm hold. Gene produced pictures.

"Look at these," he commanded. "This is what they do in Ecuador after a first solo. They drain oil from the engine of the airplane you just flew and pour it all over you." A photo waved in front of my face. In it, a small mob clutched a new pilot. One of them tipped a small bucket over the new aviator and poured a stream of hot, black oil over his head. "We're going to do the same to you." Then he grinned. "You'll stink for weeks."

Hands grasped tighter. A rag covered my eyes. They picked me up and laid me on the pavement.

"Here's the first taste," Gene menaced. Warm liquid covered both my forearms. Oil indeed, I could smell it. I really was going to stink for weeks. And everything I wore would be ruined.

"Take off my boots! Take off my boots!" I shouted.

"Too late! Now we're going to drench you!" voices jeered. Rolling and dragging noises. Something big.

"Take off my boots!"

They ignored me.

"Easy with it."

"Got it?"

"Ready?"

"Don't get any on you."

"Take off my boots!"

"Here goes!" they shouted and cheered.

At the same time, hands suddenly released while cold liquid poured, drenched, splashed and covered me. Cold? I ripped off the blindfold and sprang to my feet. A now-empty rain barrel lay on its side. I was soaked with water, dripping, standing in a puddle. My kids laughed and danced. Regina grinned. The hangar helpers and maintenance guys clapped and cheered. The other pilots slapped my back hard, splashing everyone close.

THE TENT

Eighteen years before arriving in Ecuador as a missionary pilot, I left the US Marine Corps and a failed marriage. I returned to college disillusioned, searching for something to fill the hole gnawing in my gut. I gravitated to other lonely people and into the hippie lifestyle.

"Hey, Danny," I asked my college roommate one afternoon. "Do you know what we get for one hundred thirty dollars a month?"

"No, what?"

"We get stiff walls," I answered.

"Stiff walls?" he asked, puzzled.

"Yeah, stiff walls," I said, rapping the living room wall of our apartment. "We could set up a tent in the hills behind the campus, trade stiff walls for floppy, and save the rent money."

Impeccable logic proved irresistible. A garage sale yielded a six-foot umbrella tent. A visit to the surplus store produced heavy cotton cloth that we painted with a mixture of waterproofing and green dye. When dry, Danny moved the couch and chairs out and I set up the tent on the living room floor. During the next couple of weeks, we cut the tent sides and sewed the cotton into sleeping wings. Then we sold our furniture and gave notice to the landlord.

Palomar College in San Marcos, California, sat amidst open hill country covered with sage, chaparral, sumac, and an occasional scrub oak. About a mile from campus we found a sumac clump large enough to shade and hide the tent.

A visit to the county records office revealed the name and phone number of the landowner. We called, explained that we were military vets going to school on the GI Bill and needed inexpensive housing. "May we set up a tent on your land?" He agreed with a few reasonable conditions like no drugs, booze parties or dirt-biking.

We cut an entry path into the clump's interior space, then leveled the dirt for a flat floor. The site provided a view across a little valley, fresh air, and the hoped-

for shade. A week later we set up the tent and moved into our floppy walled home.

We hung our clothes in the middle section like a common closet. Then we each claimed a wing for our cot and sleeping bag. After turning off the lantern on our first night, the moon shone bright, casting branchy shadows on the ceiling. The floppy walls breathed in and out with the rhythm of the scented evening breeze. The last birds chirped briefly as they settled down and a coyote sang in the distance. Clean air, hard work and the sounds of nature quickly put us to sleep.

A drop woke me. Small and not too cold, it landed exactly on the tip of my nose and spread slowly down either side. I opened my eyes and peered hard into complete darkness. The moon had set. A quiet but constant pattering filled the night and I sensed, rather than saw, a looming presence just beyond my face. Carefully, without turning, I reached for the matches next to my cot. A scratch, then a brilliant flare leaped out and illuminated a dark green mass three inches from my face. My eyes focused close, just in time to see a second drop form, fall, and follow the first. Fully awake, I suddenly realized two things. First, the pattering signaled steady rain. Second, the roof of my wing bulged down, suspending 30 or 40 gallons of water.

I slid left as flat as possible, stuck the match into the lantern and turned the valve. Nothing. Of course. All the gas in the line had burned when I turned it off. I stretched my right hand across my chest and tried to reach the pump. I could neither reach it nor turn on my side to get any closer. The match went out.

"Rats!"

"Waz happ'n?" Danny asked from his side of the dark.

"Don't get up!" I ordered.

"Huh?" he asked, still mostly asleep.

The gentle pattering turned to a roar and the bulge strained tighter, closer. I found the flashlight and flicked it on. The one slow, small drip multiplied into 20 faucets as the token waterproofing gave up. Water poured over me, my cot and the lantern.

"What's going on?" Danny hollered.

"Stay down!" I commanded. He bolted up, head-bumped the twin bulge over his cot, then bounced back down. The water soared up, paused high, then dropped and didn't stop. Yards of cold, wet, leaking canvas smashed down, tearing the stakes out of soft mud. His entire wing collapsed in a surprised, thrashing mix

of tent, cot, water, sleeping bag and Dan. That pulled over the main pole, followed by the center tent section and then my wing. In moments our proud castle disintegrated into a soggy mass indistinguishable from the mud underneath it.

At 1:00 a.m. we slipped a muddy mile through the torrent to the campus parking lot. There we dripped the rest of the night huddled in my car. The next day we went to Sears and bought a real tent.

We enjoyed a few months of idyllic life. Black starry nights and chaparral-scented morning mist offered themselves as precious jewels. It was a private world to which I admitted only a chosen few. And when overwhelmed by emptiness I couldn't understand, I closed the door and found a measure of peace.

FINDING FREDDY

Even though ceremonially initiated by the team, my training continued. Most new pilots needed three to four years of skill-building to safely operate out of all 130 strips. I flew the easy "B" strip milk runs for a month, then Gene scheduled the next lesson.

"Say again?" I asked in Spanish. The answering voice in my helmet earphones still made no sense. We sat at the end of the gravel runway, engine idling, heat rising, frustration building.

Gene shook his head slightly, looked toward the control tower at the far end of the airport and pushed the push-to-talk button on the control yoke with his right thumb. "Okay, we'll watch for the inbound traffic," he replied in Spanish. "We're ready for takeoff."

"Alas Zero-Four, you are cleared for takeoff," the tower responded.

At least I understood that. After eight months of language school and three months in Ecuador, I still struggled with Spanish. On good days, I understood most of the words, but assembling them into coherent messages took deliberate thought. On bad days, like that day, it was just noise. Especially over the radio.

"Let's go," Gene said.

I looked up once more along the path a landing airplane would use if sneaking into the pattern unannounced, saw only empty sky, so pushed in just enough throttle to get us rolling. As the main wheels reached what I judged to be the runway centerline—there was no line painted on the pebbles—I applied light right brake pressure to swing the tail to the left and then stopped and looked down the length of the 5,000-foot runway.

I poised my right thumb under the last switch of our mechanical checklist sitting atop the glare shield. Before calling the tower, I had pushed up four of the five switches as I completed the items labeled above each one. The fifth switch—EMERG PROC, ABORT, EFS—reminded me to review the emergency procedures for aborting the takeoff, for engine failure immediately after takeoff and for how to use the emergency fuel system.

I chose a building halfway down the runway as an abort point. If everything still looked and felt good when we reached it, I'd continue the takeoff. If not, I'd chop the power, push hard on the brakes and stop. The runway's length made it an almost academic exercise; without power, we couldn't roll to the end. Still, it was good practice. Other strips were shorter.

I pushed the fifth switch up and a green light labeled TAKEOFF illuminated. The same switches also had labels beneath them (if all were pushed down, a green bulb labeled LAND would light). Helped when things got hot and busy.

I pushed the throttle in slowly and the airplane started to move. The lumbering ka-thump, ka-thump, ka-thump of idle gave way to unmuffled roar. On a short strip, I'd hold the brakes and let it come up to full power before starting the takeoff roll. Here that wasn't necessary. We started moving and as the rudder became effective for steering, I slid my feet down the rudder pedals, toes off the brakes, heels on the floor.

We were light, so the tail sprang up and we rolled level on the main wheels. The view in front changed from mostly sky to mostly runway pointing to mountain. My back pressed into the seat as the propeller driven by 285 horsepower finally grabbed hold. Spinning blades chewed off more air, biting, gulping, devouring, flinging it all backward, pulling us forward. I felt more connected, not a passenger in a machine, but an equal partner in the mystery of flight. We needed each other to do this. The crunchy sound of tires rolling over sandy gravel stopped suddenly. The wings took the weight.

I kept the airplane low and level over the runway in ground-effect, that place where airflow over a wing very close to the surface gives extra lift. Power still sounded, smelled, looked and felt good. I moved my right hand from the throttle, down and back and grasped the flap control lever. It stuck up like a giant parking brake lever between the two front seats. A push on the end button with my thumb released the pressure and I lowered it one notch, which raised the wing flaps from 20 degrees to 10 degrees. A glance to the top left of the control panel showed the airspeed climbing. And decision time came quickly. I looked down at the abort point. I could pull the power off, force the airplane back onto the ground and still stop before running off the remaining runway.

Everything still good, so my thumb pushed the flap release again. I lowered the lever all the way to the floor, relaxed back-pressure on the control wheel and allowed the airplane to accelerate to a speed called "Vx" or best angle. That yielded the most height gained for the shortest distance traveled over the ground—the steepest climb angle. As we reached Vx, I pitched the nose up to hold that airspeed and used the excess horsepower to climb.

The first ascent after breaking free of Earth always produced the most drama. Suddenly we could see over rooftops. The ridge ahead no longer cut the sky. A higher ridge hiding behind it rose up to take its place. The ground between the two, now exposed, revealed more of the river between them. I loved the transition from earth-realm to sky-realm. Ground things, dirt-side affairs, flatland business faded. Their cares, thoughts, and priorities dutifully retreated to their assigned compartment, forced to wait until summoned again. Sky cares, thoughts and priorities rose as the airplane rose—mental, precise, facts and numbers, but accompanied by feelings, insights, and inspirations thin and rarified like fine air, not heavy sand, clay or stone. Surviving in the sky required an engineer's attention to detail. Living in the sky required a mystic's heart for the Spirit. The trick, of course, was finding the fine balance between the two.

At first, the engineer had the duty. With my right hand, I pulled back slightly on the throttle to reduce to max-continuous power. I could run the engine all day at this setting and not hurt it. I let the airplane accelerate to "Vy," the best rate of climb speed, then held that new, higher speed. "Vy" gave the most altitude gain in the shortest time but was still steep. Neither efficient for getting anywhere nor cooling the engine, I allowed the airspeed to accelerate to 100 knots yielding a good cruise climb.

When we reached 400 feet above airport elevation, I started a left turn and continued climbing perpendicular to the runway—crosswind leg. A moment later, after checking again for clear airspace, I made a second left turn and flew parallel to the runway now nearly 1,000 feet below—downwind leg.

The tower operator called on the radio, "Alas Zero-Four, say your estimate for Pitirishka."

Gene's thumb started to move to the push-to-talk button on his wheel but hesitated. He looked at me. This one I understood and answered, "Shell Tower, I estimate Pitirishka at two, two." That meant I calculated reaching a specific electronic intersection in the sky at 22 minutes past the hour.

"Affirmative, Zero-Four, change to Approach Control frequency," the tower instructed.

"Roger, Zero-Four changing to Approach," I answered.

It seemed almost presumptuous placing a controlled airport with separate tower and approach radio frequencies this close to the end of the world. The Shell Oil Company built the strip in the 1930s to support their oil exploration in the Amazon Jungle to the east. When they left because existing technology wouldn't allow them profitable operations, the airstrip remained.

The town and airport sit on a plateau above the Pastaza River canyon where the Andes Mountains meet the Amazon Jungle. From there the terrain tumbles in stages to cliffs, deep river canyons, rolling hills, then finally rests as a flat expanse stretching to hazy horizon. Mild temperatures prevail—60 to 80 degrees—but the humidity averages 95% from the drenching 21-feet annual rainfall.

Civilization's self-definition ended at the town of Shell. Roads—of sorts—ran north and south parallel to the mountains, but not east into the Amazon Jungle. That immense creature controlled its domain, brooking only limited, fitful access by intruders on their own feet or wing. And even that came with no guarantee of safe passage. Yet, presumption remained civilization's trait. A behemoth might live next door, but we humans automatically assumed its territory was ours, believing the creature simply didn't know it yet.

"Amazonas Approach, this is Alas Zero-Four, climbing to five thousand, five hundred feet," I called.

"Alas Zero-Four, Amazonas Approach, copy you climbing to five thousand, five hundred. Report reaching Pitirishka," they responded.

"Affirmative."

Pitirishka lay 20 nautical miles (23 statute miles) southeast of Shell on an electronic highway defined by the 151 degrees radial from the Pastaza VOR (a VHF radio navigation beacon). Before the signal faded into static 30 miles out, it served as a local highway, funneling traffic onto a defined path. Traveling that route, I reached Pitirishka and made a right turn to head south down the Upano valley.

We headed toward my next checkout airstrip, called "Twenty-fourth of May." The Ecuadorians—and other Latin American countries—often named streets and places after important historical dates. The 24th of May 1822 marked their official separation from Spain as they formed part of an independent country called "Grand Colombia," which later split into present-day Venezuela, Colombia and Ecuador.

The 1,600 by 40-foot gravel-and-dirt runway sat perpendicular to a cliff overlooking another small river. Infrequently used because the Shell-Macas road ran nearby, it still served as a good emergency strip along the Upano valley route and provided a good first step in learning the area. We practiced a half-dozen landings and takeoffs then headed back to Shell.

As we passed Pitirishka, I flew the airplane, absorbed in doing pilot-things correctly. Gene's attention, however, focused on the radio crackling with extra chatter. Then he said suddenly, "Freddy's missing."

"What?"

"Freddy's missing. They're asking other planes to listen for him on the radio," he explained. Then he called approach control. "Amazonas Approach, Alas Zero-Four."

"Alas Zero-Four, Amazonas. Go ahead," they replied.

"Where was Freddy flying?" Gene asked.

"En route from Quito. He was supposed to arrive here over an hour ago," the controller answered.

"Roger, copy that, Amazonas. Has anyone looked in the Pastaza pass?" Gene asked.

"Negative," they responded.

Gene stabbed upward a few times with his left thumb as he radioed back, "Okay, we have enough gas to take a quick look. We'll start climbing to 8,500 feet."

"Roger, Zero-Four, thank you. Report overhead Shell."

Freddy, from North America, headed up a jungle air service called "Los Solicianos." They supported the Catholic mission effort in southern Morona-Santiago province with a few single-engine aircraft at their main base in Macas. Macas, the provincial capital, was the next town a car could reach 50 miles south of Shell in the Upano valley.

Freddy, himself, usually flew his favorite airplane, a twin-engine Piper Aztec with six seats and retractable landing gear. It was bigger and faster than anything in our fleet, not ideal for the bush but good for executive-style transport between cities. Amazonas Approach told us he left Quito earlier that afternoon with the Ecuadorian Minister of Education and other passengers aboard, but never arrived in Shell.

I added power, opened the cowl flaps for engine cooling, and raised the nose to climb. With just two of us on board and less than two hours of gas, we were very light and reached 8,500 feet by the time we got to Shell.

Gene turned to me. "I'll work the radios and do the looking. You fly the airplane."

"Okay, I've got the airplane. You've got the radios and are the observer," I confirmed.

Gene keyed his microphone button on the wheel. "Amazonas Approach, this is Alas Zero-Four overhead, level at 8,500 feet. We estimate Canelos *[another electronic position]* at one, two."

"Alas Zero-Four, Amazonas. Copy Canelos at one, two at 8,500 feet. Report reaching Canelos," the controller said.

As we passed over Shell, the wide flat jungle plateau abruptly ended at the Andes Mountains. Ahead, a wide wall blocked our way except for an opening where the Pastaza River flowed out. Up to that point, our path followed the river. But I moved the plane to the right, giving Gene a better view of the canyon's foothills. He twisted to the right in his seat and looked squarely out his side window. I looked ahead, followed the canyon's turns and set the power to climb again as we entered higher terrain. I monitored engine temperatures and watched the airspeed and altimeter. At that power setting, we climbed at a predictable rate. But, if I had to pitch up to a slower airspeed to continue the same climb rate, that would indicate descending air. A little was okay. A lot was not. I continually kept enough room on the left side of the airplane to turn around within the canyon and head back downhill if necessary. We had a good division of labor. Gene looked for Freddy. I kept us alive.

As we neared the town of Baños at the high end of the pass, Gene said, "Let's turn back, we don't have enough gas to look anymore." I concurred as did the clock and fuel gauges.

I closed the cowl flaps, turned left to cross the river, and set up a descent to match the lowering terrain. In clear, smooth air I would normally allow the airspeed to build up, recapturing some of the time lost during the slower climb. Instead, I reduced power so Gene could search the convoluted, tree-covered hills more thoroughly. The jungle could swallow a lot without burping.

The next morning 30 of us assembled in the Shell Airport's main terminal building—pilots from the military, commercial charter companies, and two mission flight services. We quickly found places within a gaggle of hastily gathered chairs. An army aviation officer stood in front of us next to a large map perched on an easel. On the clear plastic sheet hung over it, colored lines marked multiple zones. He called the impromptu meeting to order without the normal introductions and accolades. He reviewed the known: the plane took off from Quito shortly after 2:00 p.m. the day before. The Minister of Education, his assistant, his son, two other passengers, and Freddy were aboard. In Shell, several schools had assembled their students for a special ceremony, but he never arrived. The officer also confirmed that Quito Approach Control lost radio contact with him shortly after he departed.

Each organization received search sector assignments based on the number and capabilities of aircraft they made available. We brought two, each with a pilot and observer. Gene and I paired up again and took off shortly thereafter with full fuel tanks—and lunches.

The Pastaza River gorge runs northwest from Shell to join the main central valley of the Andes which runs approximately north-south. Baños sits where the two meet. Heading north from there, two major cities, Ambato and Latacunga, occupy the valley before coming to Quito. Our assigned sector lay along the mountains on either side of the central valley between Baños and Latacunga. With the same division of labor—I flew, Gene looked—we followed the contours of the foothills and lower mountains. Other crews searched the valley floor.

Finding survivors seemed unlikely, but hope propelled the search. Our grim purpose contrasted with a strange beauty. We usually flew to get somewhere, to reach a destination for a purpose. The in-between geography—called "flyover" country in the US—often receded to an inconvenient obstacle blocking our plan. But our operational rules that day prohibited me from searching. I flew according to what Gene wanted to see, kept us from running into anything, and managed the airplane systems. I moved with the terrain. The hills spoke to the valley below and mountains above. I watched clouds grow atop a ridge where the wind rose up one slope and disappear as it descended over the opposite side. I saw herds of sheep and llamas, small mud-brick farms and mountain villages that had known human presence for thousands of years. I also viewed hilltops, draws, and meadows, probably untrodden by human foot for those same years. The jungle's beastly, dense, wet wildness gave way in those upper elevations to thin, crystalline, ethereal loneliness. Man inhabited mostly the border between the two.

We searched all day and found nothing. We returned each to our warm meals and safe beds. But the objects of our hunt remained in whatever state they now found themselves amidst the dark, cold, wild night. Some marveled that so many searching eyes failed to discover them. I thought it marvelous that we actually expected to find anything. A Piper Aztec seems big only when parked next to a car or when a new pilot prepares to fly two tons of machine, gas, and payload for the first time. Airline passengers, on the other hand, scoff and dismiss it as a puddle-jumper. And compared to the convoluted rolls, ridges, and valleys of the Andes, such a vehicle was a pebble, a speck hidden, lost in the vastness, unnoticeable not through disdain, but unavoidable insignificance.

We anticipated resuming our quest the next day, but the military canceled the search. An Army helicopter pilot located the wreckage on the sheer cliffs of an extinct, blown-out volcano called Rumiñahui, just south of Quito. A farmer high up the lonely slopes of that mountain provided the key clue when he reported a dozen soccer balls bouncing down the mountainside toward his field. No one lived above him.

Post-accident investigations reveal a pilot's decisions in cold light for all to examine and judge. The thoughts and intents of his or her heart remain less clear, but always invite the inevitable question of "What was he or she thinking?"

It turned out Freddy thought a lot. Unfortunately, his starting assumptions led to invalid conclusions. Freddy flew his capable airplane skillfully. But air traffic's infrastructure accommodated neither his desires nor his schedule. The official Instrument Flight Rules (governing flight inside clouds, solely by reference to instruments) prescribed routes between Quito and Shell. The minimum altitudes allowed varied between 18,000 feet in the highland valley and 15,000 feet in the Pastaza River gorge. Those rules guaranteed separation from both the terrain and other aircraft also flying inside the clouds.

Freddy's plane didn't have a supplemental oxygen system installed, and he reportedly considered it unbecoming to ask government officials to wear the masks in any case. That forced him to fly at lower altitudes to avoid his passengers or himself passing out from hypoxia. Investigators searching his aviation documents found charts detailing custom instrument flight routes between Quito and Shell. They depicted precise procedures that granted him illegal success many times. He chose 12,000 feet as his highest altitude. But that provided no margin for ridge crossing or mountain avoidance. Nor did it consider others who might fly the same route at the same time. Freddy would either report that he was flying at the correct, higher altitudes or else tell controllers that he was flying according to visual rules which required he be able to see out the window—which he couldn't.

After takeoff from Quito and departure to the south, Freddy claimed he was clear of clouds. Instead, he entered a large storm and slammed himself and his passengers into Rumiñahui's sheer cliffs while climbing through 11,000 feet.

CLOSING SHELL

Friday afternoon. The last two planes inbound. No flights pending for the weekend, just emergency standby. Spooling down, winding down. Each of us pilots thinking weekend thoughts—home, wives, kids, chores, church. I tilted my chair back, propped muddy boots on the desk as I finished the day's paperwork. Pancho stuck his head into the pilot's ready room, looked for Gene.

"Capitán, Eugenio," he said after finding him. "A soldier's here asking for you."

Gene raised an eyebrow. Pancho shrugged. Gene slid his chair back over the hard tile floor, stood and walked to the lobby. A moment later he returned, open envelope in his left hand, a single sheet of typewritten stationery in his right. He read the letter again as he walked, the furrow between his eyes deepening. He stopped in the middle of the room, stared at the page again, then looked around at us, shaking his head.

"You're not going to believe this," he said, shaking the paper for emphasis. "They're closing the airport for paving."

"When?" we asked almost in unison.

"Monday!"

"Which Monday?" I asked.

"Three days from now!" he answered.

"This Monday?" we chorused.

"Yep." He shook his head again.

"For how long?" John asked.

"Doesn't say here. But it took them two years to pave Macas." Like Shell, Macas had a control tower. Unlike Shell, it received regular airline service once every weekday. Paving made sense for them. Paving for Shell? Nice? Yes. Essential? Not really. But we were just guests.

We stared at each other a moment more, then everyone spoke at once.

"That's crazy!"

"They can't do that!"

"How will our clients work?"

"How will people out there get back?"

"What about the commercial operators?"

"What about the military?"

"How are we going to cover emergencies? People are going to die!"

"We've got to move our operation to Tena," Gene said.

Everyone stopped talking.

"Tena?" I asked.

Tena, a larger city than Shell, and the capital of Napo province, lay 60 miles north. And, like Shell, it sat along the eastern edge of the Andes Mountains bordering the Amazon Jungle. Reaching it by air required an easy 30-minute flight north. The same trip overland offered two options, both presenting greater challenges. The mostly paved route took 10 to 12 hours—if everything went right. The route went west from Shell up the Pastaza River gorge to Baños, then north to Quito along the Pan Americana Highway. From Quito it turned east, out of the highland valley, then climbed and crossed the Andes divide via a high pass. From there it descended down a jungle canyon to Baeza. There it split north and south like a "T." Tena lay another 60 miles to the south where the canyon finally opened at the junction of two rivers—Rio Anzu and Rio Napo.

The alternate route was the unpaved road north, direct to Tena. That required only four hours—if everything went right—of dusty shaking, rattling and pounding.

Tena's airport tucked into the northwest corner of town. Its dirt runway was 3,200 feet long with good approaches on either end—huge by our standards. But it had no ramps, pavement, operators, or activity. Well-trod footpaths crossed the runway's weedy pebbles in several places, more like unkempt park than aerodrome. Water and electricity ran only to a small, two-story control tower–shaped building. Its sole occupant, Baltazar, carried the indifferent demeanor of a political appointee, but dutifully answered Unicom radio calls for airport information and accepted filled-in flight plan forms.

"Yeah, Tena," Gene confirmed. "We've got to set up a temporary base there. It's either that or we shut the program down."

We looked at each other again, realizing we had no choice. Gene assigned tasks. Abandoning kick-back weekend plans, we spooled up rather than down.

Saturday, we loaded a rented truck with fuel drums, pumps, a radio, a battery and solar panel along with other big stuff and sent it north to Tena. Next, we flew three airplanes and drove a Chevy Trooper to the Tena airport. We claimed an area about 50 feet from the runway, on the same side as the tower building. Any farther away put us in danger of taxiing into the mud. After cutting back the weeds, we drove stakes into the dirt for three airplane tie-down spots parallel to the runway. Then, to the right, we set up a fuel cache with six 55-gallon drums and the hand pump under a tarp. But where could we put tools, oil cases, and parts?

Panchito Cunalata, at barely five feet tall, grinned widely as we voiced the question. "Cappy [we were all 'Cappy' to him], I'll take care of it." Machete in hand, he disappeared into jungle trees that began 20 or 30 yards farther away from the runway. A few minutes later he reappeared dragging a newly cut, four-inch diameter by 20-foot long pole. He dropped it by the fuel drums then returned to the trees. Back and forth he went until he'd accumulated a pile of similar poles. After that, he walked across the runway to the street outside the airport gate, flagged down a small pickup truck taxi and headed to town. Forty minutes later he returned loaded with a dozen basketball-sized rocks; a pile of 8-foot, 1-by-6-inch planks; and a box of nails.

The apparently uneducated hangar helper then directed our

crew of highly trained pilots. We unloaded the rocks and placed them in a small rectangle as he directed. Then he dug depressions for the rocks closest to the runway to make the tops level with those placed five feet farther away and down the slight slope. Next, he cut the poles into measured lengths, arranging some in a rectangle that sat upon a rock foundation. Within a couple hours, he cut, lashed and nailed the log pile into a shelter large enough for four fuel drums, two tool boxes and a stash of parts and supplies. He fashioned a lockable man-door in the back and a wide front-window opening with a counter. A hatch hinged at the top closed the window when down and provided shade when propped open. Corrugated roofing sheets completed our fuel shed. The result looked more like a ticket booth but worked.

As a finishing touch, he cut a 30-foot pole. We nailed a small pulley at the thinner end and strung 60 feet of 3/16-inch cord through it. Then we raised the pole vertically with the cord hanging from the pulley and placed the pole's fatter base into a yard-deep hole. Some of us held it straight up while Panchito and the rest packed stones and dirt into the hole. We tied the center of an 80-foot antenna to the cord, pulling it to the top of the mast, then staked either of the 40-foot ends as far as we could from the pole, creating exactly the same kind of antenna we set up in the villages. Our "Inverted V" antenna's high angle of radiation served our application well. The 11-year sunspot cycle was at its minimum, lowering the part of the ionosphere that our shortwave signals bounced off of. That meant our most effective communication range was less than 200 miles—perfect for our operating area.

The black coax cable dropped from the antenna's high center down the pole and then into the fuel shack. Inside we placed a car battery and the same kind of two-way shortwave radio we used in the villages. We tied a solar panel atop the roof and fed its output to a voltage regulator that charged the battery. Thanks to Panchito, we had a working operations base in one afternoon.

We still faced two big challenges: staffing and aircraft

maintenance. The drive from Shell to Tena over the brutal dirt road took over four hours if we encountered no landslides, fallen bridges, strikes, protests, flat tires, or flooding. Daily commuting was not a practical option, nor was moving families. Fortunately, the one missionary in town had a contact that led us to a large, partially constructed, two-story cement house a half mile from the airport. It had a roof, windows installed in the first story, electricity and water connected, and lockable doors. We rented it, then purchased wooden bed frames, mattresses, a small kitchen table and some chairs to furnish our castle.

Tena provided power and water on a rotating basis. The water was the more predictable, coming on for two to three hours late every afternoon or early evening. That made showering easier. The pila, an open-topped cement tank used for washing clothes, sat just outside the kitchen door. We filled it with 100 gallons of reserve water for flushing toilets, washing dishes or taking bucket showers if the city water didn't appear.

We connected sockets to the wires sticking out of the ceiling and screwed in bulbs, which gave us light when we had electricity—usually, but not always, for a couple hours in the morning. We also bought gas lanterns for evening light.

Once we had a place to live, we split into two teams of two to three pilots each. One team drove to Tena Sunday afternoon to be ready for the Monday morning radio contact. Midday Wednesday, the second team arrived to take over and stayed on duty until Saturday afternoon. We couldn't cover Sundays, even for emergencies. That rubbed our service ethos raw and motivated even more prayer for the health and safety of the folks living in the jungle. Our hangar helpers elected to work one-week shifts in Tena, then take one week off after returning to Shell.

Operating out of Tena turned into cultural adventure. The Ecuadorian military moved some of their Shell-based aircraft to Tena. When they staked out ground next to us, we found ourselves elbow to elbow with their pilots, our C-185s parked next to their De Havilland Twin Otters and Pilatus Porters. We ate dinner at the same restaurant—Mama Emma's—a couple of blocks from the airport. And everybody spoke Spanish. All the time. We worked with Spanish-only speakers all day. We socialized and ate with Spanish speakers every evening. We spoke Spanish in the house every night as a courtesy to our national hangar helpers. By the time we finished operating out of Tena, aviation Spanish became as fluid as English to me. I even started dreaming in Spanish.

Aircraft maintenance challenged us the most. No power and no compressed air precluded basic tasks like engine compression tests and tire inflation. No hangar left us at the mercy of the equatorial sun. Any uncovered tool or part grew too hot to touch. Fortunately, the wings offered shade for breaks. We also spread open maintenance manuals and tools across the aircraft floor. I draped a towel over my head and neck, then secured it in place with a baseball cap. That combination plus a long-sleeved shirt provided sun protection but turned me into a sweat fountain in the 95% humidity.

Rainy days, though cooler, turned the ground into a slippery, gravelly mess that precluded thoughts of opening engine cowlings, inspection plates, or tool boxes. We could still place manuals on the aircraft floor—if we could find room in the fuel shed for the seats—but drenched hands and arms dripped water across paper pages and parts. Working on engines required a ladder, introducing slippery steps to already slippery handles. Someone else holding an umbrella sometimes helped—until moving to get a better tool grip put the back of my neck directly under the small canopy's runoff, sending surprisingly cold water down my back.

The limited room for inventory in the fuel shed also hampered us. The part or tool we needed to get a plane back into the air inevitably remained in Shell. Sometimes Dave Bochman, our maintenance director, sent spares or special equipment with the relief crew traveling north. Other times he'd send it with a client or on the bus with a hired helper. As an army traveling on its stomach, our small contingent of God's air force demonstrated that a reliable support pipeline feeding competent maintenance could make or break a flight operation.

The move also challenged our clients. Initiating flights from Tena put us farther away from their base in Shell as well as their regular jungle destinations. Some curtailed their flights drastically. Others drove four hours from Shell to make a 30-minute flight only because they had no other option.

The patients we brought out of the jungle on emergency medical flights suffered the most. A public health facility existed in Tena but didn't even equal the limited facility in Puyo (Pastaza provincial capital five miles from Shell). The mission hospital in Shell itself was the same four-hour ambulance ride away—when we could arrange one at all. Some patients opted to wait at home, hoping or praying for recovery, rather than make that overland trek.

The ride over that road was bad. After two months of two trips a week, I happened to need the telephoto lens stowed in my travel bag. I pulled the lens out of its case. It rattled. Rattle? Not supposed to rattle. But nothing looked wrong. I hadn't dropped it. I removed the front lens cap and looked in. Scratches crossed the inside of the main lens. I opened the cap at the mounting end. Same thing. I held it up to the light and looked through. Like stones in a jar, a thousand pieces crammed into a jumble. I rotated the lens, the mess tumbled. Then I tilted it. The mass slid like scree on the side of a volcano—a disappointing development. Then I reflected that if macroevolution were true, given enough trips my lens should reassemble itself, re-polish and coat the glass, and upgrade its light sensitivity by an f-stop. Seemed unlikely.

Operating from Tena also opened an alternate perspective on the jungle. Starting from Shell, the changing contour of the hills as they migrated from the Andes, across the Cutucu Mountains and then on to the flat jungle were like our home neighborhood. But from Tena, we crossed the same territory from different angles. The first time I flew a long north-south route felt like entirely new country. The hill shapes, river courses, even sun angles seemed fresh, almost foreign. Out the right window, as I headed south, the familiar peaks near Shell seemed a far away, mysterious place.

Then a surprise. Two months after opening our temporary base, we learned the paving contractor had completed the first 1,000 feet of the northwest end of the Shell runway, and Gene asked the Shell airport director for permission to use the new section. Because we were accustomed to strips that length, but with rotten surfaces and obstructed approaches, he said yes.

Parking, however, was another matter. The first taxiway exiting the runway was 700 feet from the threshold, well within the useable thousand feet. That gave us access to the public DAC ramp so we could at least get off the runway. But without tie downs, electricity, and water we would be in the same situation as in Tena.

A friend rescued us. The owner of a longtime commercial air taxi operator, TAO, offered us the use of his currently unused Shell hangar. The same taxiway we would use to exit the runway continued past the public ramp right up to the airport property line where a large gate barred further passage. Just beyond the gate lay the main road passing through Shell. Across the highway, another two-part gate granted access to TAO property. The huge hangar offered, once again, the luxury of shelter for airplane parking and maintenance, electricity, water, and lockable tool and part storage. Not only that, a large above-ground fuel tank and pump remained operational.

We dismantled our ops shed, loaded the big cargo aboard another large truck and sent it to the TAO hangar. Then we wrapped up affairs with the landlord and flew the airplanes to Shell. Parts and tools returned to our own hangar down the street at the other end of the airport.

Of course, we had to modify our procedures. Getting to and from the runway required the biggest adjustment. When ready to taxi, two hangar helpers went ahead of the airplane, opened gates on the TAO side of the road, and stretched two flagged ropes entirely across the highway over to the airport side. Then they opened the airport gates as well. After confirming that all auto traffic stopped, they signaled for us to proceed. We taxied from the ramp, across the road, and onto the airport. The helpers behind us closed the airport gates, removed the ropes, allowing traffic to pass, and closed the TAO gates. Once we completed our pre-takeoff checks on the public ramp, we called the tower for takeoff.

Our clients, glad to have us back in town, overlooked many minor inconveniences. And we got to live with our own families and sleep in our own beds once again. The stress level dropped. Almost too far.

A couple weeks after moving to TAO, I loaded the plane for a long flight. David Gualinga, a Quichua church leader and evangelist, sat in the copilot seat to my right. We both had lots to do and needed our "A" game faces on. I took extra care starting because extra people moved about the ramp. I followed the pre-taxi checklist carefully, then signaled for the helpers to prepare the path across the road. As I started taxiing, I looked carefully toward my left where I planned to go. All extra people clear, I spotted exactly where I'd turn to head for the gate. Wanted to be sure I gave the corner of the hangar a wide berth. Also wanted to avoid a dip where the paved ramp changed to older, gravelly asphalt.

David pounded my arm frantically. As I turned from the left window toward him, I saw Pancho on a ladder fueling one of our planes just 20 feet in front of me. I stomped the brake pedals hard, bouncing the tail wheel up a foot, pulled the throttle back and stopped. Pancho, wide-eyed, mouth agape, stared at me, frozen in place. It took a moment for the enormity to sink in. I was but seconds from chopping him to pieces, destroying two aircraft and starting a major conflagration. I shut down the engine—there was neither room to turn nor presence of mind for anything else. I needed time and space.

We pushed the plane backward, pointing it toward the gate. I asked Pancho's forgiveness. He graciously granted it. Then we all prayed together, thanking the Lord for David's timely intervention. I took a cooldown walk around the hangar, resolving to look where I was actually going more than where I planned to go. Recomposed, David and I reboarded and completed our flight.

Burned Out

On the 5th of May, it came to an end. Danny and his girlfriend, Lorrie, drove to Tijuana, Mexico, for the "Cinco de Mayo" celebrations. I lay on my cot, pummeled by a flu's high fever. Midmorning, I dimly realized ten times more birds than normal crowded the sumac bush over our campsite. Their shadows hopped across the tent roof in time with their excited chatter. A few minutes later, Justin, my black Labrador, started barking. Then I heard animated voices.

"I think they're up this way," said one.

"No, they're farther down the hill," said another.

"Listen! I hear their dog barking. I bet they're over by that clump." No one from outside ever visited, but the voices sounded like outsiders. Even sitting felt like a bad idea, let alone confronting hostile strangers. But I pushed myself up and shuffled outside. I found them at the end of our path in a standoff with the dog.

"You gotta get outta here now!" said a tall man I recognized from the college maintenance crew.

"Why?" I asked, struggling to keep my eyes open in the bright sunlight.

"Look!" He pointed into the hills. A huge wall of gray-brown smoke filled the sky. Flame tops cavorted from behind a ridge.

I ran back to the tent, put on shoes, grabbed my wallet, untied Justin, and hustled down the path. They followed an old jeep trail and drove within a quarter mile of our campsite. They came just to warn us. So much for secrecy, but I was grateful.

The local fire department gathered at the maintenance building to strategize how to save the campus. In 15 minutes I rode into the field with other students and townspeople. The professionals attacked the bigger blazes with four-wheel drive fire trucks. We volunteers beat out smaller fires in the short grass with old brooms and spotted new blazes hidden in the smoke. After a few hours, the fever left as I sweated out the flu.

The main fire wasn't out, but the campus was safe. That gave me a moment to think about the tent. I found a couple friends to help, so we navigated the jeep trail with my old station wagon. Amazingly, the fire hadn't touched the campsite. Shifting wind had carried the fire in another direction, but it shifted again. Now it moved across the valley toward the hill base below us. We raced down with three shovels and spent five minutes trying to fight it. Twenty-foot flames roared above us. The rock-hard ground rendered shovels as effective as spitting. We threw everything, including the tent, into the back of the wagon and raced back down the hill. Ten minutes later, fire swept through the site.

Many blamed the "hippies living in the hills" for starting the fire. Fortunately, all of us could prove we were out of town when it started (I was in Los Angeles and returned sick, not knowing anything about it), so we were quickly cleared. Official investigation eventually identified the cause as careless picnickers.

Danny returned to find our campsite and chaparral on surrounding hills reduced to black and gray ash. We needed a place to live. Hidden, protected campsites were suddenly scarce. Local property owners were understandably nervous. We spent the next few weeks living out of the back of my station wagon. Every evening we drove to a clump of eucalyptus trees atop one of the few remaining unburned hills. It offered beautiful vistas overlooking the campus and surrounding fields. But we deemed it unwise to set up a permanent site or even light the lantern. We unpacked and set up our cots in the clearing next to the car every night. We each had a piece of plastic nearby in case of rain. At dawn, we stowed it all in the car again and drove away.

Then we discovered the state park on the beach at Carlsbad. The regulations said campers could stay 29 days in a row, then had to leave for at least one night. After that, they were permitted to camp for another 29 days. Dan and I, along with a few other citizens of San Marcos Hills, moved on the same day into adjoining campsites. The park featured hot showers and restrooms. And our site lay just a few yards from the ocean. It wasn't free, but we could afford the rent. Besides, what was a 20-minute commute when we lived at the beach?

Life there should have been good. But sunsets, predawn runs along glassy surf, wave rhythm, ocean motion, sun, and wind, neither singly nor collectively, could heal my emptiness. They made it worse. They existed in peace, but a peace they could only display, not share. I scratched to get into life, but the universe wasn't listening and no one opened the door.

Every Day, Any Day

The sun barely cleared the horizon, but the dim hangar couldn't hide knee-high tires or cargo pods under the bellies. The Cessna C-185s and C-206s looked like what they were—work machines. Pancho and I pushed the large doors open. Their groans admitted morning's first glare and, like a starter's gun, broke the morning silence.

I read the day's schedule, helped push out a C-185, then joined the chorus of fuel orders and cargo instructions fired to rushing hangar helpers. The flight coordinator gave me his first plan revision, searched for two other pilots, then ran back to his radio link with the jungle villages.

When I came to MAF from suit-and-tie, commercial aviation, there still lay hidden in my subconscious the popular image of the bush pilot—macho hot-dogger, defying the laws of physics to achieve impossible feats. Instead, I found commitment to do a difficult job safely in an unforgiving environment. The laminated, preflight checklist in my hand, for example, contained the standard Cessna items. But extra entries made it clear that some things, like stopping, rated special emphasis. One entry detailed checking the Rake Brake. My right thumb could flick a switch below the throttle and drop one end of a tough, steel rake from the tail. When combined with the regular aircraft brakes, it cut the airplane's stopping distance in half. Our regulations required it to be operational before flight, but it was for emergencies only. Use in earnest meant extra paperwork and an interview with the chief pilot.

The day started with a flight from Shell to a cluster of villages, say Charapacocha, Kusutka, and Iñaywa, then back to Shell. That required 2.1 hours. We flight planned a C-185 to burn 15 gallons per hour, so I needed 32 gallons, plus the mandatory one-hour reserve, for a total of 47 gallons for that flight. But, before putting it on board, I checked that the planned loads of people and cargo wouldn't make me too heavy for any of those takeoffs. About 70% of the 120 strips we used had departure weight limitations.

The C-185 was loaded to gross, at 3,350 pounds, with 3 passengers and 450 pounds of cargo and waddled duck-like to the runway. The tower cleared me for takeoff on Runway 30. I pushed the throttle in and a ring of moisture condensed in the prop arc. The acceleration was slow, but the tail eventually came up and I lifted off. I made a left downwind departure and climbed to 7,500' at Vy (best rate of climb speed) plus 10 knots to keep the engine cool.

I radioed Pancho with my time in the air, number of passengers, cruising altitude, hours and minutes of fuel on board and the ETA (Estimated Time of Arrival) at my first destination. MAF regulations required position reports on any leg more than 30 minutes long as well as before each landing, after landing, and when ready for takeoff. If something went wrong, someone knew within minutes.

Jungle navigation required a disciplined, systematic attitude. No navigation radio beacon reached beyond 30 miles from Shell. Few prominent terrain features marked the flat jungle beyond the Cutucu Mountains. The airstrips were tiny scratches cut among 150-foot trees. They often remained invisible until one minute out. If we flew under a 500-foot ceiling, we might be a quarter mile to one side and still miss the field. We held an exact heading for a specific time to reach a point we knew we could find. After identifying it we changed course for the next known point and so on. This method took a few minutes more than a direct course, but required far less time than hunting for, and not finding, the destination.

For the first leg to Charapacocha, I flew a heading of 133 degrees for 25 minutes. That put me over the junction of the

Copataza and Pastaza rivers. Then, I turned right to 120 degrees and started a gradual descent along the Pastaza River. The runway there lay perpendicular to the river and coming in over the water offered the best approach. But at gross weight, there was no possibility of a go-around once I flew within a quarter-mile of the runway. So, I usually made the steeper approach over the hill at the other end. The runway was long, 1,740', and the surface like hard beach sand. A low spot in the middle filled after a hard rain and stayed soft for a day or so after.

Our typical strip was 1,300' long, slippery because of grass or mud and had at least one obstructed approach. Past that they were all different. The airstrip directory we carried aboard the airplane gave detailed information about each authorized landing site, but it took a new pilot a couple of years to learn them all.

After touchdown at Charapacocha, I added power to taxi to the plaza. My two passengers that day, an Ecuadorian couple, got off while I knelt in the wet sand and unloaded 200 pounds of cargo from the pod. The government paid the teachers and specified a minimum curriculum. But missionary Lloyd Rogers selected and trained the teachers, supported them during the school year, and asked us to transport them. He also provided uniforms, supplemental food, and medicine for the children. Cesar and Roscio worked for Lloyd and supervised several schools. They made a good team and I enjoyed working with them. Cesar loved to ride as "copilot," but Roscio got airsick every time she flew. Even so, she displayed the most enthusiasm for their work.

A hundred pounds of cargo remained in the pod and another 150 pounds was tied down in the back. It and my remaining passenger were scheduled to get off at my next stop, Kusutka. I calculated my takeoff weight, confirmed fuel quantity, checked fuel for water, picked up the mail and completed the other items on the list.

Loose kids presented a perpetual hazard. Once, a two-year-old crawled, unseen, all the way underneath the airplane. He then stood immediately behind the prop. A horrified dad waved, caught my attention, then raced to retrieve the errant toddler. After that, I always flicked the starter to bump the prop, but not turn it. That made enough noise and shake to scare anybody who snuck too close.

I hollered "libre!" (the Spanish equivalent of "clear!") and bumped the prop. A second look around the area, combined with a glance at the gathered faces outside, convinced me all was clear. I hit the boost pump to 12 gallons per hour, released it and cranked. The big engine lumbered back to life. I taxied to the far end, swung the tail to the left, and lined up with the runway.

Our regulations required planning every takeoff so we could lift off within the first 70% of the available surface. We also picked an abort point that allowed us to chop the power and still stop on the remaining runway. At a few short, slippery strips on hillsides, we passed this point when the wheels moved. Next, we picked both our departure path and where to put the airplane if the engine quit after takeoff. These were different at each strip and required that we knew where to go ahead of time. If we waited until needed, we were too late.

We installed markers at most of our strips that indicated the 50% and 75% points along the runway to help judge our progress during the takeoff roll. At only 2,840 pounds I lifted off before the halfway point and climbed above the trees as I passed the 75% marker. I turned right to 290 degrees for the 18-minute flight to Kusutka, but the dispatcher had a surprise for me.

The village of Libertad radioed for a medical evacuation flight. I was only 10 minutes away, so I turned back to the left to 249 degrees. A soldier's temperature stuck at 105 degrees for four days and he lapsed into and out of unconsciousness. The doctors, trying to diagnose by radio, wanted him taken to the military clinic at Taisha, another four-minutes flight time away. They feared he would die if carried six hours over slippery jungle trails.

I found the Makuma River and followed it downstream and landed at Libertad. As I shut down, the patient's friends appeared where a trail opened onto the strip. They carried him on a stretcher fashioned from blankets and poles. I moved my passenger for Kusutka to the seat behind me and had the patient's wife sit in the back seat behind him. Then I removed the copilot door (it had quick-release hinge pins) and all the seats on the right side of the plane. These went into the pod along with the rest of the cargo. This left me a clear aisle the length of the cabin. We laid the patient on the floor, with his head where the copilot seat had been. Finally, I secured him in place with cargo straps and replaced the door.

After takeoff at 3,110 pounds, I turned to 285 degrees for the military base of Taisha and was surprised to see scattered showers sprouting to the north. That could affect later flights. Focusing again on the present, I entered the pattern and found a military De Haviland Buffalo (twin-turboprop cargo plane) parked exactly in the middle of the 3,600' grass runway. The normal procedure at this strip was to land anyway, using less than half the runway. I circled and saw soldiers still unloading and the engines shut down. On base leg, I looked for anyone on a straight in approach, completed the mechanical checklist, landed and taxied up into the Buffalo's shadow.

We placed the young man on a real stretcher carried by other soldiers. Then I saw the Buffalo's crew returning. I couldn't hide my plane from their prop blast, so I asked to take off first. They said, "No problem. Go ahead." The professional aviator community in Ecuador was small, friendly and helpful. Miles of inhospitable terrain between high mountains and dense jungle motivated us all to care for each other.

I turned the tail toward the big plane, taking off away from them. With my plane's gross weight at 2,860 pounds, wheels left sod and I easily cleared the trees I'd just landed over. As I climbed for the 10-minute flight to Kusutka, I saw showers merging into an advancing gray line.

Lying but a degree south of the equator, we didn't receive the regular parade of fronts as in North America. The Amazon Jungle occupies almost half the distance from Ecuador to Africa. It sits squarely on the equator where the northern and southern hemisphere sections of the atmosphere collide in a region called the Inter-Tropical Convergence Zone. That malevolent beast, the Amazon Jungle, manufactures whatever weather it wants, anytime it wants. Receiving weather observations from four dozen villages twice a day, while somewhat helpful, didn't give us much of a database. No agency computed or provided forecasts, so what we saw was what we got. The primary weather rule was: "ALWAYS keep your back door open."

I tucked in close to a tree-covered hill and flew over Kusutka. The dirt runway was hard, drained well and had one very good approach. The departure along that same path allowed a gross-weight takeoff when surface condition and wind agreed. The village was justifiably proud of their work. I landed, quickly unloaded my passenger and cargo, and was in the air again in less than 10 minutes.

It was decision time and this one was easy. I had left Shell with exactly one hour's fuel reserve because of the load. The diversion for the patient had eaten into that. Now I needed more gas to maintain that reserve. Fortunately, we maintained a fuel dump in the jungle for just this purpose only three minutes away at Makuma.

I landed, taxied up to our fuel shed, swung the tail around on the cement pad and shut down. The gas was stored in two 50-gallon drums mounted 12 feet up in the rafters. I opened a locked box on the outside wall of the shed, uncoiled a black rubber hose and left it dangling. Next, I pulled out a large, black funnel from the lockbox. Its 12-inch-diameter by six-inch-high bowl had a flat, rather than sloped, bottom. A hole in the center protruded downward to form a three-inch spout. Atop that hole, we installed a six-inch-high by two-inch-diameter filter. Carrying the funnel with me, I climbed up on top of the wing, sat to one side of the fuel tank cap with my legs dangling over the leading edge. I removed the cap and inserted the filter's spout into the opening.

Meanwhile, Calixto, our Makuma airport coordinator, laid the metal handle of the hose nozzle onto the rim of a clean five-gallon metal pail. Pointing the nozzle into the bucket, he squeezed the handle, starting a flow of aviation gasoline. When full, he released the nozzle and let it hang free again. Then he carefully picked up the bucket and carried it to the airplane, stopping just below where I sat.

Lifting the 30-pound, sloshy pail of highly flammable liquid without spilling any required our careful coordination. He had to lift it high enough over his head for me to reach. At the same time, I had to lean over and down far enough to grasp the handle securely without also sliding off the slick wing onto him, yielding potentially disappointing results.

Calixto lifted. I grabbed the handle. He held the weight until he felt me pull the bucket up, then released it. I pulled the full pail farther up and moved it over the filter. Next, I tipped it briefly to stream about a cup into the filter. I checked the color—clear green—and looked for junk—floating or sinking, as well as water drops collecting in the bottom. Then, holding the bucket's weight in my right hand, I dipped my left fingertips into the small pool then raised them to my nose. Smelled like avgas, very different from car gasoline. Finally, I watched it evaporate. Yep, it seemed to be genuine 100/130 octane aviation gasoline. Okay to put into the tanks.

I learned the trick to pouring it in. Too fast and it spills over the top. Too slow and it dribbles down the side of the bucket and spreads along the wing. Sitting in a puddle of avgas presents not only a fire hazard, it stings. I did that only once. Found it ruined my concentration on the next landing.

Refueled and in the air again, I saw an unbroken line of rain and clouds advancing from the north. I couldn't tell how deep a system I faced when seeing only the leading edge. Would it pass in 30 minutes or two days? Both were possible. I could reach Iñaywa easily before it did but taking off again might have been a problem. My cargo out of there complicated the situation.

We hauled beef from the villages to buyers in Shell as a community service. One was scheduled for that day so, earlier in the flight, I radioed an "okay" to butcher a cow. The beef from one cow was worth several peoples' yearly income. Because the meat couldn't last long in humid heat, we didn't give the order to butcher unless we knew everything was right—the buyer waited to receive it, the aircraft and pilot were available, and the weather would stay good. Usually, everything worked.

I circled Iñaywa, calculating if I'd be able to take off once loaded. The strip was 1,640' long, but trees and terrain precluded any thought of an uphill departure making it a one-way strip. That day's weather, however, forced me to choose either a downwind takeoff or reject landing at all. So, I faced two decisions. First, with the wind as it was, could I take off with the anticipated load? I'd make a final decision on the ground, but from pattern altitude, I judged yes.

Second, racing a thunderstorm is always a bad idea. But in that case, the advancing line lay many miles to the north and moved slowly. I estimated an hour or more until arrival. If everything proceeded normally, I could load and take off well before it hit. But if some unusual delay came up, I'd have to wait. A couple of hours was okay. Overnight with an airplane full of butchered beef, on the other hand, didn't present a pleasant picture.

I landed. The beef's four quarters hung ready from a log frame. The sudden weather change bothered the people as much as me. They wanted to load right away, but I needed five minutes to configure the cabin. Everyone hustled and twenty minutes later it was done. I cleared the area, restarted, and taxied uphill. A radio call to Shell confirmed visual but overcast weather. The wind remained stable while I loaded and taxied. Neither thunder nor lightning presented itself. The ceiling stayed high enough for me to take off and land again should I have to.

Taking off downwind required alert feet and sensitivity to the airplane. The apparent speed could mislead. The tail came up and I rotated at the 60% point, but as soon as I got close to treetop level my climb flattened out. This was not as good as I had planned, but still within book limits.

I gave Pancho my numbers, checked the weather again and studied the route ahead. VFR (Visual Flight Rules) was out. The dark gray meshing with the ground merged into the overcast and went as far left and right as I could see. I did a 360 degrees turn and confirmed that there was still good VFR behind me. I could turn around and easily reach several strips before they closed.

We were allowed to fly IFR (Instrument Flight Rules), but only according to strict procedures approved by our Standards and Safety Committee. They required an area of known VFR within reach, use of predetermined minimum sector altitudes until able to join the government published system, and radio contact with ATC (Air Traffic Control). Additionally, even an experienced pilot with an instrument rating upon arrival still needed 500 hours' experience in country before beginning his IFR checkout. It took that long to build a mental moving map that could be overlaid onto the paper map in hand.

When high enough I called Amazonas Approach for a clearance. I entered the soup, level at 6,000 feet, heading for the VOR (radio beacon) and waiting for the DME (Distance Measuring Equipment) to lock on. Then Pancho called. The ceiling was lowering, but fair visibility remained in light drizzle. The deteriorating trend clearly said I needed to land soon. But then, ATC asked me to climb to 7,000' and hold at the VOR because the Buffalo returning from Taisha was first for the approach.

Time to double-check the options. I asked our dispatcher to check with villages to the north. Their replies indicated the bad weather had passed them and was less than 40 miles deep. That gave me two gold-plated alternates I could reach within 20 minutes and still maintain my one-hour fuel reserve. Unfortunately, someone would have to bring me more fuel before I could return to Shell. That would mess up the day's schedule, but both were wide open back doors.

I climbed to 7,000', crossed the VOR and entered the holding pattern still in the clouds. I had fuel for two turns holding and one approach before I'd have to head for the VFR area. The rain intensified and ATC reported the visibility deteriorating. I calculated my course and time to Villano, the nearest alternate, and waited for the Buffalo. Just before I finished the second pattern, I was cleared for the approach into Shell.

The visibility was at minimums as I turned inbound. I reviewed the missed approach procedure once more and descended to 4,000 feet. I broke out at the MDA (Minimum Descent Altitude) but still couldn't see the runway. Then .2 miles from the Missed Approach Point, I saw wet asphalt shining silver in gray rain.

After landing, I shut down the engine in front of the hangar. The helpers braved the downpour, put a tow bar on the tail wheel and, before I could get out, pulled the airplane inside. Water was still running off the trailing edge onto the dry floor as I climbed out, thinking about lunch, when the flight coordinator ran up.

"Emergency in Tzapino," he said. "Snakebite. You need to get on it as soon as you can get gassed and go."

The rain slacked to a drizzle. One helper fueled under an umbrella while the other unloaded the beef. I ran across the street, grabbed my lunch in my left hand, filled out a flight plan with my right and was back in the air within 20 minutes.

Surprise!

I loved our Cessna C-180, the first airplane I soloed in Ecuador, and called her "*La Señorita Viejita*" (*The Little Old Miss*). She was like a sprightly spinster aunt. Never married, but cheerful, willing to extend any favor, always fun to be with. She flew almost as fast as the C-185, carried less weight, but handled less truck-like, more nimble.

Landing her at Conombo, gravel crunched as the big wheels touched and started spinning. The strip required gentle braking because tires had to roll over the sharp rocks rather than slide across them. But Conombo's extra-long runway gave us plenty of room. I finally stopped, swung the tail around and taxied back to the village plaza. As I reached it, I pulled the red control for the fuel mixture, and the engine shook to a stop. Then I noticed it. The hour meter (like a car's odometer) showed *The Little Old Miss* had flown exactly 12,000 hours since she left the factory. She had accumulated more hours in the air than any other plane in the Ecuador fleet.

The Indians laughed at her nickname. Even though "she" was a machine, they also understood affection for a friend. Sometimes, somehow, assemblages of cold aluminum, hard steel, and slippery plastic took on personality if not actual life. I, along with almost every other pilot, sometimes found myself talking to my plane, to a mythical "her," confiding my plan for the next maneuver, or cajoling her to climb a little faster to avoid an extra circle before crossing a ridge. When passengers asked why we pilots (both male and female) referred to our aircraft as a living being (usually female), all explanations sounded lame. I dismissed such questions with a chuckle and small wave, muttering something about funny habits and then changed the subject. Truth was, any airplane I flew often became more companion than machine. Not exactly the same as a favorite dog or horse, but definitely a cognizant partner for focused jobs.

So, while tying down cargo in the back, with no one close by, I asked her, "How many times have your wings flexed to lift a load or ride the rapids of turbulence? How many rocks, holes, and muddy strips have you been pounded into? How many miles of air have slipped past your smooth, red and white sides?"

She didn't say much, waiting for me to figure it out. I did the math. Given an average airspeed of 138 miles per hour, multiplied by 12,000 hours, she'd covered about 1,656,000 miles since new. That was the equivalent of 66 times around the Earth or three round trips to the Moon. Cars with a tenth as many miles sat rusting in scrap yards, yet she kept flying on.

I double-checked the cargo strap knots. Sometimes it seemed we spent more time tying cargo down than making the flight. On the other hand, it was good to know that same cargo wouldn't hurt anyone if I swerved to miss a kid running onto the runway. The last knot tested secure and I reflected that in her career with MAF, this old girl had carried preachers to encourage new believers; government officials to inspect anything and everything; live calves to start a herd; doctors, nurses, and medicine to fight epidemics. She had flown beef to market; food to the hungry; evangelists to the lost; delegates to conferences; and missionaries into and out of their jungle stations.

I had placed entire families—mom, dad, teens and babies—with everything they owned, inside her cabin. She carried them to a new home in 20 minutes, instead of the dangerous week-long jungle hike. She'd ambulanced sick patients to the hospital and, when well, returned them home. Doctors and nurses had flown in her cabin to train village health promoters. She helped a retired general spend a day distributing Bibles to soldiers in otherwise unreachable jungle camps. She bore snakebite victims to help in time to save their lives and delivered drums of fuel to power a

Christian radio station. I'd strapped in generators, cement and roofing for a clinic, and desks for a school. She'd flown teachers to their classes in isolated villages and delivered the mail. .

Earlier that day I flew the Ecuadorian husband-and-wife team, Cesar and Roscio Tokiton, to the village of Capahuari, waited an hour while they worked on students' Bible verses, then continued on to Bufeo where they planned to spend the night. I planned to return a day later with *The Little Old Miss* and move them to a different village to conduct another Vacation Bible School. Then I went to Conombo to move Dr. Milton Tapia over to Shiona so he could continue fighting a malaria outbreak. My other passenger was Basilio Santi, a Christian school teacher, whose severe malaria needed hospital attention in Shell.

Cargo loaded and secured, fuel checked, I stood in the wing's shade waiting for my passengers to make their way down the path. Doctor Milton helped Basilio, who shuffled more than walked. "Well, Old Girl," I said aloud, "just another day in paradise, isn't it?" The two men arrived. I helped Basilio into the copilot seat next to me, while the doctor circled around to the left side of the plane and climbed into the middle-row seat behind mine. "The needs keep coming. Will we ever finish?" I asked her as I closed the right-hand door, circled in front and checked the prop once more for stone damage.

She said nothing but seemed to know, seemed ready to fly again. I would get breaks. I could rest. My body could recuperate, even heal itself, and come to work again. Sure, a day would come when I'd make my last flight, hang up my helmet, and go on to something else. But, as sharp rocks crunched under my boots, I wondered, *How much more pounding, shaking and sliding on mud would the old girl have to endure?* Like me, she'd fly as long as possible, but metal doesn't heal. It only wears out. Eventually, she'd fly her last mission here. Then I hoped she'd retire to a weekend flier who would pamper her with a heated hangar and the best wax, ask her to fly only on sunny Saturdays, and land her softly on long, smooth runways.

I strapped in, completed the pre-start checklist and looked over at Basilio. He tried to grin through his fever while I started the engine. It occurred to me that just as he trusted me to get him to the hospital I, in turn, trusted this aged but still sparkly girl to carry us above the jungle and safely home. The weather was turning. Time to go if we were going to make it that day. I pushed the throttle forward and we accelerated down the gravel strip. The wings flexed once more as she took the weight. The wheels stopped rolling and we climbed to clear the tall trees atop the canyon wall.

#

Three years later *La Señorita Viejita* waited as I prepared for another flight. Henry Orellana flew her that morning, then the plan called for me to fly her after lunch. As he handed me the airplane's keys and flight-sheet board, he briefed me on the fuel status then said, "No squawks, everything works fine."

"Okay, I've got it, thanks," I said, accepting the airplane.

He started across the ramp toward the hangar, stopped, turned and added, "Oh yeah, it does seem to be burning fuel more from the left tank than the right. Maybe it's flying slightly right wing low. We should probably check the rigging."

That made sense. The fuel selector on both the C-180 and C-185 had four positions. *Off, Left Tank, Both Tanks,* and *Right Tank.* We always used the *Both* position that drew fuel from both tanks at the same time. If, however, the plane flew consistently right wing low, the left wing and its fuel tank would be slightly elevated and, theoretically, supply more fuel than the lower tank.

I preflighted the plane still hot from the morning's flight. As Henry said, the left wing fuel was lower than the right, but both tanks together contained plenty for my flight. No need to add more. Ambitious schedule and changing weather propelled me. I was supposed to go north, but lowering ceilings and rain made that impossible. That meant shifting to the requests from the south jungle while we could. The bad weather might also shift south. Or, it might not.

First, I flew 25 minutes to Tamantza, a long, 1,700-foot grass strip on a cliff over the Makuma River. This was one of our "90%" strips. We called it that because our Flight Operations manual dictated that we plan takeoffs to become airborne after a ground run of no more than 70% of the available strip length. However, if there was at least a clear 50-foot drop-off at the departure end of the runway, we could extend the margin to 90% of the length. Tamantza's runway ended at the edge of an abrupt 300-foot precipice. Sometimes we'd give our passengers an extra bit of safe fun by leveling off with our wheels just a foot or so above the runway. Then as we flew past the end of the strip, the ground would suddenly drop away beneath the airplane. The "90%" takeoffs gave me one of the rare opportunities to share air-life with ground creatures—an unexpected delight for them like a carnival ride, a normal way of moving through three-dimensional life for me.

From Tamantza I hopped three minutes to Mamayak, a 1,200-foot grass strip on the flats along the Pastaza River, then back up to Tamantza again. From there it was two minutes over to Makuma. On our cement platform at Makuma, I climbed up to reach the top of the wing via the built-in steps on the fuselage and strut. Using the calibrated dipstick, I checked the fuel quantity in each tank. The left was still lower than the right, but the total was more than I needed. My passengers were three Shuar men dressed for business in the city—shiny shoes, pressed slacks, collared, long-sleeved shirts, big watches, and briefcases. They not only looked better than me, they smelled better.

They wanted to go to Macas in the Upano river valley. Macas was a jungle anomaly, accessible via many hours of car-abusing gravel roads, one from the north, the other from the south. Those roads eventually connected to other roads that ran up the sides of spectacular valleys into the central Andes mountain range that, in turn, connected with the paved north-south Pan Americana Highway that served Ecuador's major cities. Macas also sported a few paved roads downtown, electricity, and an airport with paved runway and control tower.

Of course, you couldn't get to Macas from Makuma by road. There were two choices: hike for many days over the small, but rugged, jungle-covered Cutucu Mountains that parallel the Andes like satellite, baby mountains, or fly for 25 minutes.

The Cutucu's highest peaks reach 7,000 feet, but Makuma and Macas are only 29 nautical miles apart. Not worth the long climb in a non-turbocharged aircraft, and the necessary, but hard on engines, rapid descent on the other side. So, our route wound through lower river valleys and required only one ridge crossing. Not particularly hospitable terrain for a forced landing, but none of the jungle presented that luxury. This was just worse than the normal bad option.

I tied down the briefcases in the cargo area. Then the three passengers climbed into seats as I assigned them. After the safety briefing and other checklist items, I taxied onto the strip avoiding the invisible soft areas. On the way to the departure end, I called Pancho for the latest weather info.

"The sky is still clear here, Capitán. But stations farther east report low clouds moving south toward you."

"Okay, thanks, Pancho," I said as I reached the end of the usable surface. "Zero-Three is ready for takeoff, Makuma, over."

"Zero-Three ready, Makuma, over," he repeated back.

"Affirmative," I confirmed.

After mentally calculating an abort point for this takeoff, I pushed in the throttle. The acceleration felt good. Though equipped with the smallest engine of our fleet, she was quick with a light load. I completed the after-takeoff checklist, reduced power to the climb setting and lowered the nose to accelerate. At this weight, I could head straight for the narrow opening to the pass through the Cutucu Mountains and be at the correct altitude when I arrived.

The Makuma River exited the opening, glinting silver in the still clear sunlight. On the right a steep cliff rose to a 4,400' peak we called Visui. As I climbed level with it, I could see where we hoped to install a repeater to serve the villages of the south jungle with better radio communications. On the left, an equally steep, but higher wall rose above us.

We passed through the first narrow spot and entered an open area. I could turn and return if necessary or turn 45 degrees to the right and exit the mountains to the northwest. After passing sheer 1,000-foot cliffs, I'd be over flat jungle in five minutes. But Macas lay to the left so I turned deeper into the mountains.

All looked clear ahead up to the unavoidable ridge crossing. But low clouds hung over the ridge itself merging above into vague gray. Were they nearby clouds, or overcast sky miles ahead? Couldn't tell. I leveled off at the normal crossing altitude. Descent wouldn't be an option when we got there, but I might have to climb.

The visibility there was fine, even scenic, but not inviting to a flier looking for an off-airport landing site. On the right, a tangle of lower hills lay jumbled like choppy water. On the left, more high cliffs rose above us. Below, a convoluted, rocky river squeaked through twisting canyon. Even in the mountains, the beast-jungle encroached, engulfing everything except the steepest, nearly vertical terrain.

Closer to the ridge I saw no cloud openings allowing me to slip across. Started climbing toward an area in the gray that had what we called "definition," something with a distinct edge that might—or might not—be a hole making a way through. A couple minutes more and, yes, it did indeed look like a hole. But what was on the other side? More gray. Same question: nearby clouds or distant overcast? The hole seemed to be getting bigger. If I could get through it and across the ridge, all the terrain on the other side was lower, though just as rugged. How could I tell? Would there be room to go through, take a look and return if I didn't like it? Sure would help to know what the weather on the other side was really doing, I thought.

Then I realized I could find out. I had climbed higher than normal for this route, so I might be able to contact Macas Tower several miles sooner than normal. I dialed in their frequency, 123.0 MHz, keyed the push-to-talk button on the control yoke and called, "Macas Tower, Alas Zero-Three, over."

Nothing. I called again, "Macas Tower, Macas Tower, do you copy Alas Zero-Three?"

"Alas Zero-Three from Macas Tower, go ahead," came the weak reply.

"Macas Tower from Alas Zero-Three. We're in the Mutinza pass, coming from Makuma. What is your weather? Over."

The tower operator keyed his mic and I heard a roar, then his voice only slightly above the roar. "Alas Zero-Three, Macas is closed. We are below minimums with a strong thunderstorm over the field. Repeat, Macas is closed. Landing is impossible. Over."

I started my turn back to Makuma even before he finished. "Roger, Macas Tower. Understand Macas is below minimums and closed. We are returning to Makuma, over."

"Alas Zero-Three, Macas Tower. Copy you are returning to Makuma," he shouted over the rain's continuing roar.

As I leveled off on a course back through the pass, I informed my passengers who couldn't hear my radio conversation. They looked at each other with a barely perceptible shrug then returned to watching the rugged jungle pass beneath us. The Shuar laughed easily enough, even at my poor attempts at cross-cultural humor, but when faced with danger or disappointment became stoic, almost unresponsive.

Though I would have to be at 3,300 feet when I reached Makuma, I chose to remain higher, at 5,500 feet. No point in giving up altitude until out of the mountains. I radioed Shell, let Pancho know I couldn't reach Macas, gave him my estimated arrival time back at Makuma, and asked about the Shell weather.

"Still good here, Capitán," he said, "but Copataza said lower clouds are moving in there, over."

"Okay, copy that, Pancho. Thank you. I'll call when I'm landing at Makuma."

Copataza was mostly east and slightly north of Makuma, less than a 10-minute flight away, but on the far side of the Pastaza River. If low stuff was moving in there, it might be getting close. I checked the fuel gauges, though I knew the amount better than they did. Still, they confirmed I had plenty left to reach Shell if necessary. But the left gauge was looking lower than I liked. I reached down between the front seats with my right hand and felt the fuel selector, moved it slightly right and left, confirming it solidly in the detent for the "Both" position.

As we reached the exit from the narrow canyon by Visui, I turned slightly right on the last leg back to Makuma. I would normally start a descent there to reach the pattern altitude of 3,300 feet—1,000 feet above the airstrip. But as I cleared the tall terrain on my right, instead of jungle coming into view, a cloud layer below us stretched off to the east. Time to head for Shell? Perhaps. But I could see occasional holes. Maybe I could get under the layer and at least get these guys back home. I continued a slow descent, reaching 4,500' just as I reached where Makuma should be under the clouds. A large hole revealed the center of the airstrip, allowing an easy left spiral down through the cloud layer. Good visibility below, I stopped the descent as I reached pattern altitude, but continued to turn, crossing over the strip to reach the proper side for entering the downwind leg of the landing pattern. *Looking good*, I thought. I'll drop these guys off, see if there might be any passenger or cargo for Shell and head home. Didn't get everything done, but still not a bad day.

On the downwind leg, parallel to the runway, I continued the pre-landing checklist, passed abeam of my intended touchdown spot and reached for the throttle to start the landing descent. As my fingers brushed against the large white knob ready to grasp, the engine stopped. No sputter. No cough. Only the deep silence of air rushing over a once-powered aircraft.

The unexpected produced its moment of disbelief. Then

training kicked in. Five Gs: *Glide. Grass. Gas. Gab. Get out.* Glide: set up the best glide speed—at that weight, it was 60 knots. Grass: pick a place to land—how about the airstrip? Gas: fuel's on both, ignition's on both. Normally not much else to do in a stock C-180, but we equipped our planes with a custom Emergency Fuel System (EFS).

A MAF pilot (Nate Saint) in the early 1950s observed an Ecuadorian bus ascending the Andes Mountains without using its carburetor. A boy rode outside on the fender, manually pouring fuel into the manifold from an external tank. Nate wondered, "Would something like that work for a broken or iced up airplane carb?" Turns out it did work. Very well, actually. We equipped all of our piston-engine airplanes with an engineered version of his early experiment.

The one problem? Getting the EFS to work well demanded high operator skill. Our regulations required we practice using it. Every month. With a MAF certified instructor. At altitude. In good weather. Directly over a suitable runway.

Still on the third "G," my hand moved to activate the EFS. But wait. I was already in the landing pattern within gliding distance of the strip. Why not land and figure things out later? I turned left toward the useable part of the strip sooner than if I had power and picked a landing spot farther down the runway than normal to give me margin if I undershot. I held the airspeed on 60 knots, watching to see if my spot moved up or down in the windscreen. Up meant I was undershooting, down overshooting. I had options for getting rid of excess altitude. Reacquiring lost altitude, however, was another matter.

It moved down. Good. I had something to play with. I added flaps to steepen the descent angle and held the spot in a constant position in the windscreen, so went to the fourth "G," Gab. "Shell, Shell, Shell," I called, "Zero-Three landing Makuma, engine just quit, but I can make the field."

A longer pause than normal, then Pancho replied, "Roger, Zero-Three. Engine-out landing at Makuma. Standing by."

Airplanes travel faster than cars, but some things still take time to unfold, even descending inexorably toward the jungle. I completed our custom mechanical checklist, flipping down the remaining switches as I checked each item. I already knew the wind and strip conditions. Gas on both. Flaps: set. Brakes: tested. Mixture: rich. Prop: full RPM. The green light came on. Nothing to do but fly.

I crossed the runway threshold high (as planned on this approach), continued toward the spot, then started to flare. As I raised the nose, the still-spinning-but-silent propeller suddenly roared to life. What ...? The plane rose, but I yanked the throttle back to idle and we settled again, touching ground past my chosen spot. I braked to a stop and the engine continued running. Strange. I released the brakes and taxied up onto our cement pad and let the engine run.

"Shell, Shell, Shell. Zero-Three on the ground, Makuma. Everyone on board is okay. No damage to the aircraft. Repeat, everything is okay."

"Roger, Zero-Three. Understand on the ground, Makuma. Everything okay. Confirm..." Pancho answered.

"Affirmative, Pancho," I said. "Everything is okay here. I'll call again in a few minutes when I have some idea what's going on. Please ask David to come to the radio."

"Roger, Zero-Three."

I shut everything down. Sat a moment, then opened the doors. My passengers unbuckled their harnesses and hopped to the ground. One looked up at me and asked, "Bad weather in Macas?"

"Yes," I answered, not quite believing his question.

"Any idea when it will get better? We'd like to get there today."

I nodded. "I'll let you know."

"Thank you, Capitán," he said, then walked away with his friends.

I still sat, helmet on, buckled in. Very glad to be parked on our pad rather than atop a clump of 150' jungle trees. My passengers, on the other hand, had no idea what just happened. The same inconvenience that disappointed them, thrilled me. The cooling engine ticked and pinged. The gyros spun down, their lowering notes also growing fainter. The cockpit began to heat, with no passing air to cool it.

"Thank you, Lord, for your mercy and protection. This could have turned out much worse," I said aloud. No one around heard me speak. No one knew. They had things to do. Just as I did. Another breath. Again, "Thanks, Lord." I unsnapped my helmet strap, pulled it off, hung it up on the cross brace, pulled the helmet liner off my head and stuffed it into the hanging helmet, wrote the tach time on my flight sheet, unbuckled my harness, turned left in my seat, and hopped to the ground.

I turned around, looked her over, shook my head and asked, "So Little Miss, what's going on with you today? You know we almost scratched your paint." She didn't answer, so I started the examination. I pulled the top engine cowling off, then unclipped the small flashlight I carried on my belt. Shining everywhere, I hunted, probed, poked, and "hummed" like a doctor. I looked high. I looked low. I looked outside. I looked inside. I checked the fuel level—left tank very, very low, but right tank had plenty. Nothing leaking. Nothing falling off. Nothing loose. Nothing disconnected or undone. Nothing cracked. Nothing out of place. Everything fine—except, "You quit running at an inopportune time."

I walked into the airport shed and called on the radio. "Shell from Makuma."

"Makuma from Shell, go ahead, Capitán Diego," Pancho answered.

"Is David available?" I asked.

"Yes, he's right here."

A pause, then David's voice. "What happened?"

I told the story. Just the facts. Didn't share speculations on what-could-have-been. No emergency merits public display of unsettled, discomfited, uncertain, confused, or excessive emotion. Tom Wolfe's "Right Stuff" remained a reality even in missionary aviation culture.

David suggested troubleshooting points. I went back to the airplane and started the engine. It ran without problem. Sounded good, felt good, even smelled good. But after an hour of radioed instructions, engine tests, and reports back, we remained stumped.

The engine worked normally on the ground. But there was no way I, or anyone else, was going to fly it back to Shell until we figured out what happened. The only other option was to pull a plane and pilot off-line, gather instruments and tools, and then fly David or one of his mechanics to Makuma. That would cost time and money, and greatly complicate our clients' work.

I walked back inside the airport shed. Its shade blocked direct sun heat, but heavy wet air pressed in. The ever-present smell of mold wrapped around me again. Ubiquitous background bug sounds revealed their close, but mostly invisible, presence. Sweat flow increased once more without the light breeze outside. I sat in the airstrip agent's chair and lay my folded hands on the little wooden table serving as his desk. The wood felt slightly soft, not wet, but not dry either. The loose pages of his log sheets stuck to my forearms. I picked up the microphone. Deposits left by a thousand clutching fingers ran along the very top edge. But where the heel of a hand held it, and where thumb pressed the button, the dark green plastic sported high sheen. A bright green lizard did pushups on a two-by-four cross-brace. A cockroach ran out from behind the radio but jumped back as my hand brought the mic closer.

"Shell from Makuma," I called.

"Go ahead," David answered.

"I say we take a break. We're not any closer than when we started. I'm going for a walk. Maybe the Lord will give us some ideas. I'll call you in a half hour."

"Okay, understand. I'll be standing by in 30 minutes. Shell out."

"Makuma out."

I went back to the airplane, pulled on my baseball cap, then shut the plane doors. I wasn't worried about theft, but about wishful kids playing pilot, and bugs looking for nesting sites. I walked off the cement pad, shushing through tall grass toward an open area away from traveled paths. This jungle didn't allow much unfilled space. Except for river sandbars, it produced a tangled mass nearly continuous from the ground up 100 to 150 feet. But occasionally I found places to walk alone. Gringos were common enough in Makuma, so my walk attracted no following crowd. I needed space to think and listen for inspiration from the Holy Spirit.

I stopped in a rare unclogged, shady spot. "Lord, what am I missing here?" I asked aloud. I waited for a bit, asked again, but still nothing. After nearly 30 minutes I returned to the radio.

"Shell from Makuma," I called.

"Makuma from Shell, go ahead," David answered.

"I don't have any more ideas except we're missing something obvious. You got any inspiration?" I asked.

"Yeah, run the engine for five minutes in each fuel selector position then call me."

Back in the cockpit, with our airstrip agent keeping the platform clear, I started the engine once more. The fuel selector sat on the floor just ahead of and between the two front seats where the pilot could reach it with his right hand. A three-inch handle rotated a center shaft around a circle with stops at four positions: *Off* at 12 o'clock, *Right Tank* at the 3-o'clock position, *Both Tanks* at 6 o'clock, and *Left Tank* at 9 o'clock. The *Right* and *Left* positions drew fuel from either the Right or Left tanks respectively. The *Both* position drew from the two tanks simultaneously, and *Off* stopped all fuel to the engine from any tank.

I'd been running the "Both" position successfully—on the ground at least—so switched to "Right." The engine ran fine for five minutes. With engine still running, I switched to "Off," expecting it to quit in just a moment. It continued running. And running. And running. *Shouldn't do that*, I thought. Then I switched to the "Left" position. The engine ran 30 seconds, then stopped.

Finally, I switched the selector back to "Both" and restarted the engine. It ran normally.

I shared the test results with David. He paused a moment, then he said, "Check the fuel selector lever for a cotter pin going through it and the selector shaft. I'll stand by."

I looked at and felt the area where the lever fit over the end of the selector shaft. Smooth, no pin. Only a little hole where a pin could fit. I returned to the radio, told David.

He replied, "That plane left maintenance yesterday and the fuel selector lever was reinstalled incorrectly. When you selected *Both*, you were actually in the *Left* position. That's why the left tank was so low while the right tank stayed high. Pull the lever off the selector shaft, turn it 90 degrees to the right, then replace it. Before you push it back onto the shaft, double-check that the small cotter pin hole in the lever and the hole through the shaft are lined up. There's supposed to be a pin there to prevent what you experienced."

I re-dipped both tanks to confirm the quantity in each, then did as instructed. After waiting 10 minutes, I measured both tanks again. The left quantity was five gallons higher, the right five gallons lower. Mystery solved.

I took off, climbed to pattern altitude and circled Makuma for 10 minutes. The fuel gauges showed the tank levels equalizing as the engine ran normally. Too late to go anywhere else, I climbed up to 6,500', turned to a heading of 330 degrees and flew home.

Hippie vs Redneck

I stood beside a roaring, late-afternoon torrent. Droves of cars and trucks headed north along Highway 101 from San Diego. Thumb out, I hoped for a ride to our campsite in Carlsbad. A blue '57 Ford sedan stopped in front of me. The passenger door opened. The driver straightened from leaning across the seat and asked, "Want a ride?"

This presented two difficulties.

First, in 1972 two cultures divided America—Rednecks on one side, Hippies on the other. The driver was a Redneck's Redneck. His short hair provided no shade for the back of his tanned neck. His official membership badge—a hard-hat—sat in the center of the rear window deck.

I, on the other hand, represented the other side. A Hippie, my ponytail ran down to the middle of my back, and a thick goatee beard and mustache decorated my face. Stripes or fringe adorned everything I wore. I'd cut long slots in old Hush-Puppy shoes to fashion cooler sandals. A fringed leather bag hung across my chest. Did he stop to pick a fight? I wondered.

Second, while his left arm curled around the large steering wheel, his right hand firmly grasped an open beer can. While BOTH my US Marine Corps officer and subsequent hippie life proved I was no stranger to drinking, I did learn one thing. Mixing alcohol and cars spawned bad fruit. I hesitated, eyeing the silver can with suspicion.

"You want a ride or not?" he asked, punctuating his words with the open can.

"Uhh, yeah, sure, far out. Thanks." It was just past 5:00 and I guessed this was his first drink after work. And I wasn't going too far. Probably okay.

As he merged back into traffic, he glanced alternately at me and the road. He tried making small talk but stumbled over words. Swallowed a lot. Cleared his throat a few times. Took some deep breaths. Sweat stood out on his forehead. The hand holding the beer trembled. Suddenly, he started talking about Jesus—

at least he tried to. He stammered. Repeated himself.

"Oh man," I groaned inwardly. "Not again!" I wondered if I was the victim of some sort of plot. For six months someone talked to me about Jesus nearly every day. In the store, strangers pressed tracts into my hand, left them in my basket, or started conversations. At school, students I neither knew nor had ever seen, slowed to walk with me, stood in the cafeteria line with me, or sat under the same tree I'd chosen. All wanted to "share the Gospel." On the beach, the guy catching the wave next to me talked between sets or a jogger stopped his run to bring me the "Good News." I was sick of it. Why couldn't they leave me alone?

Hitchhiking to school one day, a girl I knew gave me a ride. Her 1967 Plymouth Valiant featured an all-metal dashboard. She'd plastered the Gospel message across it in neatly arranged Dymo-Tape. As I settled into the seat, this presented an immediate problem. I could only look in one of four directions. If I turned to the left and stared at her, she'd feel threatened. If I turned and looked out the back window, she'd wonder who I ran from. If I looked only out the right window, she'd wonder what I was trying to hide. The only remaining option, look ahead and try not to read—impossible for the trained literate.

On the other hand, strange things happened during those same months. I'd see a flash in the corner of my eye. But when I turned to look, I saw nothing. It happened every few days—the flash, the turn, nothing. The flash, the turn, nothing. Nothing, that is, except a yearning that struck suddenly like the whiff of exotic perfume on a downtown street. An automatic turn to look, but no princess. Just the crowd. But I kept looking. If I could see it, maybe touch it, I knew I would be in a different place.

I needed a different place. My free-falling hippie life didn't promise high-quality outcomes. Nothing good awaited at the bottom. I looked for meaning everywhere. I tried Eastern religions, mysticism, psychic phenomena, and astrology. All proved to imitate reality just enough to be called something, but actually contained nothing. Next, I turned to touchable, provable science. I declared astronomy my college major. And the math raised a logical question. Are we humans descendants of some interstellar civilization? Convinced, I changed my major to physics to help develop an interstellar propulsion system that would take us home. Intriguing challenge, but it didn't reach the sweet spot.

The Redneck stammered on. No surprise. I'd heard Christianity had some nice ideas. But, clearly, it didn't work. I'd studied spiritual truths. I knew. The

Bible? Just a collection of fables and poems—touched neither deeper truth, nor everyday life. What'd I ever do wrong to deserve this harassment? I wanted to get out, but a ride was a ride.

Oddly, while his racket continued, I wondered: If I, the enlightened one, had delved into life's ultimate meaning, where was my peace? My mind rejected his absurdities, but my heart rumbled like a ravenous beast. I thought one thing, felt another, strange thing. Wished we'd reach my stop. I considered getting out early, trying for another, less obnoxious, ride but decided I could handle a few more miles.

Suddenly the Redneck stopped talking. Glancing only occasionally at the road, he stared at me, brow furrowed. Then he tried to ask a question, his can punctuating each attempt. Beer splashed onto the seat, onto my arm in rhythm with his stammering. "Would you...? Do you...? That is, could you...? Do you...? Do you...?" He stopped, beer can still poised. Looked lost. Fearful. Then, with another deep breath, resolute. "Do you want to accept Jesus as your Savior?"

An eternal moment's shocked silence. Then we both received a huge surprise. I said, "Yes!"

Like logs blocking a mighty river suddenly exploding free, my surrender burst out, unbidden, unplanned, unstoppable.

His astonished eyes grew huge, dinner-plate round then narrowed to angry slits. "Are you serious? Are you messing with me?" Shaken can spraying at me again.

"No, man! This is far out. I can't believe it ..." My turn to stammer.

"Are you sure?" he demanded, eyes still narrow.

"Yeah, man!" I said, even more shocked than him.

"Wow! Praise God!" he exulted. He jerked the steering wheel left and braked hard. We left the fast lane, drove into the ice plant–covered center divider and stopped. He turned to me, eyes still wide, and said, "You really mean it?"

"Yeah, man!"

He tripped his way through something. Made little sense to me until he said, "Repeat after me."

"Okay," I agreed.

"Lord Jesus," he said. "I surrender my life to you."

I repeated.

"I ask you to save me from my sins and take control of my life. You're the

boss now, not me," he continued.

As I said the same words, each one sank deeper and deeper, dropping into crevices and chasms in my heart I didn't know existed. I could feel them bounce wall to wall like stones pitched into a dry well. Every hit cracked rock sides, producing geysers of water. Soon hits and splashing merged into a flow gushing from fathomless caverns.

He stopped. I looked up. His eyes, still round, moved from me up toward the sky, then left and right as if he suddenly saw a new reality. He repeated over and over, "Wow! Praise God! Wow! Praise God!" Then, as if surprised by its presence, he started at the can in his hand. Old King James English would've described his expression as, "From whence cometh this foul abomination?" Instead, he said, "I don't need this anymore!" He turned away from me to the open window at his side and flung the can, twirling and spewing out into the ice plant.

As I followed its arc, I realized he'd pulled off the road exactly where I wanted to stop. Still in a daze, I said, "This is really far out, man. Uhh, this is where I gotta get out. Thanks."

He responded, "Wow! Praise God! Wow!"

With my right hand, I pulled up on the big lever, pushed the door open and stepped ankle deep into ice plants. "Thanks again, man. This is really outta sight."

He said, "Wow! Praise God!"

I pushed the door closed and stepped back from the car. He pulled the shift lever down into first gear, let out the clutch and drove off saying, "Praise God! Wow! Praise God! Wow! ... "

I watched him merge onto the highway with the speeding traffic and disappear to the north. I looked up into the late afternoon sky. "Lord," I affirmed, "I don't really know you yet, but somehow, someway, I know you're there. I do surrender my life to you. You're the boss now. Show me what to do." I turned left, onshore breeze rushing in my ears, and looked at the sun hanging low over the sea. At that moment I knew I'd received an entirely brand-new life and would never ever be the same.

I never saw the Redneck again. Never learned his name. But I'll recognize him in heaven for sure.

FINDING MOLINO

Finding airstrips defined the difference between success and failure. I, as a pilot, might take off and land on shorter strips than anyone else, calculate more precise fuel burns, perform perfect maneuvers, speak flawless Spanish, and accurately predict the weather. But not finding the intended destination rendered all that pointless.

But if I brought any strong talent to the tough world of bush flying, it was navigation. Maps intrigued me. Since boyhood, I studied them, laid out courses, measured distances, and calculated headings. Before I ever flew, I read contour lines to visualize terrain. Where did rivers run? How did land move? Maps made sense of something too big to see, helped me find my place in a world too big to know, revealed how and where to move when all directions looked the same. I imagined approaching Earth from space, locating my hemisphere, the right continent, zooming in closer to country, region, neighborhood and street until I finally hovered over my room. Maps provided tangible evidence that I could confront an infinite universe without being swallowed. Precise navigation revealed I could locate myself, anyone or anything, not just close enough, but exactly.

The Ecuadorian government printed terrain maps at the same scale as WAC (World Aeronautical Charts) charts—1:1,000,000—but without any aviation data. So, starting with those, we made our own flight maps. We cut Ecuador east of the Andes out of their large publication. Then we divided that portion into two 12 ½" x 8 ½ " sections—one from Ecuador's northern border with Colombia to the midway point, and the other half from there to the southern border with Peru. We cut stiff cardboard the same size and slid it into a clear plastic envelope. Then we inserted the north map into one side and the southern section into the other. That gave us a stiff chart of eastern Ecuador that we could either lay flat on our laps or stow between the seats.

In the less explored jungle portions, the cartographers showed imaginary roads, named nonexistent towns, and declared phantom airstrips while ignoring populated villages and useable landing places. However, they accurately portrayed rivers and terrain. Gene (a gifted artist) painstakingly placed tiny donut-shaped black stickers at each airstrip's actual location. Then, using that map as master, he made color photocopies to carry in the airplanes. Measuring courses between the pinhole white centers of each dot proved surprisingly accurate despite the fact that, at that scale, a half inch on the map represented about ten miles of dense jungle.

We had two radio beacons in Shell, but our navigation relied primarily on the centuries-old method called "dead reckoning"— travel at a constant speed along a fixed compass heading for a measured time to arrive at a specific location. Simple. Accurate. Most of the time.

I had passengers and cargo for Molino, a village on the north bank of the Bobonaza River a half-hour flight east-south-east of Shell. The terrain along that route crossed the flat plateau for 10 minutes, dropped off dramatic cliffs, then faded to rolling hills finally yielding to the flat Amazon Jungle. Except for rivers cutting deeply into meandering valleys, one lump looked like any other lump from the air. The normal procedure for reaching Molino was to fly to Canelos—ten minutes from Shell just past the edge of the cliff—then follow the Bobonaza River for another 15 minutes. *Easy enough, but why not follow the more direct, elegant course?* I thought.

That day dawned clear, pristine. Looking over my left shoulder, I saw the first Andes ridge behind Shell. Ahead, a straight, sharp line cut the division between sky and jungle. In the entire immense, crystal clear hemisphere around us, only one small cloud marred smooth blue. Barely big enough to produce a small shower watering the trees below, it lay directly in our path. Divert around it? It was too little to produce significant turbulence.

I held the compass heading precisely. We penetrated the gray veil. The bright light immediately dimmed. Rain, loud only because of its sudden onset, peppered the windscreen. The bumps began, but my feet played the rudder to keep our calculated course directly under the compass lubber line. A few more thumps and suddenly brilliant light returned, the small, dark, wet place already a memory. And I still held the course.

Suddenly my front-seat passenger called out, "Capitán! I see it, I see it!"

"See what?" I asked.

"Masaramu, where I grew up."

"Masaramu?" I scrunched my face, disbelieving. "Are you sure?"

"Absolutely. I can see where our house was. And where I fished." His face twisted further right against the Plexiglas as he tried to keep it in sight. "Thank you for letting me see it."

We quickly learned the value of local knowledge. While I was highly trained in aerodynamics, geography, mathematics, and a dozen different forms of navigation, I also recognized I was a novice in the jungle. To me, all trees appeared the same and a path looked like a space between green bushes. To the folks who'd lived there, the same path told a complex story. They discerned the difference between leaves good to eat and those that stung. Between plants that healed cuts and those that hid snakes. They may have lacked our style of formal education, but they possessed detailed knowledge of their world. Perhaps they couldn't operate a telephone, but they could survive a week with just their bare hands. So, I reasoned, if the man said we were over Masaramu, then we were indeed over Masaramu.

How could I have gotten so far off course? I wondered. I'd calibrated the compass. I'd held the right heading. I'd marked the time. Being over Masaramu placed us on a river 10 miles north of the one I wanted and 15 miles farther east. It didn't make sense, but I had to correct course immediately. I calculated that a heading of 260 degrees held for seven minutes should fix things. I noted the time and started the right turn, going by—but not into—the same cloud.

The dearth of unique jungle landmarks made any wind aloft calculation a guess at best, but it obviously pushed me north, so I should turn more to the south. How much? I turned back 10 degrees to the left toward the south and checked the clock again. Five minutes to go.

When the time was up, I started looking for Molino. Nothing. Not even the river. I banked left, right, then flew a complete circle back to my original heading. Still nothing except broccoli-like treetops rolling off in every direction. My passengers sat typically stoic and said nothing. But I could hear them thinking, wondering. I wondered too. *Perhaps the wind is even more southerly than I calculated.* I turned another 10 degrees left. I flew another two minutes, about four miles, and looked again—left, right, full circle. Nothing at all.

Okay, time for serious thinking. First, I wasn't lost. I looked out the right window and could still see the Andes Mountains and the familiar peaks just beyond home base. Second, not only could I not find Molino, I couldn't find anything I recognized—terrain, river or airstrip. Third, fuel quantity would soon be an issue. I had to find my passengers' destination, unload them and pick up new folks—quickly. Or I could give up and return to Shell without accomplishing my mission. Besides marooning my passengers away from home for another night, messing up the day's flight schedule, and costing our program a few hundred dollars, I would have failed Navigation 101. I could handle weather or mechanical problems aborting a flight. But missing my destination on a crystal-clear day? No way.

We had a prescribed procedure if lost (I was not lost!)—fly an expanding square. I started from a base heading, flew a one-minute side, made a 90-degree left turn and flew another minute. Another turn, another minute. Another turn, another minute. Back where I began, I started two-minute sides. I watched treetops, scanned the horizon, peered through the canopy with non-existent X-ray vision. Nothing I recognized. *Was I suddenly on another planet?* After the third two-minute leg, I realized it was time to call for help. Even so, my left thumb hovered over the mic button on my control wheel. *Was I quitting too soon?* I wanted to solve this myself. There wasn't a set time I'd get off the "supervised" leash, but this wouldn't help. I could see the other guys' bemused smiles and slight head shake when they heard. They wouldn't say anything, but they'd know.

I glanced at my puzzled, but silent passengers wrapped with me in a couple hundred-thousand donated dollars of MAF property. No question, really.

"Shell, Shell, Shell, from Zero-Four," I called, casting the die.

"Zero-Four from Shell," Pancho answered.

"I need to talk to Capitán Eugenio," I said in my most nonchalant, professional, almost bored voice—important to display, even in this situation, that I still had plenty of "Right Stuff."

"One moment," he answered.

A couple minutes later, "Zero-Four from Shell. What's up?" Gene asked.

"Shell from Zero-Four. Well... I'm not lost. But... I can't find Molino. Not sure how I missed it. I'm flying an expanding square, but no joy so far. Thought you should know. Any suggestions?"

A few moments loud silence, then "How's your gas?"

"Good for now."

"Okay, follow the standard procedure. But leave yourself an out. If you have to, land someplace and we'll bring you gas," he said like it was normal.

I'd been around long enough to know how badly this would trash a day's schedule. "Okay, will do. I'll call and let you know how it's going. Zero-Four out."

"Shell standing by."

Done. And it didn't hurt as much as I feared. I was about to start another turn when we crossed a river. *Something familiar*... The jungle contains thousands of rivers. From cruising altitude, most looked alike, reflecting the color of the sky except for where they slunk under the canopy. But from the vantage points of lower altitude or the right angle, each revealed a unique color, typically some shade of brown or green. Then I realized, *I knew this color.* That meant I knew the river. I laughed. It was the Bobonaza, Molino's river. *But where was I along its length?*

I checked the river in both directions. Left, upriver, water and trees. Right, downriver, a large open space. And a paved runway. Had to be Montalvo, the only paved strip in hundreds of square miles of jungle. That meant Molino lay 17 minutes upriver to my left. I almost pushed down with my left hand to turn toward Molino. Then thought, *What about gas?* Should have enough. But, *should have* was not the same as *did have.* Instead, I turned right and entered Montalvo's traffic pattern.

Seeing pavement this far out in the jungle toyed with reality like going back in time to the Old West to find a pickup truck towing the chuck-wagon. An oil company helicopter base and Civil Aviation control tower occupied one end. The Ecuadorian military had a large base at the other. I called Shell, told Pancho that I was landing and asked him to let Gene know.

On the ground, I shut down the engine, asked my passengers to stay in their seats. I unplugged my helmet radio, opened the door, unlatched my harness and hopped out. I found 17 gallons in the right tank and 13 gallons in the left, making a total of 30 gallons. That translated into two hours of flying. Subtracting 17 minutes to Molino, another 30 minutes to Shell, plus our required hour reserve left me with an extra 15 minutes of gas. That would work.

In the air again, I headed west along the Bobonaza for 17 minutes. I found it right where it was supposed to be, a Lowland Quichua village with its strip set on a plateau high above the north bank of the Bobonaza River. Perpendicular to the main stream. Its 1,300-foot-by-50-foot strip sported a flat touchdown zone, then headed steeply uphill with a 3 degree or 5% slope. Made 1,300 feet seem a lot longer. Nice for landing but eliminated any go-around. Once I crossed the river on final approach, I was committed to touching the ground—someplace. Might as well be the airstrip.

I landed, dropped off my relieved passengers, unloaded the cargo, sorted out the new passengers and their cargo, then took off again. A half-hour later I landed in Shell.

#

"Yeah, Mike, I can do it." I forced out a calm reply to his question about another flight, snatched the paperwork he waved at me and kept walking into the hangar. I felt like an idiot. How could I have screwed up something so simple?

I looked at the revised plan. My Navigation 101 mess up forced Mike to dump some of my flights on the other guys. The rest would domino through the week.

The busy hangar offered few refuges. I stalked into my narrow radio shop, pulling the door closed behind me. My face burned. I clenched my fists, shut my eyes and took a deep breath. I felt worthless under a despondent wave. Then I remembered I hadn't given Maximo a fuel order for the next flight. I had to keep moving to salvage some of the day's work. I strode out of the radio shop, passed Gene, and called "Forty gallons" to Maximo, who nodded and headed for my plane.

Gene came up to me asking, "You okay?"

"Yeah," I lied.

"You sure?" he asked again.

"Well, okay. I'm ticked off 'cause I couldn't do simple navigation and messed up everyone's day. And I'm still mad," I confessed, shaking my head.

"Did you go into the radio shop?"

"Yeah..."

"Go back," he said.

I turned on my heel, crossed the hangar floor and walked into the shop. Why did he want me there again? I looked around the shop rather than at the condemning scenes running past my mind's eye. There, taped to the wall shelves, hung a white three-foot-by-four-foot sign. Gene had obviously drawn it. The edges were charred. The handwritten title declared "*Map of the Lost Quichua Civilization.*" He'd drawn a little airplane following a convoluted route twisting all over the jungle. At various positions, his map subtracted or awarded points for my decisions such as "*Storm—lose 1 point.*" Or, "*Call Gene—gain 3 points.*" I laughed despite myself. The plain truth? Christ condemns no one. Not even me.

FLIGHT COORDINATOR

I stood at the plane's open door. My helmet hung in the cockpit, its cables dangling down to the headphone and microphone panel connectors. My navigation notes hung from the small clipboard attached to the center of the control wheel. Tanks contained fuel. Net and straps restrained cargo. Passengers paced. My flight plan was an hour old, yet still I waited. No rain. No wind. No sky. Only treetop cloud merged seamlessly upward into featureless gray. Where's the ceiling? Ten feet up? Ten thousand feet up?

Mike, John and Pablo Weir (Finish pilot loaned to MAF-US) walked over from their aircraft also waiting on the hangar ramp. The Amazon Jungle laughed, disdaining forecasts, but we stared east anyway, desperate to eke meaning from the nothing before us.

"See anything yet?" Pablo asked.

"Nope," Mike answered.

"What about above the ridge? I think I see definition," I said.

"Definition? Where?" they echoed. Definition meant one shred of cloud differed from another. Enough definition meant clearing. Clearing meant flying. And we had to fly.

"There, just above the peak." I pointed. "It extends to the left, over the lower jungle. See how that area is slightly lighter than the rest?"

"Nope," from John.

"Yep," from Mike.

"Maybe," from Pablo.

We spent the afternoon until too late to fly, forcing definition where none existed. Made me glad I wasn't the flight coordinator.

So, by the time my turn came, I should've known better. Part of me knew it to be a hard, most thankless, frustrating, "enemy of all/friend of none" job. That part wanted to hide in the airplane, saying *"Just let me fly."* Unfortunately, the "manager" part of my nature secretly liked the idea of planning, giving directions, having some say about what we did every day. So, despite hidden misgiving and because I wanted to pull my weight, I accepted my first rotation as flight coordinator.

We lived in Puyo, a neighboring town that marked the end of the road. Only five miles away, the dirt and gravel road, rutted by almost daily tropical deluges, challenged us with an uncertain traverse every morning. Most trips took 20 minutes of bouncing, bucking, slipping and sliding. But sometimes, like the morning we found a large delivery truck perpendicular to the road, sitting atop the cement railings of a bridge spanning a creek, we drove the alternate, Madre Tierra road. That route required 45 minutes to an hour.

Everyone depended on me—the Flight Coordinator—to assemble the day's flight plan before they arrived. So, it was still dark on the equator at 5:15 a.m. when Regina and I rose. After our prayer time, we awakened the kids at 6:00 to be together for breakfast. My contracted taxi arrived at 6:30 and I reached the hangar at 6:50—if everything went right. A 7:00 I conducted the morning radio contact. For the next 45 minutes, I received weather reports, emergency medical flight requests, routine flight requests, missionary shopping lists, questions about family members in the hospital along with other messages from three-dozen stations scattered throughout the jungle.

We faced three major challenges. First, flying cost so much that we combined requests wherever possible. Second, we received more requests than we could handle. Third, weather, emergencies, mechanical glitches, and pilot availability played their wildcards any hour of any day.

Missionaries, NGOs, and government agencies usually planned a week or more ahead. That gave me enough information to draft a basic plan. The national church, while also receiving top priority, employed a more spontaneous style. And the villages presented their requests fresh each morning. So after the morning contact, I tried to merge the draft plan, new requests, current and anticipated weather, pilot availability, pilot qualifications, along with aircraft availability and performance. Airstrip takeoff limitations complicated that further. I tracked each aircraft's probable takeoff weight by subtracting progressive fuel burn as well as increasing and decreasing cargo and passenger loads at each strip along the route. I had to be sure I wasn't asking a pilot to exceed any given strip's limitation. His legitimate rejection could unravel an entire combination.

A typical plan involved leaving Shell with a full load, flying 30 or 40 minutes, then dropping off and picking up passengers and cargo at three to six airstrips five to 15 minutes apart in the same area, then returning a full plane back to Shell. A pilot's normal day included two to four such combinations. Ideally, I presented him with his whole day's schedule in the morning. But because the day's actual activity rarely unfolded as anticipated, the plan functioned only as a starting point. As the wise man said, "No battle plan survives first contact with the enemy."

#

The morning provided exciting, hectic fun. Pilots and helpers weighed passengers and cargo, preflighted and fueled aircraft, gathered mail and stray children, and wrestled with last-minute mechanical problems. I waded into the midst of controlled pandemonium's sea, changing, canceling, or creating flights as weather, emergencies, and plan mods forced themselves upon us.

Fashioning efficient combinations of passengers, cargo, and schedules represented only half of the Flight Coordinator's job. Left unsaid lay the hidden "rest of the story." I also carried the responsibility of ensuring each flight paid for itself.

All of us focused our talents, aspirations, desires, and

equipment on one cause: to serve Christ and the people he sent us to reach. Everything else was secondary. Profit neither interested nor motivated us. Obedient service did. We were missionary beings, equipped, sent and supported by networks of family, friends, and churches. Nonetheless, we charged people to fly themselves or their cargo for two reasons.

First, while the same networks supporting us personally also supported our work, their donations covered only part of our flight costs. Other expenses such as fuel and locally hired hangar-helper salaries required additional funding sources.

Second, charging the jungle folks helped level a tilted playing field. We came in like winged angels dropping from the sky, bestowing the largesse of magic transportation upon whomever we favored. We made the rules, held all the cards, chose who flew and who did not. We wielded great power.

The indigenous jungle residents lacked power. They had nothing we needed or desired. Charging a token fee allowed them to retain some power, some control, some dignity. It gave them options. They could say "I choose to travel today," or else, "I think I'll stay home today."

The Latinos living in the towns and cities, while somewhat influenced by that attitude, faced a different challenge. Their prevailing attitude said anything costing nothing was worth nothing. It remained a bauble to be retained, forgotten, or tossed at whim.

Determining a fair "token fee" challenged us continually and led to a complex fare structure based on a combination of the client's purpose and ability to pay.

Purpose: Did the client support or work with the church, say as a mission or national ministry? Or were they more neutral, offering humanitarian aid, say as a medical team or water engineers? We did not fly for any person or group we knew opposed the church.

Ability: We determined rates according to the client's ability to pay. On the high end, we occasionally accepted commercial flight

requests as a community service. After confirming that none of
the commercial air-taxi services could or would conduct the flight,
we agreed to do it for the going commercial price. Next were
government agencies and NGOs. In the middle, expat
missionaries paid a subsidized rate. The national church enjoyed
a greater discount. On the low end, we charged emergency
patients and their companions nothing. Nor did we inquire about
their beliefs or purpose. If someone was hurt or sick, we did our
best to get them to medical help quickly.

After an hour or so, hangar confusion subsided, and I had time
to process the morning's requests that couldn't be handled
immediately, modify the later part of the day, and do a remake of
the next day's schedule. And by that time the radio crackled with
pilots asking: "What should I do with the four extra passengers
for Cangaime?" or "Should I wait for the missionary that won't be
ready to leave for another hour and, by the way, needs to go to
three extra places on the way home?" Also, the hospital called
saying, "The patient for Panientza can go home today after all.
We're bringing her over now." But that flight left 15 minutes after
they earlier said the patient wouldn't be discharged today.

In the mid-third of the day, my scheduled airplane returned
from its early trips. If all went well, Pancho had already weighed
passengers and cargo, had them standing by to load, and I had
presented a fuel order and completed my flight-plan. At that
point, I stuck my flight coordinator's hat in my back pocket and
tried to give full attention to piloting. Sometimes I turned the
radio off to concentrate fully on what I was doing. I learned—the
hard way—that in the air, being a pilot still came first.

#

The first lesson arrived on a busy but gray day. The lowering
ceiling dogged our takeoff from Makuma. Missionaries Duane
and Lois Holmes made it to the plane on time, but the storm front

advancing from the north ignored their demanding work of setting up the church conference in Surikentza.

Farther south, scattered believers called in favors to care for kids, tend gardens, and feed animals. Then setting out, women hefted stuffed baskets onto their backs. Men walked ahead, machetes ready to counter attacks of man or beast. After days on trails, they waited, along with Surikentza's residents, for our arrival. So we took off and climbed, racing the indifferent monster threatening to close the jungle for days. I tried to cut minutes.

Surikentza lay amidst a flat treetop sea. Any place looked like any other place, so we normally reached Surikentza by first flying 19 minutes from Makuma to Huasaga, a large military, grass airstrip. Overhead, we'd turn left and fly another six minutes to Surikentza.

But not that day. After clearing Makuma's trees I headed straight for Surikentza to save three minutes.

The gray ceiling pressed us low. Made it hard to see airstrips carving only narrow slits in the 100' tall jungle canopy. They were visible only when seen end-on.

Two minutes out I started looking—no airstrip. A minute later I looked again—no joy. Another minute—nope. Once more— nothing but treetops. Was I short, or did I fly past? No time for guessing, I turned right, toward Huasaga. After seven minutes, no Huasaga either. I could see how to return to Makuma but couldn't find anything I sought.

I started a standard search pattern—only treetops everywhere. Then I spotted an airstrip. Neither Huasaga nor Surikentza nor any place I'd visited before. I landed anyway. On the ground, a man responded to our beckoning.

Through the open window, Duane asked, "What strip is this?"

"Pumpuentza," he laughed.

I located it on my map, plotted a course and took off. Over Huasaga I turned to the standard heading and Surikentza appeared six minutes later. Cutting corners to save three minutes cost me 15 minutes.

The second, more impacting lesson came on a subsequent Flight Coordinator rotation. I flew the second half of the day trying to complete a simple combination. Dodged rain showers. Wrestled windy turbulence. I juggled that with managing the afternoon's plan modifications on the radio as I flew. As I descended final approach in a C-185 to Sarayacu—a one-way landing strip—I noted through the rain-spattered windscreen that I dealt with a quartering tailwind. I continued my conversation with another pilot trying to sort out a change, then returned my attention to the landing.

I touched down on the main wheels, got on the brakes, and started to lower the tail. The wet grass was ice slippery. The quartering tailwind not only pushed me faster, it also moved me toward the left edge of the strip. I tried to steer with brake and rudder, but the plane continued to slide. Finally, the brakes started grabbing, slowing the airplane, but I couldn't get back to the centerline. Slower still, almost stopped, but far over to the left, the left main gear suddenly sank deep into soft mud. The tail sprang up, but I didn't have enough airflow over the elevator to hold it back. The nose plunged down, burying one prop blade in the goo and stopping the engine. The tail stuck up in the air and I looked out the windscreen down at muddy grass.

I made the radio call. Then, while awaiting John Lemmon's arrival to rescue and investigate, with his permission as Chief Pilot, I solicited village help. A C-185 on its nose towers unimaginably high, a tall, tall signal of shame. Tossing a rope over the tail wheel and pulling enough to drop it risked breaking the tail, rendering the aircraft immediately un-airworthy.

A dozen men gathered. I explained the procedure, divided them into pairs, then showed them where to place their hands on opposite sides of the fuselage. We tossed a rope over the tail and pulled gently until the center of gravity barely shifted. Each pair of helpers took the weight with hands high, then slowly lowered their arms. As the first pair did that, the second pair began with arms high, then the third pair and so on. In a moment we gently set the tail wheel onto the soft, grassy mud. Finally, we pushed the airplane across the strip and up to the drier, firmer loading area.

John arrived a half hour later. He asked questions. I answered. We walked the entire strip from where I touched down to where I stopped, measuring lengths and angles, noting where I got on or off the brakes, where I started sliding and the left main wheel finally dug in. The airplane, however, showed no sign that anything had ever happened. The prop blade was clean, not even scratched. We measured both blades and they tracked true, well within allowable limits. When the brakes began grabbing on the landing rollout, I had pulled the power back to idle so the RPMs were down. And the soft mud was stone free.

After diagraming my path and inspecting the airplane, he asked more questions. I answered. The cause was clear. I'd divided my attention so much, I barged into a marginal situation, not perceiving the obvious.

We ran the engine. Everything looked, sounded, and smelled normal with all gauges in the green. Next, we conferred on the radio with Dave Bochman, our Director of Maintenance. He asked his own set of questions. We answered. He confirmed our measurements fell within operable limits and we jointly determined the airplane was safe for a ferry flight. I took off and returned to Shell empty.

Even though the engine ran perfectly, we pulled the airplane offline. A short time before, MAF adopted a policy requiring a complete engine teardown for all sudden-stoppage incidents regardless of measurements or exterior condition. That messed up the schedule for two months and rewarded me with extra paperwork.

But my incident had a small, positive effect as well. When I first arrived in Ecuador, the Flight Coordinator position rotated among pilots on an indefinite basis, but typically lasting about three months. Getting out of the position happened when either a vacation, a journey to Quito for flight physical renewal (every six months), or furlough came up. The other out came when the pilot's wife begged to have her husband released from the job so the family could regain a life.

After my incident, we tried swapping the role every week. That was nice for the Coordinator but didn't work so well for the clients. We lost too many details. Next, we tried rotating every calendar month but modified that to every four weeks. That gave our users better service, but still pushed the pilot's sanity and safety too close to the edge. Several months later the Lord provided a better solution—a full-time coordinator.

Alan Lindvall transferred to Ecuador from another MAF Latin American program. An ex-Air Force C-141 pilot and veteran MAF missionary pilot, he chose to relinquish flight status but still wanted to serve on the field.

He expressed a servant's heart through focused attention. Coupled with excellent Spanish, it allowed him to better understand our clients' needs—spoken, unspoken, and even unrealized. They quickly learned he cared enough to invest time listening. His extensive flight experience enabled him to gain maximum utility from our pilot/plane combinations without promising service we couldn't provide.

Into the Pit

Air blasting from the vent dried my shirt soaked with sweat, not rain. The Outside Air Temperature gauge read 105 degrees on the ground in Charapacocha. But, at 6,500 feet, it was down to 80 degrees—just enough lower to feel cool. But, "cool," just like "dry," was a relative term in the Amazon Jungle. That day was the first operable weather after a week of continuous rain. Foggy gray had been suddenly replaced with piercing sunshine and hard blue sky. The hot air absorbed moisture from the soggy jungle, turning it into a clear sauna.

The hangar was full that morning—mostly people who just wanted to go home. Seven days in our waiting room made everybody cranky while dozens waiting the same seven days in the jungle called insistently on the radio asking about their flights. So, it was a day for polite but focused hustle. Our duty flight coordinator's schedule featured a series of complex, interdependent combinations that required perfect weather, complete passenger cooperation, no emergencies, motivated pilots and would be marvelously efficient if it all worked.

So far it had. The stop at each strip demanded the same rapid cycle without forgetting something or offending anyone: Land on a waterlogged strip without running off the end or getting stuck. Help the passengers out of the plane. Unload cargo from the pod that stayed there. Untie and unload cargo from the cabin that stayed there. Confirm that I had the correct passengers for the next stop and that their fare was covered. Load their cargo into the pod. Load the basket too big for the pod into the cabin and tie it down. Help the passengers into the plane. Talk with the man in the middle row who now wanted to go to a different strip than originally requested. I couldn't go there that day, so he got out. I unloaded his cargo from the pod. Someone else took his place, but he also had a basket of fish that fit only in the cabin. So, I asked the rear-seat passengers to get out, untied the cargo, squeezed his in and tied it all down again. The rear-seat passengers re-boarded and I confirmed that everyone was strapped in, gave them the standard safety briefing and closed the rear doors. A woman interrupted my climb into the pilot's seat saying she forgot to include part of her husband's luggage. I climbed back down, opened the pod and gently inserted a gallon of chicha concentrate, its squishy mass wrapped in banana leaves tied with vines.

I'd left Charapacocha 15 minutes before with a full load—four passengers plus 350 pounds of cargo. If I could reach Shell, refuel, re-cargo and be back in the air again within 45 minutes, I'd still have time to move the medical team from Conombo to Nuevo Corrientes, then pick up Cesar and Roscio from Bufeo and get back to Shell with 10 minutes to spare before official sunset. Tight, but doable. As long as everything went right. I looked out under the right wing to the northeast. I was going that way next and the weather usually came from that direction. The sky was clear all the way to the horizon, so those conditions should hold for the rest of the day.

Copataza slid below the left window, the drying mud strip already showing a bit of orange tint from a sinking afternoon sun.

"Shell, from Zero-Seven," I called on the radio. After a few years, my aviation-specific Spanish flowed as easily as English.

"Zero-Seven from Shell, go ahead," Pancho answered.

"Zero-Seven reports position Copataza, level at 6,500 feet, maintaining my estimate for Shell."

"Roger, Zero-Seven. Position Copataza, level at 6,500 feet, maintaining your estimate for Shell," he confirmed.

Then I added, "When I arrive, I'll need a quick turn-around. Two of the passengers continue on with me to Conombo. Please have the other passengers and their cargo weighed and ready to load. I'll need 45 gallons of fuel and I'd like someone to present the flight plan for me. Also, call the doctors in Conombo and let them know that we're still moving them to Nuevo Corrientes today. I'll bring the fresh vaccines with me. Then, call Cesar in Bufeo and tell him that we're getting both of them out today."

"Roger, Capitán. We'll have everything ready."

Then, I called again. "Shell from Zero-Seven."

"Go ahead, Zero-Seven," he answered as if he had nothing else at all to do.

"Pancho, a special favor, please. Can you put a bottle of mineral water in the freezer for me?"

"Of course, Capitán."

"Thanks, Pancho." The average jungle humidity was 95% and routine temperatures were 90 degrees or higher. I sweat a lot. The Indians smiled and pointed discreetly when my shirt was soaked while loading cargo. They giggled when it dripped off my chin and laughed unashamed when it dripped off my nose. I got so dehydrated I could drink a whole liter of mineral water without stopping. If Pancho put a bottle in when I asked, it would turn into a marvelous icy slush when I pulled it out in 30 minutes. Of course, if I was delayed, it would explode after 45 minutes. That would mean another half hour carefully extracting glass from ice and packages. I didn't have an extra half hour but knew I'd be there in time. The day's impossible but essential schedule was going to work.

I checked the engine gauges—all in the green. Fuel quantity—correct. Heading—324 degrees, Altitude—6,520 feet. I didn't push the control wheel but thought it forward. The VSI (Vertical Speed Indicator) dipped slightly below zero and the big hand on the altimeter crept lower. I recalculated my estimate for the next reporting point. I'd arrive exactly on time. I looked behind me to the right as far as the shoulder harness permitted. The passengers seemed content. One dozed, the others searched the treetops for something familiar. Everything was according to plan. Everything was good. Mentally, I was several miles ahead of the airplane, planning how I would enter the traffic pattern. The impossible but essential schedule was going to work.

"Zero-Seven from Makuma?" A not-Pancho voice invaded the headphones in my helmet.

Makuma? I wondered. All the village radios were set to a different frequency. Makuma was a rare exception that also had the airplane channel. But it wasn't contact time. *"He shouldn't be here at all,"* I assured the correct procedure portion of my pilot's thinking. Still, a small, unbidden worry formed.

He called again. "Zero-Seven, Zero-Seven, Zero-Seven from Makuma. We have an emergency."

We were the ambulance of the jungle, so emergencies were a normal part of a normal day. So much so, we were unknowingly tempted to treat them like they were also normal for everybody else. I put aside the worry and immediately started calculating a heading and elapsed time to get to Makuma from my present position. Even before I answered, I calculated 195 degrees, 12 minutes. Then, I remembered. I couldn't add even one more passenger. I was completely full. And, two of these passengers were continuing on with me to Conombo. There was no way I could pick up anyone. Confident with my unassailable plan, I answered. "Makuma, from Zero-Seven. Go ahead."

"Capitán Diego, we have an emergency here. You have to come now." The voice sounded worried, genuine.

"Makuma, from Zero-Seven. Okay, Calixto, what's the emergency? " I recognized who was calling. The Makuma airstrip served several villages as well as the original mission station. Its operation and maintenance had been turned over to a local association that, in turn, hired a local resident to coordinate flight requests and operate the radio. It was a busy place, a gateway to a larger, outside world. The position conferred prestige upon the holder and we always tried to confirm the authority and responsibility that went with it. Calixto had held this job for several months. He was friendly and seemed to understand what both the pilots and passengers needed. There was a growing mutual respect.

"Capitán, we have an emergency. You have to come now!" he repeated.

"Okay, Calixto. I understand you have an emergency. What is it?"

"It's very serious, Capitán. You have to come now!"

"Calixto, my plane is completely full. I don't have room for anyone else. Tell me what the emergency is and I'll get help to you as soon as possible."

"It's very urgent, Capitán. You have to come now!"

I wasn't getting any more information from this conversation. Makuma had passed behind my left wingtip and was now getting farther away—14 minutes was my revised estimate.

"Calixto," I responded, trying to control rising irritation and still sound reasonable. The longer I lived here the more relaxed I became, but there was always a background tension. Our cultures were so different that we foreigners dreaded making the unforgivable blunder, the one that the dark corner of our imaginations told us would undo decades of missionary effort and, perhaps, condemn an entire generation to further darkness and despair. I paused, silently asked for guidance, and continued. "I don't have room for anyone else on this flight. But I need to know what the emergency is so I can call a plane from Shell to help you."

"You have to come now, Capitán. It's a grave, grave emergency."

"Calixto, do you have a patient?"

"A patient? Yes, we have a patient. Very serious. Very grave. You have to come now."

"Who is the patient and what's wrong?"   ·

There was a pause, then, "The patient is a man and he's very bad. You have to come now!"

"Okay, Calixto. I understand the patient is a man. I don't have room for a man on this flight. Can he wait until tomorrow?" As I talked, I realized that none of the other planes would be able to reach Makuma today. If I didn't get the patient, he'd have to wait until morning.

"No, no Capitán. He won't last until morning. He'll die before then. You have to come now!"

"Calixto, I don't have room for a man on this flight. I'd have to leave my passengers there, in Makuma, but they have to get to Conombo today."

"Capitán," Calixto continued. "You have to come now! The patient is a 12-year-old boy. He will surely die if he doesn't get to the hospital today."

Boy? I thought he said *"man."* A hundred indelibly memorized emergencies flicked behind my eyes, but in front of my heart. I looked at my passengers again. *Where did convenient necessity rank with life necessity? I guessed it didn't really.* I banked left and eased the nose over into a high-speed cruise descent. The gentle twist of my left wrist and slight forward pressure exerted by my left elbow were immensely powerful. That barely discernible motion would maroon my four Atshuar passengers for at least a day in a Shuar village. It would delay another village of 73 people from receiving their vaccines for a day. If bad weather prevailed tomorrow, the last village in line might be missed entirely. Would anyone get sick because of that? Cesar and Roscio would have to spend at least an extra night in the jungle and would miss their meetings tomorrow in Quito. I didn't know what that might mean for them. And, it would set our schedule back by days. All the people I was going to move this afternoon would have to wait until the morning, which meant we couldn't get as many other people moved tomorrow as we should. They'd have to spend an extra day or two in Shell—if the weather didn't get bad again. What would that mean to them? Or, perhaps, my slight but powerful effort would save the life of a 12-year-old boy.

"Okay, Calixto. I'll be there in 14 minutes. Please have the patient and a companion ready. Also, see if there's someone there who will give my four passengers a place to sleep tonight and something to eat."

"Thank you, Capitán." He sounded relieved.

I called Pancho with my revised plan then flew the descent. Aloft, while cruising, the earth and sky have their own personalities—beautiful and expansive. The affairs of men are remembered as a story read long ago. The sky, however, is a different place with a different kind of time. Pilots receive permission to visit and, if they wish, may even listen to the songs. Sometimes, the words are the sweetest pain or the saddest joy and sometimes there's a smell or a flavor or just the right note or, occasionally, even a glimpse of what our real home is like. In the descent, though, the ground below changes back to the world where people live, to homes and beds which slowly become clearer as we remember that we're temporarily constrained by time, space and mortality.

I landed, braked to a stop. The transition from graceful soaring to ponderous waddling was complete. I radioed Pancho that I was on the ground in Makuma and taxied to the ramp.

I swung the tail around on the concrete pad, switched off all the electrical power and pulled the mixture control. As the engine shook to a stop, I turned off the magnetos, opened the door with my left hand and unstrapped my helmet with the right. Helmet off, I flipped the seat belt and harness release, pulled myself up on the windshield brace and hopped to the ground. Not graceful, but quick for the emergency at hand. I tried to explain the situation to my passengers while we were in the air, but they didn't seem to understand—or perhaps didn't want to—that they'd have to stay in Makuma for the night rather than where they planned. They stared at me blankly as I hurried the explanation again while looking for my patient.

The normal 20 or so folks stood around the ramp. And that was odd. They weren't clustered around the cargo shack looking distraught. They weren't wailing. They weren't doing anything but chatting in the shade.

"Calixto!" I called. "Where's the patient?"

Silence and no Calixto.

I was tempted to holler again but did not want to appear

angry—a far bigger sin in that culture than sleeping with the wrong spouse. I could insult the dignity of his position with a careless word, gesture or tone. The door to the cargo shack was open, so I strode around the airplane and entered. Sunlight leaked into the darkness between the vertical plank walls. I peered into the gloom, my eyes not yet adapted.

"Calixto?" I called again with a reasonable coworker, inquiry, tone.

"Yes, Capitán?" He answered calmly, looking up from the radio in front of him. No worry. No hurry. No stress. Easy, as if I'd merely stopped by to chat. Pleasant friendly. Mildly surprised.

"Where's the patient?" I asked.

"Patient?" he responded with a quizzical look.

"Yes. You know, the patient you just called me about."

"Patient? What patient?" he asked, genuinely puzzled.

"The patient you just called me about," I repeated in my very best professional but friendly tone.

"Patient?" he wondered aloud, tasting a foreign concept never before considered. He looked around with slightly furrowed brow as if searching for a hat mislaid the day before. "Patient?" he wondered again, got up from the stool in front of the radio and moved with small steps between me and the still-open door out onto the platform. "Anybody know anything about any patients here?" He asked in Spanish, not Shuar. Everyone looked at each other. Shrugs and shaking heads. He turned back to me, still standing outside. Smiled, held it a moment then said, "Sorry, Capitán. There's no patient here."

"But you just called me. You said there was an emergency here. Where's the patient?"

"Sorry, Capitán. There's no patient here," he repeated.

"Why did you call me?" I demanded with my very best cross-cultural smile punctuated with gringo clenched teeth.

"Sorry, Capitán. There's no patient here," he repeated a third time without denying calling me.

"But..." I stopped. I didn't know what to ask, what to say.

He pointed in the culturally normal fashion with puckered lower lip and lifted chin to my passengers who were trying to untie their cargo and asked, "Since they're staying here, you can take three passengers I have for Shell. They've paid their fare." He waggled the bills at me. Three Shuar men stepped out of the growing crowd. They wore clean shirts, pressed trousers, shined shoes, big watches, and sunglasses. Each carried a packed duffle.

Disbelief and denial have a strong narcotic effect. I stared, gaping with open mouth at Calixto. He smiled again, tried to hand me the money. When I didn't accept it, he took the bag from each man and walked around to the plane to load them in the pod. I stared at the empty space he vacated. Slowly, ever so slowly, I realized the full truth of the lie.

"Calixto," I called quietly, still, with glacier calm, cold and hard. I turned to follow him. "We need to talk. Over here. Alone." The now interested crowd followed. We drew far apart from them—three feet, a long distance by their standards. I turned my back to them, faced him squarely and said, "You called me and said there was a patient." Only a silent smile and gaze from him. "But there is no patient, is there?"

"No, Capitán. I don't know anything about a patient."

"But you want me to leave my passengers here and take these three with me to Shell?"

"Yes, Capitán. They need to go to Puyo to shop."

A barbed claw sunk into the bottom of my heart, firmly attaching a hard anger. On the outside, I did my job, as a pilot, as a missionary. I went through the standard, culturally sensitive procedure of saying no by saying yes. "I would really like to take your passengers," I lied. "I can see that this flight is important to them. Unfortunately, the plane is full and it just wouldn't be safe to take anyone else. Besides, I've already made a previous promise to these men." I indicated that they should reenter the plane. "And, I have to honor that promise. So, while I would really like to help your passengers, I'm unable to do so at this time. Perhaps the next flight will have room."

"Very good, Capitán," he accepted, not disappointed, but satisfied. He turned and spoke to the three men in Shuar. They shrugged, retrieved their bags and walked off. Calixto, still smiling, asked, "Do you have room for some mail?" He wasn't embarrassed, nervous or anxious, but rather looked and sounded the same as dozens of times before. He wasn't upset. He didn't look guilty. He didn't act sorry. His day was moving at the same slow easy pace as always.

I was incredulous, numb and furious. I couldn't speak. He lied to me. He trampled the rights and welfare of others—not just me. He deliberately deceived me, ruined the day of dozens of people and, perhaps, endangered the lives of a hundred others. He knew what he had done, but he didn't care. What kind of worthless person would do that? I couldn't look at him, but just replied very quietly, "Sure, I can take it." He handed me the small bundle. I took care not to touch his hand. He became something unclean, hateful.

I checked my own internal pilot's control panel and switched my emotion circuit to the "off" position—just as if I were flying a seriously wounded patient. There was work to do. The original passengers climbed back into their seats. I fastened their belts, climbed in, fastened mine and sat a moment. A basic principle of life was dying within me. My opportunity to be free came, but I hid and let it go by choosing, instead, to feed on bitterness. The flight back that day was technically fine. The rest of the day's schedule was indeed trashed, but we recovered by the middle of the following week. I spent the last half hour of the day picking glass slivers out of freezer ice.

My flights for the next few weeks were also technically fine, but I didn't talk much except to snap or complain. My prayer life evaporated. I was mad at everyone about everything. Finally, even I couldn't stand myself. I walked into the jungle to holler at God. I was mad. *It wasn't fair. What wasn't fair? Good question,* I thought. I didn't really know, but I felt cheated, betrayed. Finally, after I ran out of words and breath, God had a turn. He showed me that I was still mad at Calixto for lying to me, not to mention the collateral damage he caused to so many other people. And, he added, I hadn't forgiven him. The fact that Calixto neither asked for nor felt the need for forgiveness seemed to be incidental to the Lord.

I judged Calixto not worth forgiving because he lied to me. But the Lord reminded me that even though truth-telling was normal to my culture and not to Calixto's, our value to God was not based on what we did or didn't do—only on who God said we were. And Jesus paid the same price to redeem Calixto as he did to rescue me. If Christ forgave Calixto, I had no choice. I did the same. Life and flight improved dramatically after that.

First Flight

My first hint of new direction appeared in the first days of my new life. I drove a country road to school, and on each trip I passed a small sign pointing to a narrow lane winding up over the crest of a hill. Each time it beckoned, like a timid child seeking an adult's attention. It pointed with no promise. Just the single word, "Airport," called me, poking a deep place, enticing me to respond. I ignored it for a long time. But one morning I turned left and headed up the hill.

The trees opened. A small, neat building waited, single story with a couple windows. Beyond it, northern San Diego county spread out—rolling hills, groves, a sprinkling of houses. I twisted the knob, pulled the half-glass door open and walked into a new world cleverly disguised as the old. A long counter ran over a glass display case, a small desk behind, a black felt sign with slots for white letters on the wall, a couple small clipboards with keys dangling.

A pleasant, middle-aged woman sat at the desk speaking with a tall man standing next to her.

"May I help you?" she asked, turning from her conversation to greet me.

"You can't see the airport from the road, but I drive by the sign often. Just had to see what was up here. What do you folks do?"

She stood, pushed back her chair, stepped forward, smiled, and placed clasped hands on the counter. Proper, attentive, business-like smile. But her eyes told a different story. Neither challenging nor taunting, they gleamed with light from a different place. "We teach people to fly," she said.

An hour later I left, late for my morning class, minus my life savings of $136.36. I bought a block of 10 one-hour lessons. What did it matter that I was barely out of hippie life and worked for room and board caring for avocado groves? The sky enchanted me.

A couple days later I arrived in morning crisp air for my first lesson. The same woman, Barbara Whipps, led me through the office, out the back door onto the airport ramp. Two small airplanes waited, parked side by side like cars, but tied to the ground like horses, lest they run off. The wings were on top and a single propeller and motor in front sat atop a single wheel. Farther back, two more wheels on legs stuck out sideways from the bottom of the body. It looked like a big tricycle with wings jutting off the sides and the long tail out the back. It seemed, at the same time, tiny, toy-like, and exciting. So... these things really fly, I thought. And I get to go with it?

She introduced me to the first one, calling it a Cessna 150 (pronounced "one-fifty") named N51172, like a palomino named Blaze. Immediately I wanted to get on and ride.

But first came what she called, "pre-flight." We stooped under the wing, opened the doors. Then we circled the plane, methodically confirming everything necessary to get and keep us in the air was attached and likely to remain that way—wings, tail, wheels, propeller, oil in the engine. A lot of stuff to remember.

Finally, we entered, she on the right, me on the left in what I guessed was the pilot's seat. Most of the instruments clustered there, while the right side of the panel stared back mostly blank. But a duplicate control wheel protruded out and another set of twin pedals sat on the floor.

Barbara picked up a white laminated card with lists on both sides—the "checklist," she called it. She read each item aloud, explained, then adjusted the control, turned it on, or confirmed it was off, locked, or merely present.

"Altimeter," she said, reaching across the cockpit in front of me to tap the round glass face of an instrument. "This tells us how high we are. It's like a clock, but with only 10 numbers instead of 12. The little hand indicates thousands of feet, and the big hand tells us hundreds of feet. Turn this little knob that sticks out the front until the needles read the same as the field elevation, 708 feet above sea level," she said, turning the knob until the little hand was just shy of the white "1" and the big hand was just past the "7."

We completed the long list, then she said, "Okay, time to go," pointing at the ignition key in the bottom left corner of the panel.

"You want me to start it?" I asked.

"Yep. I'll work the throttle and hold the brakes. You just turn the key then let go when the motor starts. Just like a car."

I twisted the key, the motor caught, and the propeller spun, shaking the plane in time with its pocketa-pocketa sound. She pointed at the oil pressure gauge, pulled the throttle out so the engine idled at 800 RPM, then turned to me and said, "Go ahead and rest your feet on the pedals but keep your heels on the floor. They turn the nose wheel. Push the left pedal and the plane turns left. Push the right pedal and we go right. If you lift your feet up and push the top of the pedals, they work the brakes separately—left for the left wheel, right for the right. Push them both at the same time to stop straight ahead but try to steer without using the brakes. I'll take us out of the parking spot and show you how it works. You can try when we're on the straight part of the taxiway."

Her left hand rested on the throttle, her right on the control yoke. She pushed the throttle in slightly and the engine sped up. We moved forward and turned right toward a straight asphalt road with a solid yellow stripe down the middle. Seemed odd not turning the control wheel. In a moment we straddled the yellow line. "Okay, you steer with the pedals now. Keep us centered on the yellow line. I'll work the brakes and throttle."

I pushed the left pedal and we veered left off the line, then I pushed right and we crossed it going the other way.

"Smaller movements. This thing steers more like a tricycle than a car," she said.

I tried again, using gentle pushes, weaving across the line.

"Better. You're getting the feel now."

We reached a wider paved area at the end of the taxiway. "Okay, I've got it," she said. We slowed, made a sharp left turn to face the runway and stopped.

"Here's where we do our last checks before takeoff." She pulled up the plastic list again, read an item, pointed at or adjusted something, then said "Check" as she completed each one.

Finally, "Okay, let's go."

We're really going to do this, I thought.

We moved onto the runway, a wider asphalt road, and stopped, now straddling a dashed white stripe. "You're going to do this, but I'll be on the controls with you."

"Me?"

"Yep, you. You can do it, you'll see. It's easy.

"Make sure your heels are on the floor and push only the lower part of the pedals. When we start moving, keep us pointed down the runway, centered over the line. Put your left hand on the control wheel but keep your right hand in your *lap. I'll work the throttle. Keep the control wheel level and pull back gently when I say so. Got it?"*

"Uh...yeah... I think so..."

"You'll do fine. You'll see. Here we go." She pushed the throttle all the way in so only the black knob stuck out of the panel. The engine changed from big sewing machine to resolute push. Not the surge of acceleration I expected, but we moved forward—faster, faster. Felt odd over the line. This sure ain't a car, I thought. The panel rattled. Everything jiggled, shook.

"Airspeed's alive," Barbara said. The airspeed needle wiggled off the peg, moved around the dial.

Faster. Quicker shaking.

"When it gets to 60, pull back on the yoke. Pressure only, no movement."

40. 45, 50, 55, 60.

"Ok, back pressure."

I gripped the yoke tighter.

"A little more," she said.

I pulled. The hard plastic pushed into my left fingers. Nothing happened. Suddenly, but subtly, the wing took the weight. Smooth. Rattle gone. In front, the trees eased lower. To the side, the runway moved beneath us. We were flying. I was flying. Click. This was it. In that instant, I knew what I wanted to do, was supposed to do, would do.

Conferences and Kids

Residents of the jungle villages we served built their houses near a large stream or river. They devoted the land immediately surrounding the village to gardens or *chacras*. Beyond that lay the hunting areas that expanded year by year as their population grew—or they over-hunted game.

No roads connected the villages, only narrow paths formed by people feet or animal paws. Trails traversed boggy ground, centuries-old layers of decaying trees, river gravel bars, threaded between thorn-spiked brambles and vine-covered trees. That put villages a hard day's walk or more apart—a day for indigenous walkers who knew where and how to step. Foreigners needed double that. Village water came from the river. They had no electricity, no telephones, no communication with the outside world except for the solar-recharged, battery-powered two-way radios we installed.

An average village had 80 people. Little ones had as few as 50, while a big population center might flaunt 120. We normally moved people by ones, twos or threes along with their baggage and cargo. But three or four times per year, a church group or medical ministry planned a large conference and requested that we fly everyone there. This presented interesting challenges. Our safety rules still applied, but the emphasis changed from packing people and cargo combinations to carrying as many people as possible. We limited luggage to what fit in the pod under the airplane or the small cargo area behind the seats.

A few weeks before the event, the host, say the Shuar Church Association, radioed us specifying the conference location, beginning and ending dates, bad weather alternate dates, and any logistic flights needed for food, equipment, or outside presenters. They also sent a list via our jungle mail system of authorized attendees (or open slots) organized by village—two from this village, one from that, three from another, etc. List size ranged from 20 to 250 people, but the typical gathering called 50–100 together.

The pilot scheduled for Flight Coordinator duty during the conference started his planning days ahead of time. When he received the list, he worked up combinations to bring the most people to the conference location with the fewest number of flights while leaving operational capacity for bad weather delays, unplanned mechanical issues, and medical emergencies. Then he began looking for full-load requests from Shell out to a strip in the conference area, as well as from the conference area back to Shell.

On the appointed day, weather cooperating, we took off early. Like bees swarming over spring flowers, we buzzed from strip to strip across the jungle. At each village, we compared our list of authorized delegates to the folks asking to board the airplane. We collected their payment, a token fee in local currency equivalent to $5.00, or else two live chickens wrapped in vine-tied banana leaves with only their heads protruding. I stowed their fare (most paid in chickens), weighed and loaded luggage, strapped them in and gave the safety briefing. We took off, heading either to the next pickup strip or, if the plane was full, to the conference location.

After landing, our excited passengers poured out and looked for family, friends, and ferreted out housing and food. A village hosting an event doubling their population accepted a tremendous burden no less complex than a North American "gala." Despite living memory of revenge killing by spearing or beheading, most conferences ran well, sparse on offense and long on harmony. The indigenous jungle folks' transformation from Stone Age savagery to modern civility in two to three generations amazed me. My culture spent centuries doing the same.

We walked around the airplane (perhaps detouring to an appropriately secluded bush to "drain a tank") closing and checking then hopped back into the office, started the engine and took off empty to gather from another village cluster. Back and forth we shuttled, stopping only to wait out passing weather or refuel—for bigger conferences we staged fuel drums at the conference strip. We ate lunch as we flew.

Conferences started when most of those invited arrived, then lasted three to five days. Depending on the organization conducting the meetings, they included worship and singing, large sessions for everyone, and smaller specialized breakout groups. This was a big deal to them. Really active folks might get to a conference every year. Others, once or twice in their lifetime. They called those activities "conference." We called the same thing "church."

Finally, when there was just enough time left to pick up any prearranged load and reach Shell before sunset, we headed home. Then, three to five days later we repeated the process in reverse.

#

Once a year we supported our biggest—and my favorite—conference, Camp Kid flying. That was an all-hands-on-deck affair. We stockpiled our fuel cache, tailored airplane maintenance schedules, set family vacations, and adjusted furlough start and stop times to accommodate the special flights. We fueled and loaded the planes the night before, arrived at the hangar before dawn to preflight, then put on our "A" game faces for full-court press.

I double-checked the pod door closed, then stepped up into the cockpit. Three of the other four guys did the same. Mike wanted to confirm a brake disc still had legal thickness, so went to his toolbox for a caliper. Probably okay, but easy to misjudge. Better check. In our business, meticulous was a key to life.

For Camp Kid flights, we took off empty, flew to our destination, loaded up and returned to Shell. Then we repeated. All day, sunrise to sunset. And the next. And the day after. And maybe the day after that, too. Depended. We prayed for good weather and no emergencies. Tried to move rapidly, but not do anything stupid.

The tower radio announced official airport opening for the day, so I joined our parade of C-206s trundling out to the run-up area at the runway head. The early morning guys in the tower weren't accustomed to this much traffic at 6:00 a.m. But their radio personas remained professional, though I imagined them reaching for extra coffee during the brief intervals between transmissions.

"Shell Tower, Alas Zero-Eight," John called after takeoff.

"Alas Zero-Eight, Shell Tower. In the air at one-one *[11 minutes after the hour]*. Change to departure frequency," the tower instructed him.

"Shell Tower, Alas Zero-Eight changing to Departure," John answered.

"Shell Tower, Alas One-Zero ready for takeoff," Job called.

"Alas One-Zero, Shell Tower. Cleared for takeoff," the tower said.

"Shell Tower, Alas One-Zero. Roger," Job answered.

"Alas One-Two, hold short of the runway, departing traffic," the tower instructed me.

"Roger, Alas One-Two holding," I confirmed.

Back and forth, the scripted dialog set the beat, moving our airplanes step by step from ramp, to runway, to sky. One after another we took off, climbing into rising sunlight. Then, as we left the traffic pattern, each pilot turned to his respective heading and the Camp Kid games began.

Every summer, Plymouth Brethren missionaries, Lloyd and Linda Rogers, along with their Ecuadorian team, conducted a week-long camp for sixth-grade jungle kids. To qualify, the kids learned six new Bible verses every year starting in first grade. If they mastered all 36 verses when they completed sixth grade, they received an invitation to camp.

Near the end of the school year, we pilots tested the students and recorded the names of those who passed in each village. Spanish served as our lingua franca but was a second language for all of us. So, Lloyd and Linda equipped us with multi-lingual cards for each of the 36 verses. Students could recite them in any of five languages—Spanish, Waorani, Shuar, Atshuar, or Quichua. An English translation was also included for our benefit.

During my first summer as a Camp Kid pilot, we brought out 175 sixth graders. A few years later, that number grew to nearly a thousand. Lots of work, but I loved flying them. They reveled in life, not yet acquiring their elders' stoicism. At the village airstrips, they spoke whisper-soft, peering, pointing, touching tentatively, watching me for any sign. In the midst of adult conversations, my raised eyebrow snapped their extended hand away from handling anything delicate or dangerous and back to their sides. But at my smile, their pointed fingertip on fuselage become flat palm rubbing cool aluminum, with faraway looks that asked, "What's it like to fly high and fast and far?"

I called out the names of the load's passengers. They stepped forward into the center of the circle that greeted every flight. Eyes bright, but tentative. Excited, but wary. Eager, but cautious. Each one carried a small bag barely bigger than a bread loaf, all they'd need for a week away from home. I knelt down to place their luggage easily, loosely, barely filling the cavernous pod. Then stood again to orchestrate passenger loading.

Any big kids? Some sixth graders reached teenage years before their circumstances allowed them to complete the course. Some flights drew only 11–13-year-olds. Others included a tall young man, more adult-size than kid. He grinned, embarrassment banished by the promise of flight and camp.

I directed him, because he was the heaviest, to the copilot seat. I pulled my helmet cable out of the way and slid my seat all the way back. Then I showed him how to crawl across and sit. He started that process while I surveyed the rest of the load. Because of their size and weights, I could legally and safely fit another six kids into the four remaining seats. I could've fit the seventh, but she wasn't present. Fortunately, a second flight was scheduled for her village.

I asked two kids to go around to the right side of the plane and wait at the cargo doors, then directed the other four to sit, two to each middle seat. After buckling them in, I joined the waiting pair and helped them into the aft-most seats and harnesses.

Inside the airplane, they still spoke softly, but with eyes now dinner-plate wide. Most had seen airplanes, but not yet ridden in one, had never moved faster than a run nor higher than a tree. I double-checked all belts and harnesses then gave the safety briefing. I tried to look into their eyes to see if they understood instructions that could, if something went badly, save their lives. Some met my gaze, others did not. Their culture did not value direct eye contact as mine did, so I looked for creative ways to check what they learned.

I spotted a middle-sized, moderately confident-appearing kid who seemed to follow my litany, then asked her, "Can you show me how to open this door?"

Surprised, she hesitated a moment, then reached over with committed resolve, pulled up the first lever correctly to unlatch the forward cargo door. She turned her hand the other way and pulled down the second red handle to unlatch the aft door. She looked back at me, questioning.

"Very good!" I exclaimed and clapped. "You are very intelligent. Thank you."

Everyone clapped with me. She smiled, then looked down. Her compatriots grinned and laughed. Then they returned to whispering mode while waving to family outside the window. I closed the door, went through the checklist, then yelled "Clear!" out my open window. I watched the crowd for anyone moving toward the airplane and for their expressions. If all looked at me, then my blind spot under the engine cowling behind the propeller was likely clear. If one or more looked toward the nose gear, however, I called again. If I got grins or thumbs up, I proceeded. Otherwise, I opened the door and leaned or got out to check. The excitement of celebration, special event times, made everybody careless. Stories of a few tragic people-and-propeller encounters fed my imagination easily.

Engine start always brought the kids' attention forward. Lighting off 300 horsepower shook the whole plane, seats, cabin, wings, everything. Up until then, their only moving seats were tippy dugout canoes. There, they floated on top of the powerful river, but now they sat inside the beast, wondering, "Is it going to eat me?"

All checks done, lined up with the runway, engine loping in steady idle, I checked the small sea of faces behind me once more. Everyone still in place, somewhere between wondering and eager. I pushed the throttle in and navigated takeoff. Above trees and obstacles, I glanced aft again. Leaving Earth, faces and hands plastered against windows, some pointing at river bends maybe recognized, others at occasional village clearings amidst the sea of trees. As we climbed, looking down upon the tops of flying condors and parrots fascinated them. Above the clouds, faces changed from amazed to mesmerized as we soared in a never-imagined realm—deep blue above, brilliant white below, only occasional holes revealing the dark land hidden beneath, a distant home temporarily set aside.

Of course, not all my kid passengers enjoyed idyllic flights. On other days, hard days, painful days, some rode in agony as patients crushed by falling trees, slashed by errant machetes, or bitten by venomous serpents. A few left life while still in the air—an 11-year-old boy drowned in his own vomit while within sight of Shell, and some infants succumbed to dysentery's dehydration. But not that day. On that day they marveled at sights that would fuel lifelong dreams.

When we arrived in Shell, camp counselors awaited. As soon as the propeller stopped, they approached the airplane, clipboards and pens ready.

"Everyone in this group's from Numbaimi," I told Cesar.

"Very good," he said. Like clumping kittens, he attempted to gather all six kids together before they scattered. He had their attention and moved the group away from the airplane and into the hangar.

"Arturo?" he asked.

"Here," the tall teen responded.

"Rosalia?" Silence. "Rosalia, are you here?"

"Yes sir," one of the smaller girls responded.

Cesar continued calling and checking names on his list. I was amazed that he and the team knew the kids so well. For much of the year, we flew the counselors to the scores of villages scattered over hundreds of square miles of jungle as they administered the Compassion International school child program. Attentive and committed, they demonstrated fierce compassion to invest themselves in the young lives all but unknown to the dominant Latin culture and its official schools.

Lloyd and Linda successfully lobbied the Department of Education to actually place the legally mandated and promised teachers in the villages. The government ran the schools, but Lloyd and Linda provided uniforms, books, medical aid, and supplemental food.

Toward the end of the day, the kid crowd grew faster than ground transport could shuttle them to camp. The girls continued moving as a dense gaggle, but the boys scattered, had to be called back, clumped briefly, then scattered again. And, while they grew up seeing airplanes, it was quickly apparent they'd never seen cars. Giggling, whispering knots stood in the middle of the road pointing excitedly at oncoming lights, wondering why they got farther and farther apart.

When the counselors finally rounded them up and took them to camp, it was also obvious that they'd never seen electricity nor running water before. Don Chapple, the camp director, said they had a particular fascination with valves. Some deep compulsion drove the kids to turn every valve they saw to its opposite extreme every time they saw it. The same with switches. He said that made camp infrastructure maintenance interesting.

The camp offered all the typical camp activities: games, food, crafts, practical life-skill classes, and how to deal with the encroaching outside world. Then at night around the fire, counselors explained the verses the kids had spent six years learning. Like shining more and more light in a dark room, they slowly connected the verses with God's story and the kids' part in it.

Many surrendered the running of their lives over to Jesus every year. Even during the one short week, they found unexpected peace and purpose. And then, when they returned home, their enthusiasm bubbled out. Just being their new selves affected everyone around them.

Life and Death

BUFEO

The call came at a bad time. We'd loaded the airplane and buckled in three passengers. I was just climbing into the cockpit.

Pancho hurried up. "Capitán, emergency in Bufeo! Snakebite. Pregnant woman."

I stopped mid-climb. "How long?"

"Two, maybe three hours ago."

Our eyes met, knowing. Snakebite victims had a 50% chance of survival if they got medical help within four hours. Bufeo lay 45 minutes east, but the sun set in two hours. The rest of our fleet was too far away. This plane and I were her only earthly hope—if I left now.

Pancho dropped to his knees and unloaded the pod. I hopped down, hurried around the plane, leaned in the 206's big cargo doors, untied knots, and told travelers they weren't going home today after all. While they scrambled out, Pancho and I piled cargo on the ramp. I removed two right-side seats and prepared a patient bed on the floor with pad and straps. Then I checked all doors were latched, people and cargo clear, wheel chocks removed. In the cockpit I forced myself to slow for each checklist task, wiping sweaty palms across knees. Checklist, engine start, checklist, taxi, another checklist. Run up, one more checklist. Takeoff. Fast climb east to 5,500'.

Forty-three minutes later I inspected Bufeo from above. The dancing windsock said I'd have a gusting tailwind for landing. Fun. The approach was, indeed, like juggling cats. But I hit the right spot, braked hard and lurched to a stop. Not smooth, but accurate.

Wailing. Amazon Jungle residents knew only two states of health—well or dying. The woman they carried on a blanket was clearly not the former. Baby swelled her belly, poison her leg. I jumped from my perch, ran around the plane and opened the big doors. Their gentleness laying her on the pad contrasted with the cacophony storming around us. Hands reached from the pressing crowd, touching her, touching me. Husband stood there, hollow and ashen, his wide, unbelieving eyes asking, "Can you help?"

I strapped her in, looking for the first time. Young, like my bride with our first child. Suddenly, tears from some hidden locker—unbidden, neither professional nor controllable. "Let's pray," I managed. The wailing stopped. In new silence I asked Jesus for healing, committing mother, baby, and father to Christ's mercy.

Medical evacuation flights really hurt during my first term. Once turned loose with an airplane in the jungle, I felt I had to be both counselor and pilot. During orientation phase, I could busy myself preparing the airplane to receive the patient. The instructor pilot handled talking with the village, the family, and supervising gentle loading.

Once on my own, however, I carried the full burden. Bleeding, broken bodies themselves didn't make me squeamish—physiology fascinated me. But empathy sometimes threatened to overwhelm me. After loading a patient, I'd pray with him or her and the family members. Tuning into their pain, their confusion, and their fear often opened some deep emotional gate. I thought it was up to me to comfort the family, encourage the patient, even to know how to treat them. My inability to do all that all the time made me feel useless as a servant of Christ.

I'd choke up, unable to speak. My eyes would fill with tears, blurring my vision. Occasionally I'd have to sit several moments in the pilot's seat pretending to deal with technical matters while I composed myself enough to fly safely.

During our first furlough I prayed a lot about that (and other field life issues). After some weeks I felt the Lord asking me, "Did

I call you to be a counselor?"

"No," I answered.

"A doctor?" he continued.

"No."

"A pastor, perhaps?"

"No."

"What did I call you to do?"

"Fly airplanes," I answered.

"Exactly," he affirmed. "If you're trying to do someone else's job, who flies the plane?" He showed me I must remain faithful to my calling and leave space for others to be faithful to theirs.

Back on the field a few weeks later, I tried a new procedure. When retrieving a patient, I talked with the family, prayed for the patient, then reached up to my mental control panel and turned my internal "Emotion" switch to the "Off" position. After that, I served best by forgetting about the patient and focusing on my job. Neither empathy nor tears would serve them now, only good flying.

So, with them, I repeated the now familiar drill—closed doors, cleared the area, obeyed more checklists, and took off. During our climb west to 6,500', I radioed Pancho for a waiting ambulance. En route I looked in back. Still alive, eyes clenched, she gripped her husband. We landed 10 minutes before sunset and sent them to the mission hospital.

God granted them (and me) mercy. A month later she, with new baby sleeping in a cloth pouch against her chest, returned home alive.

PISTA DOCS

Medical flying accounted for almost half our flying. We were the jungle's "911" service. We flew doctors, nurses, dentists and health promotion teams into the villages. We also provided emergency air ambulance service to bring patients out to medical help. They suffered the same sorts of illness and calamity affecting developed areas, but the most frequent calls were for tree problems—falling onto people, or people falling out—machete wounds, snakebites, birth complications, burns, dynamite injuries, and dehydration.

Most emergency calls came via radio. We had two regular radio contacts every day—7:00 a.m. and 1:00 p.m.—but as our radio system grew in villages covered and capability, a call could come at any time.

If I was in Shell when a call came, I could prepare a patient space ahead of time with a pad specially cut to fit on the right-side cabin floor. In the C-185 I removed the copilot and right middle passenger seats. In the C-206 the right middle and rear passenger seats came out. In addition to the pad, MAF designed a restraint system that protected a patient lying down almost as well as one secured in a seat. If the call came while I was in the jungle, however, I couldn't provide the pad, just the safety straps.

When I arrived at a strip to extract a patient from a wailing village, our 80/20 rule confronted stark reality. The 80/20 rule said we responded to 80% of the air ambulance requests because 20% of those requests were actual emergencies. However, when confronted by 60 distraught people, all of whom knew for certain that Maruma Nayapi—wife to the chief man, mother of a dozen children, the village's favorite aunt and counselor to all—teetered at death's door, it was difficult to say she only had a cold and didn't need an emergency flight. Some days the 80% threatened to overwhelm us. We were pilots, not doctors.

Rescue came from two directions. First, Miriam Gebb, a missionary nurse, expanded a village health promoter program. She selected and trained men in several villages to administer first aid, train residents in best hygiene practices, perform basic diagnosis and administer simple, over-the-counter remedies for common ailments.

Second, we and the neighboring Catholic air service entered into agreements with the Ecuadorian Ministry of Public Health to provide air ambulance service in the jungle. The Catholic air service focused on the southern portion and we concentrated on the northern.

As part of that agreement, the ministry of health provided what they called, "*El Doctor de la Pista,*" or literally, "The Doctor of the Field." A better English phrasing rendered it, the "Airstrip Doctor," or, as we shortened it, the "Pista Doc."

The ministry of health required all new medical school graduates to serve in rural medicine for one year before receiving their license to practice medicine. They designated the airstrip doctor position as a rural medicine post, so we received a new doctor every year.

The Pista Docs, anxious to get on with their specialties or start a private practice, accepted the mandatory assignments with mixed feelings. Life on jungle's edge wasn't the end of the world, but they knew they could see it from there. Then there was the matter of working with us "foreign evangelicals." Some arrived cool, but professional, while others displayed open hostility. Fortunately, even if they didn't warm up to the jungle, they grew to respect our commitment to serving its indigenous residents. Some requested assignment extensions, a few became believers.

We were wary of such close government involvement, but quickly recognized the boon their help brought to us and the jungle people. At first, the Pista Doc spent half a day at the Soliciano's hangar, then half a day at ours. But since we responded to 90% of the emergency flight requests, and built them an office and small infirmary, they transitioned to spending the entire day at our hangar.

Immediately after the regular morning and afternoon radio contacts, the Pista Doc got on the radio and polled the same stations. He or she screened the calls, then authorized, differed, or denied a flight to pick up the patient. They also conferred with the village health promoters on routine medical issues. Finally, when an emergency flight arrived in Shell, they examined the patient and performed triage as necessary. Within a year most of our medical evacuation flights carried people who genuinely needed emergency help.

The pista doctors faced a daunting challenge. They diagnosed the ailments and injuries of patients they could neither see nor touch. They worked via a village radio operator communicating in his second language who, in turn, found him or herself surrounded by distraught family and friends. Their work saved many lives, but occasionally they made a bad call.

DANIEL'S SON

Kusutka lay in the corner of a small, flat valley two miles south of the Pastaza River in Shuar territory. I landed there to drop off passengers then continue on five minutes south-east to Makuma to pick up other passengers and cargo for Shell. But as I prepared to leave, Daniel, a village resident, stepped from the small crowd and asked, "Capitán, can you look at my son? I think he needs to go to the hospital in Shell."

"Did you talk to the Pista Doc on the radio this morning?" I asked.

"Yes."

"What did she say?"

"He didn't need to come out. I should ask the health promoter for pills for infection and swelling."

Thinking both of my squashed schedule and of those who abused the system, I said, "I can only carry patients the Pista Doctor authorizes. If she hasn't approved an emergency flight, there's nothing I can do."

Worry etched deep furrows on an otherwise characteristically stoic Shuar face. He looked at the ground, then raised his eyes to mine. After a moment he asked, "Please, Capitán. Just come and look at him."

"I'm not a doctor ..." I equivocated, but tilted my head toward the village, adding, "Let's go see him."

I followed him off the airstrip, over a log spanning the small drainage ditch, down a mud path between two split bamboo huts and into a third. A small fire smoked in the center of the dirt floor. To the left, a 12-year-old boy lay on his back atop a folded blanket set on banana leaves. I stepped between the fire and the boy then knelt by his left side. Even in the dim, smoky light, I could see the problem. His entire left side from toe to shoulder was swollen double size.

"What happened?" I asked.

Daniel answered, "A few days ago he tripped while playing soccer and cut his leg on a rock." He pointed to an angry red gash just below his left knee. "Now he can't stand, or bend his leg, or arm. He says he's hot, then cold. Doesn't want to eat. Sometimes cries. Sometimes talks nonsense. And his skin burns."

The boy opened his eyes as I touched his forehead—hot, but no sweat. His eyes wandered, didn't seem to see me. He shivered, then closed his eyes again. Though not a doctor, I didn't think a couple pills would fix this.

"Okay," I said either on impulse or inspiration. "Let's take him. Can you carry him? I'll get the plane ready." Palpable relief washed over Daniel's face. As I started outside, I turned back and said, "Bring your shoes and ID papers. You have to come with him."

"Yes, Capitán," he said, standing quickly, pulling shoes off a peg and stuffing a plastic bag into his pocket.

"So JR," I asked myself, hurrying down the path back to the plane, *"what have you done?"* The Ministry of Public Health wouldn't pay for an unauthorized emergency flight. And, taking these two meant I couldn't pick up the Makuma passengers and cargo for Shell. Besides messing up their plans, it meant I had no way to pay for the leg back to Shell. If my boss didn't agree either, then I might have to pay for the whole leg myself. "Well, so what?" I said aloud as I reached the aircraft.

Daniel and another man carrying his nearly rigid son arrived just as I finished stowing the seats to make room for him to lie flat on the airplane floor. I had no patient pad with me, but they brought the blanket. I folded it to fit between the C-185's seat rails. Then, working to bend his nearly rigid left arm enough to allow entry, we laid the boy in place. I fashioned a safety restraint from cargo straps. Then his father climbed into the middle-row seat behind mine.

After finishing checklists, with the engine running and in position, I made only the obligatory pre-takeoff radio call. I'd have time to field questions and protests while en route to Shell. In the air, I radioed again with the normal litany of destination, time estimates, altitude, remaining fuel, and souls on board. Then when Pancho asked why I was heading back to Shell rather than Makuma as planned, I asked him to have an ambulance ready when we landed. Mentally I prepared for a meeting with my boss, and a confrontation with the airport doctor.

I wasted a lot of good worry. All agreed I made the right call—my boss when I explained, and the Pista Doc when she saw the boy. The hospital doctors said delaying medical treatment for another day would have killed him. Six weeks and a dozen surgeries later, he and his dad returned home.

SUNDAYS AND HOLIDAYS

Medical emergencies refused to confine themselves to regular work days, so we followed two separate, rotating duty schedules to cover emergency standby on weekends and holidays.

The weekend duty pilot's responsibility covered Saturday and Sunday. On Saturday the duty pilot and one hangar helper split radio contacts, loading, and fueling.

On Sunday, the duty pilot stayed home or attended church, but listened to the hangar radio for emergency calls during the official half-hour blocks—07:00 to 07:30 and 13:00 to 13:30. If he flew, his wife or another prearranged person came to the hangar for radio flight following. On his own, he also determined the weather, preflighted, loaded, fueled, and called the hospital in case they were ready to discharge a patient for a nearby strip. He wrote out his flight plan, rode the motorcycle or drove a car to present his flight plan at the far end of the airport. Then he returned to the hangar and loaded any passengers. After that, for a break, he flew.

After picking up the patient, he asked the flight follower to call an ambulance, landed, unloaded the patient either onto the hangar gurney or, if ground transport had arrived, moved the patient there. If the hospital couldn't send ground transport, he went out to the road to hail a taxi. If no taxis passed by, he used one of our program cars and took the patient to the hospital himself—after he put the airplane away and locked the hangar. If another call came at the afternoon contact, he repeated the entire process.

The holiday routine followed the same pattern as Sunday, except that it always felt lonelier. Two sets of holidays—US and Ecuadorian—sometimes complicated matters. US Thanksgiving often surprised the jungle folks and Ecuadorian Independence Day snuck up on the North Americans.

We pilots expected to cover one or two holidays per year. I did Christmas a few times, either from Shell or Quito. We worked the family routine around radio contact times. Then, as I sat before the radio, ears awash in static, I prayed, "Lord, please keep everyone in the jungle safe, healthy, and honest today."

ANDRÉS

One Christmas I sat in my living room, adorned tree behind me, front window view before me. In the distance, a towering storm moved slowly across the Amazon Jungle. Wind lashed treetops. Rain drenched leaf, ground and animal. Monolithic, powerful, and oblivious to the affairs of men, it advanced inexorably to assault the Andes Mountains.

But the affairs of men continued. The distinctive crack of the long propellers fitted on our C-185s announced Mike's takeoff. I, however, turned as Regina shepherded excited kids to the awaiting gift pile. Always a good time. Always a special time. Always the essence of Christmas—the generosity of giving, the humility of receiving.

Meanwhile, during our fun, a rare giver never made it to the hospital but died aboard Mike's airplane. Andrés Mashient succumbed to cancer at 60, having lived among people who rarely reached 50 before accident or spear claimed them. No one recognized the infirmities of old age until too late.

He and I spoke no more than a half-dozen words in the same language. I came from middle-class America. He came from the Atshuar tribe of the Amazon Jungle. I studied science, math, literature and flying in college. He learned nature's ways, spear making, and the art of ambushing animal and man. I pursued an aviation and business career. He practiced witchcraft and revenge killing. I met Jesus as a hitchhiking hippie. He encountered Jesus in a dream.

The Lord transformed Andrés from fierce warrior to compassionate father. Afterward, he spent years seeking out those he'd orphaned, rescuing those he found. He brought them together, raised them as his own, and shepherded them as they married. When they, in turn, became parents, they stayed with him in the village named after him—Mashient.

To me, Christmas meant star-crowned snowy nights, hot chocolate, carols, and lighted trees. Andrés saw snow only as the white peak of a distant volcano. His peoples' music had just three notes. He drank chicha made from pre-chewed yucca, ate bananas, giant catfish and tapir. His Christmas differed from mine in all respects—except one.

Andrés possessed nothing to give. Instead, he imitated our Father by giving himself to father the fatherless. He broadcast God's goodwill to lost boys and girls. He gave what he could not keep to the powerless who could not repay. He understood the art of giving.

Still here on Earth, I, of course, rejoiced that he delighted in the undimmed goodwill of the Father of Christmas. And I did revel in our Christmas celebration, dim shadow though it might have been. But I confess, Andrés was my deep friend and I still miss him and how he taught me the art of Christmas.

ANDRÉS' GRANDDAUGHTER

A few months later, in the air, I admitted I couldn't push the airplane. And neither wish nor will sped it faster than physics' laws allowed. But I extracted all they contained. I lowered the nose, added power and settled on a high-speed, 200 foot per minute descent. My front-seat passenger raised an eyebrow at the change.

"Emergency in Mashient," I shouted over engine noise. "Snakebite."

He nodded understanding.

I recalculated: 12 minutes away, I needed to dump 4,000 feet of suddenly extra altitude without shocking the engine or popping eardrums. Easy to do normally, but not when moments stole life. I increased descent rate to 350 fpm and added more power. "Lord," I prayed, "Get me there now!" But no airstrip appeared, and the jungle slid below at the same predictable pace.

On the ground, the radio's first reports proved true. The 12-year-old granddaughter of Andrés, the former village chief and my friend, writhed on a blanket next to the plane. Venom rampaged unchecked swelling her arm green and black well beyond the vine tourniquet squeezing above her right elbow. Conscious cry alternated with unconscious convulsion as I strapped her into the seat behind me. No time to move cargo. No time to make a patient's pad on the floor. No time left for her. Only half those treated within four hours of a bite survived. They had carried her six hours to the airstrip, then waited 20 minutes for me. I was looking at 35 minutes to Shell and another 10 to get her into a doctor's hands.

In the air again, max continuous power and a flat climb still yielded only what creation's constraints permitted. No supernatural performance surge, no divine tailwind. She flailed behind me, then wailed. Flail, then wail. Flail, then wail—but weaker.

At Shell, a car pulled up as the propeller stopped. I jumped out, unbuckled and lifted her silent body, then turned and placed her onto the back seat. Was she still breathing? The car moved off the ramp and onto the road to the hospital. In the quiet, I sighed, "Lord, I did all I could, but she really needs a miracle," then repented for the implied rebuke.

Two days later, I greeted the morning's passengers. In the normal crowd of dads, moms, babies, baskets, and bags, a familiar face caught my eye. A bright, smiling girl sat, swinging dangled legs, waiting to return home to Mashient. Miracle indeed.

COCA FAMILY

Despite our best efforts to pretend otherwise, air ambulance flights always twisted something inside. We pilots watched doctors' cool, nurses' compassion, and of course, followed our aviator's code of always having the "Right Stuff," always unperturbed, in control, calm, collected, almost bored. We wanted to help, were there to help, were trained to help, but some medical evacuation flights challenged our calm core.

Stationed at our Quito base high in the Andes Mountains, I responded to an emergency call from the north-eastern jungle town of Coca. The small city, at only 800 feet elevation, lay at the junction of two major rivers, Rio Napo and Rio Coca. It marked the frontier between two distinct economic regions—rich, developed oil fields to the north and wild untapped potential to the south. Coca resembled a North American "Wild-West" town, attracting anyone seeking opportunity. Its airport featured a 7,500-by-90-foot paved runway and operating control tower.

The call came from the Ministry of Health hospital saying only that the patient had suffered severe burns in an explosion. After taking off in the Quito-based aircraft, a C-206, I climbed northeast to go around the north side of the 19,000-foot volcano Cayambe. Once out of the Quito valley, the Andes foothill ridges disappeared under a low cloud layer. I flew in excellent visibility well above them, so stayed at 13,500 feet in visual conditions. But that could change quickly. I passed the great mountain, Ecuador's third highest, on my right, looking up at its permanent snowcap. Its last eruption occurred in 1786. Then, when I could see the jungle, I turned right, rounded the corner and headed southeast directly toward Coca. I started a high-speed cruise descent and got a clearance from ATC (Air Traffic Control) to penetrate a lower cloud deck over the jungle. Forty-five minutes after taking off from Quito's Andean heights, I landed in the depths of the Amazon Jungle.

I taxied off the runway close to the gate opening onto the road. Just as I got out of the airplane, an ambulance arrived, opened the gate, and drove around to the right side of the airplane. I opened the main cargo doors and indicated the pad I'd prepared.

An attendant walked over, handing me a thick stack of papers. Thick stack? Patients usually had one, perhaps two forms. I asked. He explained. The family was butchering a pig. As a normal part of the process, they slowly turned the carcass over a hot fire to burn the hair off the skin before cutting it into pieces. It was a big pig and they needed a bigger fire. A family member tossed a gallon can of kerosene onto the fire. But the can contained gasoline.

The explosion killed one child immediately. A second died en route to the airport. The rest had second- and third-degree burns over most of their bodies. They needed expert treatment quickly to survive, treatment the frustrated Coca medics couldn't provide.

"Lord," I said aloud in English, not caring if the driver heard or understood, "I need your help to help these people. I'm not set up to carry them all. But if I don't ... more will die. What do I do?" I closed my eyes and waited a moment. I walked to the ambulance—a small pickup truck with a shell over the bed that covered bench seats along either side.

The mother lay on a stretcher in the middle. Dad, two kids, and the baby sat on the benches. Bright pink startled me. The explosion had burned off most of their brown skin. They stared silent, shocked. I closed my eyes again, set my internal emotion switch to the "Off" position, opened my eyes, and tried to smile.

I had two problems. First, where to put them? No room to lay them all down. Second, how to get oxygen to them? The flight back would take us to 16,000 feet, maybe higher. They might not survive a half hour at that altitude. I needed three airplanes and a medical staff. Not just one plane and me.

Their arrangement in the truck provided a clue. We laid the

mother down on the pad. I seated the father in the copilot's seat next to me and the three-year-old boy in the middle-row seat directly behind me. Then I put his eight-year-old sister in the left-side rear seat behind him. She was in the best shape of them all, so I asked her to hold the baby, a normal task for her.

All six oxygen masks were aboard, and the tank was full. I connected them all to the built-in system and helped them place the masks on their faces. I didn't have a small mask for the baby but showed the girl how to hold it onto the infant's face.

They winced as I buckled their harnesses. When I gave the required safety briefing, dad nodded feebly, mom's eyes stayed closed, the girl in back seemed to follow, her brother stared at nothing. I struggled to keep my emotion circuit turned off, reminding myself only professional flying would help them. I had to hurry but also forced myself to slow down, do each step in order and not skip any.

In the air, I set max continuous power and calculated a climb rate to get me to the minimum required instrument crossing altitude—16,000 feet— just as I reached OLMEDO intersection.

ATC cleared me for the route. But when I reached OLMEDO, the clouds had risen. Not a problem—unless there was ice. The temperature sat in the middle of the icing range, so I asked ATC for a higher altitude and they gave me 18,000 feet, which kept me in the clear.

After passing Cayambe again, then turning southwest directly toward Quito, holes appeared in the clouds below, revealing clear air over the city. Past the higher terrain, ATC gave me a descent. A few minutes later, after the frequency change, the tower agreed to call the HCJB hospital for two ambulances and gave me landing priority ahead of another aircraft. I landed and taxied onto our lumpy, borrowed ramp.

Everyone seemed no worse, but I left the oxygen on until the ambulances arrived. Then, with the medics' help, we removed the masks. As we pulled them away from their faces, remaining original skin peeled off with the masks. In a few minutes they left aboard the ambulances and I was alone with my thoughts and five rubber masks to clean.

House Calls

Son and Father

Bruce Mertz, a missionary doctor, seemed oblivious to our flight. How could anyone ignore surrounding beauty and three-dimensional life? After locating Corrientes, our next destination, I glanced toward the copilot seat. Head down, he read a photocopied article, then compared it to a page in his bound notebook.

We'd just left Bufeo after nearly an hour on the ground while Bruce examined his patients. Each suffered from Leishmaniasis, a tropical disease spread by sand-fly bites; it caused growing skin ulcers, always growing, usually disfiguring, and sometimes fatal.

Now on the short, nine-minute flight to his next batch of subjects, I thought he'd take a break. But no. His research into possible treatment options absorbed all his attention. He raised his head briefly when I tapped his shoulder and pointed, looked at the village we circled and returned to his notes.

Not a problem really. He concentrated on his work, I focused on mine. We didn't come to Corrientes (literally, "currents") often, so I flew an extra lap around the pattern to double check its condition. The 950-foot long runway was shorter than most of our strips, its 39-foot width only slightly more than my C-180's 35-foot wingspan. I definitely wanted to stay in the middle of the strip. Lying in a range of low jungle hills and built onto the side of a knoll, it offered only one way for landing—uphill, and the opposite downhill direction for takeoff.

The surface looked dry, but the grass high. Okay to land, but how much would it affect takeoff? We were light with just Bruce, me, and his treatment bag on board. I lined up on final approach, held the spot, and touched down three airplane lengths in from the end. I rolled uphill a short distance, stopping by the large turnaround area midfield on my right. The residents had cut into the low bank creating a rectangular parking area with exposed dirt walls on three sides. An airy stand of tall thin trees topped the bank. The entire surface of the runway and ramp lay covered in knee-high grass. Wet, it would've presented a dangerous problem, but dry, only a nuisance if attempting a heavy takeoff.

A few residents emerged from the trees and descended the short stairway carved into the bank. We accompanied them into the village. Along the way, Bruce explained he came to examine only his patients today. Could they call them? One of the men spoke to a gaggle of kids, who then scattered with their invitations.

We entered a thatched roof pole house. More kids vacated a simple bench, then Bruce and I accepted the offered seat. Bruce and the health promoter chatted for a few minutes until Bruce's patients arrived. As in Bufeo, I could see the disease in various stages—from a small scrape on a forearm, to a man's ravaged face, nose mostly consumed.

He spoke with each one, sometimes in Spanish—their second language—other times through an Atshuar interpreter, asking questions, listening intently to their answers, then writing in his notebook. An hour later, he finished. We rose and, with a small entourage, descended the dirt stairs, then swish-swished our way back to the airplane. I retied Bruce's single bag, accepted a couple small parcels and mail from residents. After more goodbyes, we returned to the air, heading west toward Shell.

#

Three months later, to the day, Bruce and I flew together again. This time his father, an ophthalmologist, rode with us. Our first stop, the Shuar village of Panientza, lay on the south bank of the

Cangaime River just eight miles from Ecuador's southern border with Peru. A long-simmering territorial dispute between the two nations made not crossing the border a high navigational priority. Unfortunately, that part of the Amazon Jungle was far enough east of the Andes Mountains to appear Kansas flat—from the air, one part looked exactly like any other area within 20 miles. Fortunately, we flew on a clear day that easily allowed finding the Cangaime River's distinct bend at Panientza. And Panientza's large airstrip—1,800 feet long by 50 feet wide—provided an obvious beacon itself.

In a larger C-185 this time, I taxied to the unloading area and helped the two doctors disembark. After re-securing the remaining cargo, I took off again to take an HCJB missionary to the village of Shiramentza just two minutes flight time north. After dropping him off, I returned to Panientza in time to help the doctors.

Bruce had assembled his research patients, but his father's visit was a surprise. When I walked into the hut from the airstrip, they were still trying to organize how the ophthalmologist could examine patients. He spoke neither Spanish nor Shuar, while none of the local residents spoke English. I turned out to be the solution.

We set up the impromptu eye clinic in a thatched roofed, partially walled house. Sunlight streamed between the split bamboo wall behind me. A similar wall closed off the far end of the house. The walls on my right and left, however, were completely open to the outside. Fortunately, the hard-packed dirt floor didn't produce much dust.

Three of us sat on benches arranged on three sides of a small table. The fourth side of the table pressed close to the bamboo wall. On one side of the table sat a village man fluent in Shuar and Spanish. To his right, at the head facing us, sat the doctor, who spoke only English. Continuing around to the doctor's right, I sat, speaking English and reasonable Spanish.

The first patient approached the doctor, who rose,

surrendering his seat. The patient sat and described her symptoms in Shuar. The man to the doctor's left faced me across the table and translated the patient's Shuar into Spanish. I, in turn, faced the doctor and translated into English. Then the doctor asked a question in English. I repeated it in Spanish. The man across from me spoke to the patient in Shuar. The patient then answered in Shuar ... and so on.

Panientza was a bigger village, so Bruce needed two hours to complete his exams. That gave his dad time to see a remarkable number of patients. To some, he recommended reading glasses (not available in the jungle but added to a list for the next villager's trip to a town with a store). To others, he prescribed medicine the health promoter could administer. And to still others, he recommended hospital treatment. The health promoter noted those also for later coordination.

As Bruce finished, his dad and I wrapped up the eye exams. We all boarded the airplane, took off and headed 40 miles almost due north to the Shuar village of Iñaywa near, but not on, the Huasaga River. Bruce studied his notes. His dad watched the scenery. I reflected that this 20-minute flight to our new destination would take weeks to complete on foot.

We landed on Iñaywa's long, 1,600-foot, one-way, uphill airstrip and repeated the pattern set in the south—Bruce examined his study's patients, while his dad, a Shuar-Spanish translator, and I conducted another eye clinic. We finished an hour later and made the 30-minute flight back to Shell.

MIRIAM

I knelt on the cement ramp outside the hangar. The sun beat down from a clear sky and the heat rose, washing over my face. Two days with neither rain nor clouds drew latent moisture from tree, grass, and ground, turning Shell into a sauna. Trucks, buses and cars passed over the dirt road in front of the hangar, churning up a high ribbon of dust that drifted, depositing grit everywhere. If those conditions persisted for a third day, we would declare a drought.

Fortunately, the C-185's big wing provided enough shade so Miriam Gebb and I both had room to sort her medicines and medical instruments. As an HCJB missionary nurse-practitioner, Miriam oversaw village health promoter training. Her program included conducting short clinics in her students' villages to treat patients not sick enough for an emergency evacuation.

Miriam devised a clever storage system to safely carry her valuable cargo. She found a store in town selling thick, rubberized plastic dishwashing tubs about 18 inches long, 10 inches wide and 6 inches high. The brightly colored tubs—red, orange, green, blue—had a handhold slot cut into the lip at each end. One of the hospital's maintenance crew cut plywood sheets with rounded corners and varnish finish that fit into the top of each tub. To that, he added a 20-inch-long by 2-inch-wide plank. Miriam covered a full tub with the wooden top. Then she inserted a plank through the slots, holding the top firmly in place.

We sorted according to her directions, covered and fastened a full tub, then I placed it into the C-185's cargo pod. After I pushed in the eighth and final tub, she handed me her "just in case" overnight bag. We were headed for Molino, so I loaded a couple homeward-bound passengers into the airplane, put their cargo into the pod and fastened the door. Miriam, a bush air-travel veteran, climbed into the copilot seat and buckled her harness. I climbed up the other side of the airplane, strapped in to my office and wondered, *Is it right that I feel more at home in the sky than on the ground? I get to do life in three dimensions AND serve you too, Lord. How can that be bad?*

Miriam chattered as we flew. A cheerful, smiling woman, she seemed happiest when working the hardest, when serving those least able to help themselves. Thirty minutes after takeoff we circled over Molino. I landed and taxied to a wide spot mid-field that allowed me to get off the runway, leaving it open in case someone else needed to land. We exited the airplane, greeted and shook hands with our hosts. Then we headed toward a larger thatched roof event center built up on the plateau next to the strip rather than down by the river with the rest of the village.

Kids carried Miriam's tubs to the temporary clinic the health promoter had set up for her visit. A crowd of patients already formed and waited for her attention. I walked farther up the airstrip hill to a small cabin with closed walls of split bamboo. It housed the village radio and battery, guarded by a solid, locking door. The solar panel sat atop the roof and the antenna support pole towered above that.

Rats sometimes chewed insulation off wires, so we enclosed both radio and battery in heavy wooden boxes. Then the village authorities moved the radio into the enclosed cabin. But the resourceful rodents attacked again. I had to replace the two battery connections—easy—and the mutilated antenna connection— difficult.

Thirty minutes later I returned to Miriam. A crowd, larger than when I left, waited outside her work area. The health promoter sat with her while she examined patients. A couple helpers regulated the flow. Somehow, despite twisted, muddy, thorn-edged paths, word spread quickly that a medic had arrived. The people literally came out of the woods, more than I ever imagined lived nearby. For many, Miriam was the only medical person they would ever see in their lives. So, the visit was important. Unfortunately, it wasn't the only important thing we had to deal with.

I checked my watch. We had to take off in an hour. That meant propeller turning in an hour, not starting to say goodbye. Miriam's schedule listed a meeting back in Shell. Other passengers, equally eager to get home, waited for me to fly them. But jungle folks measured time differently than North Americans. Minutes mattered to me. Hours made me sweat. They exhibited far greater patience. Their smallest practical time increment spanned a quarter day.

Fifteen minutes passed. Miriam and the health promoter examined patients. The crowd remained the same size. Another 15 minutes passed, but no let up.

"Miriam, I think it's time to activate our plan," I said to her in English.

She looked up from a patient, nodded, then pointed in Indian fashion with her chin and pursed lips, saying, "You can start taking the tubs I put in that corner."

I picked up two already there, walked to the airplane, slid them into the pod and returned. A minute later she pushed a third tub into the code area. I placed a top on, secured it with a plank and took it to the airplane. As she continued talking with patients and the health promoter, I shuttled tubs. Finally, she looked up, saw no tubs, then said to those still waiting. "I'm sorry, but the pilot said we have to go now. You know how they are."

They all turned toward me and nodded, echoing the common knowledge of a pilot's role as "bad guy." We walked to the plane, I loaded two passengers headed for Shell, their luggage, cargo for market, bags of food for high school students in town, and the mail. Miriam took her seat. I sat in mine. In a few minutes, we were in the air again, flying to the next need.

PAYING FOR IT

Flying dreams sounded good, but I remained a penniless hippie. Danny moved out to live with his girlfriend. I relocated the tent from the beach to a field a mile from school. An older widow lived in a farmhouse and rented a room to a fellow student. She needed extra income but had no other room to rent. Instead, she allowed me to set up my tent under a tree in her front yard a half mile back from the country road. I laid out six pallets, two by three, then set the tent atop that platform. My rent included use of the bathroom and kitchen in the house. It also included connection to a long extension cord.

My GI Bill covered fees at the community college, books, gas for the motorcycle, and food. Most days I ate a bowl of granola, powdered milk and water in the morning, a 25-cent green salad at the school snack bar for lunch, and a 50-cent yogurt for dinner. I needed more.

About the time I moved from the beach to the farm, I met a man who just returned from a year in Italy learning to make jewelry using the lost-wax casting method. Ancient Egyptians receive credit for its development, but other cultures used it as well. The Bible's Old Testament records two artisans, Bezalel and Oholiab, who brought that skill to the Israelites in the desert. They used the technique to cast bronze, silver, and gold pieces for the tabernacle. Hundreds of years later King Solomon employed Hiram to cast huge pillars for the temple using similar methods.

The process intrigued me. He agreed to train me. First, I created the object, say a ring, entirely out of wax. Then I attached wax branches to the ring, bringing them together like a tree trunk. Next, I placed the assembly into a short length of steel pipe. I filled the pipe with a fine plaster mix, being sure to leave the very end of the trunk sticking out the end. When the plaster dried, I fired the wax/plaster mold in a kiln to harden the plaster and burn off all the wax. When done, the mold contained a cavity in exactly the shape of my wax original. I placed the hot mold into a large centrifuge. Next, I put pieces of metal—

bronze, copper, silver or gold—into its crucible. I then used a torch to melt the metal into a shiny, molten puddle. After scraping dross off the top of the puddle, I spun the centrifuge. That slammed the metal into the mold, filling every opening and crevice. When the centrifuge stopped spinning, I used tongs to pull the still-hot mold out and thrust it into a bucket of cold water. The hot mold boiled the bucket full of water into steam and, at the same time, dissolved the plaster. That left an ugly tree with a ring in its top. Finally, I used fine hand tools to cut the ring out of the branches, then smooth and polish the metal into the final piece.

Allie, the farm widow, allowed me to move an old camper from the back of her property over to a spot 10 feet from my tent. I ran another electric cord and soon had a small workshop to practice my newly acquired skill.

My ex-roommate saw my work and asked me to make rings for his upcoming wedding. The first set I made looked good but fell apart when handled. I created a new wax master, then reused the gold to cast a new set. The second try not only looked better but stayed together.

A few days later another couple on campus asked me to make their wedding rings. And then another. And another after that. I never advertised, but individuals and couples tracked me down to make pieces for them. I never lacked work. Before long, my biggest challenge became managing study, jewelry making, and flight lesson time. Even though, as I later learned, I woefully undercharged for my work, jewelry making provided enough income for me to complete the Private Pilot license course within three months.

GIDEON FLIGHT

Smooth, even gray overcast spread in early morning light as far east as we could see from the runway's end. "Not sure this'll work, Rusty," I said to the tall man beside me. "Let's see what the villages report."

Rusty nodded, glancing sideways at his white-haired companion, retired General Bolivar.

I walked back into the hangar and stopped at the radio desk. The Flight Coordinator began the morning radio contact. Villages started reporting.

"Villano, medium ceiling, no rain."

"Moretecocha, medium ceiling, no rain."

"Molino, medium ceiling, no rain."

"Conombo, medium ceiling, no rain."

"Nuevo Corrientes, medium ceiling, no rain."

No word, of course, from our destinations—all military bases. But the village reports painted a weather picture worth checking. We'd be in clouds a lot, but the *medium* ceilings would permit a visual descent down to our minimum allowable altitude. The regulations governing flight in instrument weather conditions over this part of the Amazon Jungle were deceptively simple. The few radio navigation aids defined broad sectors, each with its own minimum descent altitude. Let ATC (Air Traffic Control) know your present position, cruising altitude, intended route, and estimate for next checkpoint and you were good to go. When you neared your destination, descend to the minimum sector altitude. If you could see the ground, keep going. If not, turn around, climb, and go home. The system worked well enough for Amazon Jungle airspace where we'd be the only airplane in hundreds of cubic miles of cloud. It didn't protect us from drug runners sneaking a shortcut from Columbia to Peru, but they'd be a risk even in a more robust system.

Only three of us on this flight, so earlier I unfastened the C-180's aft bench seat, folded its legs, then tied it flat up against the aft bulkhead. Since this airplane had no cargo pod, I filled the cargo area behind our seats with several cardboard boxes, securing them under the net.

Rusty's just-in-case bag lay under the net among the boxes. Mine occupied the customary pilot's spot under my seat. I offered to stow the general's gray cotton bag, but he asked to hold it. Looked small enough, so I said okay.

Rusty climbed into the copilot's seat. The general chose the center-row seat behind him, expertly fastening his lap belt and shoulder harness. Made sense. One of the mods we added to our aircraft were military grade safety harnesses. He'd obviously used them before.

General Bolivar presented an enigma. He'd been part of a military junta ruling Ecuador between civilian governments and, reportedly, a likely candidate for president until he fell out of favor. Later, while in prison because of political enemies, he surrendered his life to Jesus. After release and retirement, he joined the Gideons. Now, grandfatherly looking, he spoke with soft, but direct words. Accustomed to wielding power, he offered an easy smile with no strutting.

Rusty, a North American living in Ecuador, owned and managed a restaurant in Quito called "Rusty's," with his red hair and mustache its logo. He and the general represented the Quito chapter of Gideons International. Our mission that day: Help the general distribute Bibles to soldiers stationed at remote jungle bases.

The tower cleared me to fly direct to our destination. Tiputini lay 158 nautical miles, or about an hour and 20 minutes, straight ahead. As we climbed past 4,000 feet on the way to 7,000 feet, mottled green hills disappeared. We entered the clouds, and featureless gray engulfed us. Little danger of icing this low in the tropics, but I checked the outside air temperature and turned on the pitot heat anyway.

A bit more than 10 minutes after takeoff, we reached an official reporting point, an electronic intersection in the sky, 20 nautical miles from Shell. Twenty miles farther out, the signal became too weak to use, so I switched to dead-reckoning navigation—hold a given compass course, for a given time, at a known airspeed.

Dead-reckoning flight inside featureless gray cloud, over uninhabited Amazon Jungle felt timeless, placeless, an intermediate space somewhere between imagination and reality. The buzz, crackle and occasional voice over the HF radio offered sole testimony that we were still near planet Earth. Rusty and the general dozed. I held heading with my feet and altitude with my left hand. My right index finger slowly moved across the map on my lap, approximating where I thought we were.

And just controlling the airplane inside the clouds, where ground and horizon remained invisible, required special equipment and training. Located directly in front of me, a cluster of six instruments gave me the information I needed. Interpreting their readings to achieve safe flight required a skill called "The Scan."

I looked first at the center dial—one of six aircraft performance instruments—to verify wings and nose level. From there I looked at the second, then returned to the center. Then the third and returned to the center. Then the fourth and returned. And the fifth. Then I did it again. And again. And again. Every few scan cycles, I also included engine instruments, outside air temperature gauge, vacuum gauge, ammeter, fuel gauges, radios, map, passengers, doors, weather, etc. for the duration of the flight inside the clouds.

Finally, it was time to recheck my descent calculations. Tiputini's elevation is 722 feet above sea level. I wanted to reach the standard pattern altitude of 1,000 feet above the ground (1,722 feet above sea level) before I arrived over the strip. But we were at 7,000 feet. That meant I had to lose 5,000 feet. In non-pressurized aircraft, we limited the descent rate to 500 feet per minute so our passengers' ear equalization could keep up. Descending too fast guaranteed major pain for the uninitiated. So, dividing 5,000 by 500 told me I should allow 10 minutes to reach the lower altitude. Given a descent speed of 130 knots, I then calculated we'd cover 22 miles. But dead-reckoning for so long in the clouds meant my position estimate could be 5 miles off. I had to give myself time and room to hunt for the base and its airstrip once we broke out underneath the clouds—if we did.

The terrain beneath us was entirely flat jungle, so the authorized minimum descent altitude for that sector was 2,000 feet. When I reached that altitude, I had to either encounter visual conditions under the clouds or else climb back to cruise altitude and return to Shell. Given our position ambiguity and our proximity to the Peruvian border—only 13 miles from the base—I decided to start the descent 30 miles out. That gave me plenty of time to find where the smaller Tiputini River ran into the Napo River. The military base lay at the junction.

My finger touched the 30-mile spot on the map. I eased the control yoke very slightly forward. That lowered the nose and the airplane began a descent. I then trimmed the controls to hold a constant airspeed and descent rate. Awake people compensate for pressure changes more easily than sleepers, so I woke my snoozing passengers.

"We've started our descent. Should be there in about 14 minutes," I said.

Both nodded understanding while looking intently at cloud innards the same gray as those near Shell. After a few minutes, Rusty dozed off again, but the general kept looking out the right side of the plane.

Nine minutes later we popped out the bottom of the clouds at 2,500 feet. Visibility underneath was good, better than Shell. I started hunting for rivers. The massive Napo River angling toward me from the left was impossible to miss. But where along it were we? I estimated Tiputini still about six miles ahead, but Ecuador and Peru weren't the best of friends. An Ecuadorian-registered airplane wandering across the border would not receive a friendly reception.

I needed to find and follow the Tiputini River to the junction. But would that smaller river be on my left, or right? If the wind aloft hadn't been too strong, I expected to see it also coming in from my left. Amazon Jungle rain could produce a sizable river in just a few miles. Many on the chart displayed no name. Many on the ground didn't make the chart. And often trees overhanging from either bank met in the middle, completely obscuring the water from aerial eyes. So positively identifying a specific river required a skill more resembling art.

No distinct river beneath me or to the left, other than the obvious Napo. Couldn't see much to the right, south, unless I turned that way. Instead, I turned left directly toward the Napo. I spotted a distinctive bend near some large islands matching the chart. At the bend, I turned downriver again, keeping the big water well to my left so I could see any river joining its south bank.

I spotted the military base before I saw the river union. It lay on the northeast shore just upriver from the junction which I found a moment later. I turned left again to make the base easily visible from the right side of the airplane. Then, wanting absolute confirmation, I asked the general, "Is that it?"

He looked, gave me a thumbs up, then returned his gaze outside. I turned left to circle with the strip on my side of the airplane. I saw no control tower, but the general had sent messages ahead to expect him. I hoped that constituted permission to land. Since none of us MAF pilots had ever landed there before, I chose to do a strip inspection before committing to touch the ground.

I called Pancho on the HF, giving him our position over Tiputini, then said I'd call again if I decided to land. The Ecuadorian military routinely operated Israeli-made Aravas (a 15,000-pound, twin-engine turboprop) from this strip, so a little C-180 should have no difficulty fitting in. I flew another complete circuit, found nothing amiss on the ground nor with traffic in the air. The wind favored landing to the northeast, so I approached over the river, touched down about a hundred feet past the threshold and braked to a stop using less than a quarter of the strip. I pivoted the plane around and taxied back to an open area near the main base. Because they routinely handled bigger aircraft, I had no problem fitting the plane onto the grass ramp. I taxied forward, pivoted around once more to face the runway, and shut the engine down.

Looking out to my left, I saw soldiers already approaching the airplane. Quickly finishing the shutdown checklist and removing my helmet, I unstrapped, opened the door and hopped to the ground. An officer flanked by two armed soldiers on either side called to me. I noticed they carried their rifles at port-arms, ready to use, rather than on a sling over their shoulder.

The officer asked, "Who are you and why did you land here?" No smile. Business tone. His furrowed brow said this was not the time to be cute. I hoped my pilot shirt with its gold bar epaulets declared me official, legit, and most definitely not a Colombian drug runner.

"I'm Capitán Diego, from Alas de Socorro," I answered.

"This is a prohibited military base. You can't land here. What do you want?" he demanded.

Apparently, they were not expecting us. "We received permission ... " I started.

Suddenly, his eyes widened. His mouth dropped open. General Bolivar walked out from behind the far side of the airplane, around the nose, and toward us.

"General ... " the officer stammered. "I didn't know... No one told us ..." The soldiers with him stiffened to attention. The officer saluted even though the general wore civilian clothes.

"That is not a problem, Lieutenant. Can you take me to the base commandant?" he asked, smiling.

"Yes, yes, of course, sir. Please. Come this way ..." Then looking back at Rusty and me, he added, "and your guests as well."

He leaned toward one of the soldiers, spoke quietly. The soldier ran down the path ahead of us toward the base and disappeared around a bend.

Ten minutes later we sat at a linen-covered table on the officers' club screened veranda. The base commander and several officers sat around the general, chatting, smiling. A waiter took drink orders—in the morning, this far in the jungle, our choices were water, Coca-Cola, Fanta, or Sprite. The commandant, embarrassed, apologized for the lack of a proper reception. A severe lightning storm took out the base radios a few days before. Replacement equipment was coming, but in the meantime, the base communication with the outside world happened only via messages aboard Army aircraft.

They talked of family, friends, the weather, their health. Gracious, easy, friendly. The older officers talked, the younger spoke only when addressed. But the wide eyes and focused attention of old and young revealed the general's status—a father, even a patriarch. Rusty and I sat, listened, neither excluded nor included, not military, clearly foreigners, permitted in the private realm only because we fell within the general's aura.

Thirty minutes passed. Forty. Still no motion toward the general's main purpose. Inwardly, I covered the pilot's duty of worrying about the weather. Of course, I could do nothing about it, known or unknown. This affair was going to take the time it was going to take, and the weather would be whatever it would be. When it was finally time to fly, I'd know.

Then, as if by secret, prearranged signal, the base commander said, "Shall we go then?"

General Bolivar said, "If everyone's there, yes."

The commander nodded. He and the general rose. The rest of us followed. The general turned to Rusty and said, "Can you bring back ..." he looked up a moment, calculating, "... six boxes?"

The commandant added, "This soldier here will help carry them." I accompanied Rusty and the soldier to unlock the plane and make a radio call.

Rusty and his helper collected five boxes and returned to the base. I offered to bring the sixth. No rush. We had several minutes. I radioed our plans to Pancho. He said Shell weather hadn't changed. The other guys were flying under a jungle-wide low ceiling and no one reported rain. I set my box on the ground and started closing the airplane again. On the right side, I noticed the draw cord of the general's personal bag hanging across the doorframe. Apparently Rusty had brushed it while unloading. I pushed the cord back inside the cabin and the bag opened. A long-barreled, 45 caliber, 6-shot chrome revolver poked out the mouth.

Neither the general nor Rusty mentioned carrying arms. Surprise! I was supposed to know about weapons on board. We worked hard to remain apolitical, so normally we did not carry uniformed military personnel or their weapons. We didn't want to give any reason to think we represented any part of local power structures, nor any excuse to shoot at us. I saw five empty chambers. The sixth hid behind the barrel. Behind the grip, a box of bullets peeked out.

Should I call him on it? On one hand, he was carrying a small cannon. On the other, he didn't know our internal regulations. We missed asking him, so it was our fault. I considered a moment, then pushed the barrel back into the bag, pulled the draw cord tight and slid the bag all the way under the seat. The man had surrendered his life to God, but I wondered about the world he'd come out of. *What about his high-power life had made carrying this kind of weapon normal?*

I found a crowd in a large, covered amphitheater. Seeing Rusty off to one side, I walked up with the sixth box and stood next to him. "They've got every single soldier on the base here listening," he said.

Soldiers filled all seats but the front row, occupied by officers. The general told them how meeting this invisible, but very real, Jesus while in prison completely changed his life. He challenged them to surrender their lives, to try it for themselves. When he finished, the commandant said a few words, thanked the general for coming, then instructed each officer and soldier to take one of the gift Bibles we brought.

Rusty and I, along with four soldiers assigned to help us, stationed ourselves at the exits. We pulled out stacks of the small blue books, each one a Gideon Spanish language New Testament and Psalms combination. As the military men exited, we handed each one a copy. Some glanced back to see who watched, resigned to satisfying an officer's keen observation and, deciding not to take a chance, allowed me to place the offered gift in their hand. Others, however, eagerly pulled it from mine—some just because it was a free gift, and still others because they were hungry and hoped it had what they needed. A few thanked me.

We walked back to the officers' club and were served another Coke while the commandant and general chatted. After a few moments, an officer approached with three small boxes, presented one to the general, then one each to Rusty and me. Each box contained a hand-carved model canoe, paddle and display base. The unit patch graced the side of the canoe with their designation: BS-57 "Montecristi". The opposite side displayed the Ecuadorian seal and a phrase reading: "*Hacia El Amazonas Por La Ruta De Orellana*" (To the Amazon by Orellana's Route).

"You've honored us today, General." The true sentiment was more obvious in the Spanish they spoke. The commandant and other officers addressed him as '*mi general*' (my general) or '*mi padre*' (my father). They gave him respect and affection running deeper than mere military courtesy, as much for a beloved elder as a superior officer.

In a few minutes, I repacked and secured the cargo, confirmed Rusty and the general strapped in, and took off again. This time I turned southwest to 209 degrees and headed for the Ecuadorian Army base of Lorocachi. I decided to stay under the clouds at 2,000 feet—500 feet below the clouds and a bit more than 1,200 feet above the jungle canopy. The Lorocachi base was only 57 miles away. And more importantly, my course took me almost parallel to the Peruvian border, angling in closer. Lorocachi lay on the south bank of the Curaray River just 11 miles from the border, and I wanted to be absolutely sure I remained in Ecuadorian airspace.

After takeoff from Tiputini, I passed over the massive Napo River, then started counting major rivers—the Tiputini, a smaller no-name river, the Nashiño, the Cononaco, another tributary, and finally the Curaray. The junctions and distinctive bends agreed pretty much with the chart. In 30 minutes, I found Lorocachi right where it was supposed to be, descended slightly to the pattern altitude of 1,800 feet and circled the field to check it out.

Only a bit more than half the length of Tiputini, Lorocachi at 600 meters (1,992 feet) was still big. It ran NNE by SSW and, like many jungle strips, lay perpendicular to the river. The SSW end ran into a high hill, effectively barring any takeoff or go-around in that direction. The base buildings sat tightly clustered at the river end of the strip in an area dramatically open in a dense sea of trees. A tall radio tower at the north end of the base, next to the river, dominated the entire installation.

Lines of soldiers spanned the wide grass runway every hundred feet or so. Maneuvers? Physical training? Then their motion gave them away. They cut the grass with machetes. A good action in the long run, but they prevented me from landing. *How long would I have to wait?* I began a third circuit while also calculating my loiter time. I needed fuel for this landing, a flight to a third base at Montalvo, the flight back to Shell, and a one-hour reserve. I started writing numbers, but suddenly, as if every soldier heard the same command at the same time, Red Sea–like, the legion split down the middle and moved to either edge of the strip.

The wind still came from the north, so I continued around the pattern and landed over the hill toward the river. Machete-wielding soldiers, sweaty, grass-covered, lining both sides of the runway, stared as we taxied by. I found a parking space off the runway by the guard shack at the business end, nearest the river, taxied in, swung the tail around and shut down the motor. I jumped out quickly to meet a sergeant and his armed guard. They approached quickly with eyes set harder, brows furrowed deeper than Tiputini's reception committee.

"Why did you land here?" the sergeant demanded, then interrupted my explanation. "Are you from Alas de Socorro?"

"Yes, I'm Capitán Diego with Alas de Socorro." I pointed at our name on the airplane's tail.

"Good for you. Some here said you were a drug runner, that we should shoot you down, but my officer looked with the binoculars. He said everybody knows Alas de Socorro." His officer, a captain, approached. The sergeant stiffened, then demanded again, "Why did you land? This is a prohibited military base. You can't be here!"

The captain stood behind the group, watching. Said nothing. But then, as at Tiputini, General Bolivar walked out around the nose of the airplane. The officer's expression the same—wide eyes, open mouth, something between shock and astonishment. Without looking, he said to the sergeant, "That's all, Sergeant. Your men may secure their arms but keep them here ... as an honor guard."

The sergeant spoke. His soldiers relaxed their gaze and stance toward me, but then stiffened to attention when they saw the captain salute the general. Then they accompanied the captain and general to the commandant's office.

The other officers and the base commandant offered the same deference I witnessed at Tiputini. In just a few minutes every single soldier on the base sat in another covered amphitheater and listened to the general. After he spoke, Rusty, assigned helpers, and I distributed the little blue Bibles to the soldiers as they left.

As we walked back to the airstrip, the captain explained to me that the same severe lightning storms that took out the Tiputini radios had also damaged theirs. They had no idea that General Bolivar was coming. We reached the airstrip, repacked the remaining cargo, boarded and took off again, headed for a third military base at Montalvo.

In the air, I turned left to 244 degrees for the 38-minute flight.

We flew away from the border, so I wasn't worried about Peru but decided to stay low anyway. The visibility was good underneath, but the ceiling was below that sector's instrument minimum descent altitude. Montalvo had no official instrument approach for civilian aircraft, so if I ascended into the clouds, I'd be stuck up there until I reached Shell.

Montalvo's 4,800-foot-long paved runway posed no challenge to find. The airport, a joint military/civilian facility, served several surrounding villages. Oil companies exploring in that part of the jungle used Montalvo as their principal aerial supply base, constructing the civilian ramp at the east end. The Department of Civil Aviation installed an official control tower as well. The military base placed their large taxi-in/taxi-out ramp at the runway's west end but occupied the land between the south side of the runway and the Bobonaza River.

We flew into Montalvo frequently, so we and the tower operators were well acquainted. But they did ask me to confirm that I wanted to park at the military end. I explained who I had on board. When I shut down on the military ramp, an officer and honor guard waited to greet us. This visit duplicated the others: The officers showed the general near-reverential respect. All base activity stopped. Every soldier assembled. We distributed Bibles.

I planned a direct flight back to Shell, but after takeoff I diverted to Pacayacu for an emergency flight. We'd distributed almost all the Bibles and burned most of the fuel, so I could carry the weight, but worried balance and room might present a problem. I flew 30 minutes to Pacayacu under a lowering ceiling. After landing at the 1,250-foot grass strip, I found the patient, a young woman with a badly broken arm who truly needed the flight. Though in pain, she could sit up. After confirming the aircraft center of gravity would still be within limits, I reinstalled the back seat and tied the little remaining cargo over its right end. Then I buckled the patient's husband into the left end. Finally, I placed the woman in the seat behind me. After all the normal checks, we took off.

Pacayacu was only 15 minutes from Shell, but the ceiling had lowered enough to make an instrument approach into Shell necessary. After takeoff I called approach control, who cleared me up to 6,000 feet in the soup. In a few minutes, I shot the instrument approach, broke out of the clouds at 200 feet above minimums and landed. The Gideons had returned.

Inside-Out Heart

We served a tribe the outside world called "Aucas," but who called themselves "Waorani." Their fierce reputation kept foreigners at bay for hundreds of years until the unlikely intervention of three women and a girl (see Chapter 27, *Flying Rachel*). But after the killing stopped, the outside world encroached again. So they tried a new strategy. Rather than spearing foreigners, they chose to manage the invasion. They built airstrips, then invited school teachers, doctors, and missionaries into their villages, and sent patients and shoppers out.

Anyone entering the jungle confronted a stark choice—walk for days or fly for minutes. To reach the Waorani village of Toñompade required one to two weeks on foot or 30 minutes by air. Most regular tourists came to our hangar first, but we referred them back to the commercial operators. Our government contract prohibited us from doing commercial flights unless the commercial operators didn't serve a specific strip, or they declined a request. However, that same contract allowed us to include anyone part of our mission work. So, we accepted what I called "mission tourists" if they enhanced a missionary's work or encouraged the local church.

Every few weeks a group of them arrived in Shell wanting to see the "Aucas" firsthand and visit "Palm Beach." Although they showed interest in our work and often volunteered to help, I privately chafed at their cultural insensitivity and resented their intrusion. In the four decades since the tribe first drew public attention, these well-meaning folks still didn't know the moniker "Auca" was the jungle equivalent of "nigger." And what about our mission work? We received more requests than we could handle.

We were too busy for looky-loos.

When they requested a flight, we asked for names, weights, days they could fly (changing weather and emergencies dismantled precise schedules), where they were staying (usually a guest house or hostel), then worked out the procedure for making the final go/no-go decision on flight day. We briefed them on:

What to wear—bug repellant applied from feet to waist before dressing, long pants, long-sleeve shirt, shoes okay to get muddy, and a hat.

What to bring—camera, local money in small bills, bottled water, passport copy, snacks, and 2–3 days' vital meds.

Who they'd meet—friendly people in varying stages of dress whom they should neither call "Aucas" nor whose intelligence they should underestimate.

What to expect—mud, bugs, heat, humidity, thorny plants, moldy trees, tippy canoes, offers of food they should decline, and offers of handcrafts they should buy.

Attitude—listen, learn, don't point, and smile a lot.

We explained the trip would take at least four hours and could easily expand to all day. It also offered the small, but real, possibility that weather, emergencies, mechanical issues, or political unrest might prevent us from picking them up the same day they arrived. We never took people into the jungle later than two days before their scheduled international flight. Finally, we radioed Toñompade to request a guide and canoe for the planned visit date.

On the scheduled day, the passengers arrived one hour before takeoff. If the trip remained feasible, we radioed Toñompade to confirm our arrival time. We weighed the passengers (unpopular among North American women) and their luggage. They, bigger and heavier than the Ecuadorian indigenous folks, usually filled the plane. That precluded combining the flight with other mission passengers going into the jungle, but it provided a good combination for people and cargo coming out. Normally, after landing in Toñompade, we turned them over to their guide. Then we flew to other places to do real work. We retrieved them later in the day. They were happy. I pretended.

One morning Gene called me into his office and said, "Ken and Carol Frizzell are coming to visit the Ecuador program." Ken, MAF's Director of Operations, was Gene's boss's boss. Clearly important news. Gene continued, "Take them to Palm Beach, but, stick with them all the way to the beach and back. They don't mind jungle, but they don't speak Spanish."

"Okay." I nodded, flattered I'd been chosen to fly the "Big Boss." Ken and Carol served MAF ten years in Indonesia. Ken flew the jungles of Iran Jaya and Kalimantan, helping discover and contact tribes unknown to the outside world. So, no, jungle shouldn't be a problem for them.

On flight day another couple, Lee and Bonnie, joined the tour. Five of us North Americans filled the Cessna 185. But all were slim, and an out-and-back flight required less fuel, keeping the plane's weight and balance within limits.

Early morning rain and cloud cleared, leaving leaf and branch sparkling as we climbed toward the rising sun. Quiet, intense excitement filled the cabin, eclipsing my internal grumbler. I added "tour guide" to professional pilot role and, in between required radio reports, began a running monologue over the engine roar.

"The Andes Mountains stop right here." I motioned over my shoulder with my right thumb. "Ahead," I pointed forward, "this plateau we're over now is at 3,000 feet elevation. In about 10 miles it drops to 1,200 feet. After that, it takes another 2,500 miles to get down to sea level. That's one reason the Amazon Jungle holds so much water. It's very flat."

Right on cue, we flew over the edge. One of the ladies gasped. Thousand-foot cliffs plunged beneath us into the deeper jungle below. At their base, a convoluted jumble of tree-covered hills gave way to a broad, flat valley. A river appeared before us, magically—it seemed—springing from dense forest. The Beast, watered by 21 feet of rain a year, produced an impressive river quickly, sending it pointing in the same direction we flew. *How did it know?*

"The ridges on either side of this valley," I continued, "come close together there in front of us." I pointed to a spot 20 miles ahead where the valley narrowed to a small notch. "The Curaray River runs through that notch. Toñompade, the village the killers came from, is just beyond. We'll fly through that notch and stay over the river so I can give you a good view of Palm Beach. We'll circle a few times then head to the airstrip."

Ken nodded, peered ahead almost carrying the airplane.

Ten minutes later we flew through the narrows. The river hugged the right-hand ridge, but the land opened a little to the left, allowing enough space for the village. We bent right to stay over the water. Thousands of sand and gravel bars dot the Amazon Jungle's river banks, forming wherever hydraulic law dictated. Of all those, however, only one received a name. As we reached Palm Beach, I slid the airplane left, then entered a right circle to keep it in view. Ken was in the airplane, but also on the ground and in the space between. After a couple of circles, I reversed direction to give those on my side a good view. After the second circle, I leveled the airplane and headed toward Toñompade, just a mile away.

I passed above the east end of the strip, banked steeply left, but cross-controlled the ailerons *[control surfaces on each wing used to bank the airplane]* with lots of right rudder to continue flying straight. That tipped the airplane but let me check the entire runway surface for obstructions, standing water, and soft spots. No obstructions. Good. No standing water. Good. Mud color? Dark. Not good, but not surprising. It rained midmorning. Not enough time to dry yet, so I got ready for the slip-slide dance.

#

Toñompade had its own special kind of mud. When dry, its

hard, undulating surface pounded landing gears, mercilessly ignoring even the best pilot technique. Wet, its inner animal emerged, turning potter's clay soft—sticky and slippery at the same time. At landing speeds, I could brake until the wheels stopped turning, but the aircraft would continue sliding. At taxi speeds, it turned into clingy glue clutching rolling wheels. But brake one wheel to pivot the airplane and it slid like ice. Then, once the airplane headed straight, the mud wrapped a two-inch thick grass, pebble, and clay blanket around the tires.

Not removing the blanket made takeoffs more interesting—particularly the C-185's. As the wheels spun faster, grapefruit-sized clods would spray wildly into the air, coating fuselage and wings. And a few of the bigger clumps always arced inward, splatting across the center of the windscreen. At that point an abort would break the airplane, offering the pilot no choice but to continue the takeoff. Only two solutions remained. Either find a rain shower to fly through or else land at the next short, obstructed, slippery one-way strip with forward vision blocked.

I imagined, and could almost see, a malevolent, mud-controlling intelligence clinging gargoyle-like to a nearby tree, snickering as I wrestled the airplane about. Toñompade mud required its own special consideration.

I continued turning left, leveled the wings briefly, then turned right to enter a right downwind. I chose to land east because the wind favored that direction and also offered the best go-around option. And it allowed me to position the airplane where I could park off the runway surface in case someone else wanted to land.

There were, however, two drawbacks. The first was that I'd have to pivot in the mud twice—once so I could taxi back to the takeoff position after loading passengers and cargo, then a second time when I reached the takeoff position to face back to the east. It was possible to take off toward the higher terrain to the west, but not with that day's wind, nor with a fully loaded airplane.

The second drawback to landing toward the east offered the kind of fun pilots enjoyed, but passengers not so much.

Toñompade sat in a bowl formed by a bend in the Curaray River, tight against higher terrain on the west and north with the river running parallel along its south side. To land to the east, I flew downwind leg over the river, which put the airstrip off the right side of the airplane. That made it harder to see anything or anyone on the runway. Then for base leg and final approach, I tucked into a tight right turn over the sloping terrain. I liked the sweeping view into the sides of the trees growing up the slope. I regularly saw the trees from above while cruising, and from below while on the ground, or off to the sides during approach or takeoff. But rarely could I peer straight ahead, for just a moment, into the treetop world. It was one of those private, special treats inconsequential to most, special to me. A sky creature's privilege to check on the narrow realm in-between ground pounding and soaring.

I touched down on target. Braking? Fair. Gentle pulses on the pedals kept it straight, not skidding, hardly any sliding. Slowed as I approached the east loading area. Not too many people around and none close. That let me do the first turnaround while still carrying a little momentum since pebbly, muddy prop blast wouldn't spray anyone. I shut down, reviewed the checklist, took off my helmet, opened the door and hopped to the ground.

Rachel and entourage walked up, so I introduced my passengers. The intensity of their obvious honor at meeting her surprised me. She, wearing celebrity status with gracious ease, showed them to their guide. Then realizing that I was part of the touring party, beamed at me, saying only, "I'm glad you finally get to visit the beach."

A straight line from the airstrip to Palm Beach covers just over a mile. Getting there, like anywhere in the jungle, covers more distance and requires an hour and a half. There's the walk from the strip down to the river—slower for foreigners who know how to walk trails properly. Then the inevitable "you've got to be kidding me" reaction boarding the tippy dugout canoe took its own time—particularly for the non-swimmers.

Finally convinced we could sit correctly, our guide pushed the canoe away from the bank and out into the main flow. Away from the airstrip in my pilot uniform, I suddenly felt more tourist than knowledgeable local. Water running over gravel bars made its own noise—a continuously variable background to silence. A bird called. A fish jumped. Branches hanging over the water rustled to monkey's scamper. Our guide's pole neatly pierced the water as he pushed us downstream. But still the silence. The jungle's domain. An encompassing presence, ruling hill, canyon, and river—barely tolerating interlopers, permission to pass conditional, revocable. Sometimes in the deeper brown water, we felt motionless while the overgrown banks passed us. Other times, running over a gravel bar, we seemed to surf a torrent.

Checking my watch dipped me temporarily back into time's realm, but a glance up and the jungle subsumed me. Finally, after a bend, our guide pushed us onto a large sand and stone bar— Palm Beach. The canyon walls seemed closer on the ground than in the air. Maybe the 100' trees emphasized the depth, highlighted the isolation. And no push of my right hand would bring a roar of power pulling me up and away. Flying there brought me close to the jungle, but this was different. Now I was in the belly of the Beast.

Branchy green close on the right, tall trees vying for space up the steep canyon wall. An expanse of running water to the left separated us from the opposite tree-lined bank, less steep, but still rising. Up and down river even more green enveloped river bends, cutting off any long views.

We stepped carefully along the still-tippy canoe's length to the beached bow and then onto the sand. Ken and Carol immediately walked away from the rest of us toward the center of the beach. They stood still, hand in hand, then as a couple slowly turned, taking in the panorama. They looked high, into the trees, then lower into the bush tangle that disappeared into diminishing dark spaces between the trunks. They both prayed aloud, spontaneous, unashamed by anyone's presence, eyes a little wet, but mostly intense, looking almost four decades into the past. They thanked

God they could be there, stand where Nate and the other men stood. They saw in their hearts' eyes the yellow Piper land, park. The men waiting, not fully understanding what was coming that afternoon, faithful in the family business, ready to share the Father's love.

Ken, returning briefly to the present, told me how the event had propelled him into aviation and missions. His mom read a *Reader's Digest* version of the story to the kids. Later, when he was 18 or 19, driving bulldozers and boarding with another family in Canada, the lady of the house gave him a copy of *Jungle Pilot* by Russell T. Hitt. That book nudged him toward becoming a MAF pilot. But, on that day, standing on the same beach, the reality of the five men's sacrifice, the raw beginnings of MAF's ministry, hit him full force.

I could see it in his face, how he stood, even saying nothing. Suddenly, my cynical heart melted. Its eyes opened, and I saw it too. A New Testament verse sprang to mind, saying how some people see every day as the same, but others highlight special days. Same way about places. To one, all spots were the same. To others, some were special. People have pilgrimaged for all recorded history. Why should hearts be different in "modern" times? The same Spirit touches all.

The looky-loos I resented were actually pilgrims, journeying to a special place, seeking a more tangible touch from God. These flights were not a bother, but a ministry God assigned to us. He granted us the privilege of aiding those pilgrims on their way. My private disdain morphed into open respect, resentment into welcome, bother into honor.

Finding the Big Apple

Angry black clouds dogged me all day. They seemed safely distant when I arrived at my first stop, Amuntai. Down lower than most of the jungle at 600' elevation, the dirt strip still sat above the Pastaza River. Here the petulant, rocky, winding water course gave way to brown, sluggish flow. Big, even from the air, powerful, but dull, its size offsetting any need for brilliance or beauty, it moved ponderously southeast to eventually join the Amazon River in Peru.

Although capricious wind sometimes bedeviled Amuntai, I chose to land to the south even with a slight tailwind. If I messed up the approach, the go-around path over the river was too good to pass up. Just get my wheels an inch off the dirt and there was nothing to hit for miles. Landing to the north, on the other hand, presented higher terrain.

The 1,150-foot-long strip surface wasn't too bad—sandy dirt and, this time, not too many ruts. I stopped a bit more than halfway down the strip, hopped out and helped my passenger down. The jungle residents, regardless of tribe, were athletic by necessity. Still, a lady carrying a baby could easily miss a C-185's small step. After she was out, I knelt beside the pod, opened the door and fished out her cloth-wrapped bundle. No one met her. No one came to the plane at all. Odd, but the village was a five-minute walk down the slope toward the river. Maybe coming up the hill was too much for a hot morning.

Minus one passenger and her baby, I taxied back to the approach end of the strip and took off toward the river. Out over the wide, brown water, I made an easy left turn to head north to my next stop, Bufeo.

Dark-gray, mottled with black, filled the windscreen as I climbed for the eight-minute flight. I eased the nose lower toward a level attitude for a moment to get a better look. I could see clear air for 30 miles under the clouds, but then slanted, deceptively lighter gray fell from the bases to the ground, obscuring all other color. Probably enough margin to get in and out of Bufeo 16 miles away. But someone had, indeed, let the dogs out. Their line, advancing from the northeast, promised a wet and wild afternoon for this portion of the Amazon Jungle.

Bufeo, actually 33 feet longer than Amuntai, provided a bigger challenge. A 250-foot tree-covered hill, hungry for careless fliers, defined the northwest end of the strip and dictated the single landing direction—regardless of wind. That hill also forced me to commit to touching the ground a quarter-mile from the runway. The only remaining question was: Where, exactly, would I contact dirt? Might as well be the runway.

Problem was, kids, dogs, and stray pigs could dart out between bushes after I'd passed the go-around point. If a strip offered room to roll and go, or at least touch and go, the odds were more in my favor. For a place like Bufeo, however, a frolicking five-year-old would neither hear nor see anything until too late.

#

We talked about it sometimes. During check rides or standing beside loaded airplanes waiting for another downpour to clear. "What would you do if...?"

"What would you do if you were landing at Bufeo (or a similar no go-around strip) and a dog ran in front of the airplane?"

"Depends on the size."

"Yeah, but remember it's Bufeo. You can't go around. Do you keep going straight and hit it, do you swerve, or do you try to hop over?"

The size actually mattered. One time at Montalvo, a paved

military/civilian strip 90 miles into the jungle from Shell, a small dog ran into Pablo's spinning propeller during landing rollout. The dog was so small that Pablo wasn't certain the dog actually made contact. No noise, no bump, no vibration. But he didn't see it run out from under the moving plane. He continued taxiing to the loading ramp at the far end of the strip. His passengers left. Pablo inspected the prop and wheels, saw no sign of impact or road-kill remains, so loaded his new passengers and flew back to Shell. Once he leveled off and transitioned to cruise flight, he felt a slight vibration. After landing he asked Dave, our maintenance director, to check it out. All looked good until he twisted each of the prop blades. The first was fine. The second was loose. The impact with a scrawny 10-pound dog broke the blade-stop inside the hub. Hitting a 100-pound pig would seriously damage the airplane.

The question again: "Which is better: Hit the animal and break the airplane, but (probably) stay on the strip. Swerve to miss the animal, run off the side of the strip and (probably) break the airplane. Or try to use the last bit of lift in the wing and hop over, risking either dropping in hard or running off the end of the strip and (probably) breaking the airplane?"

Lots of discussion centered around weighing the "ifs" in the one or two seconds available in such situations, but the consensus was, "best to keep the plane on the ground and moving down the center of the strip."

Then someone always asked, "What if it's a kid?"

We thought a moment, scenarios playing like videos in our imaginations' eye. Then one of us typically asked, thinking out loud, "If I *have* to choose ... who's safety is my first responsibility? The kid on the ground who runs in front of the airplane? Or the passengers inside my airplane?" We never came up with a solid, fail-safe, one-size-fits-all answer.

#

I dipped the left wing as I crossed 500 feet over the center of the strip and checked for dry or wet dirt, standing water, holes, ruts, logs, and debris. Then I scanned the borders for kids, pigs, dogs, or unusual clusters of people—especially groups of men carrying spears or rifles. I leveled the wings for a moment, pushed dog-pig-kid thoughts aside and started a left turn to fly the downwind leg, parallel to the strip. The windsock bobbed, fitful in the generally north wind at—I guessed—five knots. That would give me a crosswind from my two o'clock position on landing. The variable component could be tricky, but the headwind portion would give me a little extra margin if I had to go-around just before the abort point.

Despite being short and obstructed at one end, Bufeo's level, firm (when dry), packed dirt surface allowed gross weight landings. Departures were another matter. With no wind, we limited our takeoff weight to 3,000 pounds—a full 350 pounds under full gross weight. That was equivalent to two local adults and a luggage. My helpful five-knot headwind on landing would change to an annoying five-knot tailwind on takeoff. Hoped I wouldn't have to leave a passenger behind, but probably would have to leave some cargo. Depended on the numbers. And the weather. The advancing line still glowered miles away. We should be safe from first-gusts—the fast-moving edge of turbulent wind resulting from the strong downdraft dumping out the bottom of a storm cell. When it smacks the ground, it shoots out in all directions like a jet of water hitting a flat rock. If the storm cell is large, the turbulent line can strike miles ahead under a still-sunny sky.

So, I had to get in, off-load my passengers and cargo, pick up the new passenger and his cargo and get out quickly. The request said one passenger at 160 pounds (big for a local guy) and 200 pounds of cargo. With my remaining passenger and cargo, taking off in the available runway length with everything aboard would depend on the weight of fuel remaining in the tank, plus the exact weight of the new guy and his cargo. I could estimate the guy's weight. The cargo, however, we weighed on a handheld scale.

After tallying the weights, I'd calculate the distance required for takeoff. Then I'd add more to compensate for a soft strip (not an issue this time) and the tailwind. That distance had to add up to no more than 70% of the runway which, in Bufeo's case, would mean my wheels had to leave the ground no more than 826 feet down the runway.

When the total weight reached what the calculation said would get me off in that distance, I'd declare the airplane full and we'd go. Communicating that sometimes presented a challenge when a seat or two remained empty. But numbers ruled. Most folks in communities we served regularly were accustomed to it, even if they didn't like it. The remaining question was, Could I do all the right stuff and still take off before the storm line and its wild turbulence got too close. The time to talk and weigh cargo were the unknowns in the equation.

I completed more items on the landing checklist and passed abeam my intended touchdown point. When the end of the runway was at a 45-degree angle behind my left shoulder, I turned left to base leg—now flying perpendicular to the runway. I started a descent, added another 10 degrees of flaps and slowed to 70 knots. Then I looked straight ahead and to the right along the path where some other airplane might be making a long, straight-in approach. Clear. I looked left again to the spot where I planned to set my wheels onto the runway. Despite the nervous windsock, the air was smooth 600 feet up. That meant I'd cross through a shear layer where air from the advancing storm line crossed the lower tailwind. Gentle now, but the dark, advancing, barking pack could grab local air and shake it any way it wanted.

Held the spot to a good touchdown. Good braking. Stopped before midfield. Shutdown. Hopped down to the ground. Unloaded the passenger. Unloaded his cargo. New passenger approached. Looked less than 160 pounds. Good. Others carried three quintal sacks (like burlap bags but woven from flat nylon strands). Hmmm. One carrier dangled his sack easily. Good. Two carriers struggled with theirs. Not good.

The scale would reveal all, but I guessed some would remain behind. The delicate challenge arose once again—show my respect for the people while also obeying aerodynamic laws that played hardball. I smiled, greeted and shook hands with each man gathered, and teased a kid. I confirmed the passenger's name on my plan, then asked, "Is this your cargo?"

"Yes, Capitán," he answered.

"Good." I answered enthusiastically, "I'll check the weights and get it loaded."

"It's very light, Capitán. It doesn't weigh anything. Would you like me to load it for you?" he asked, moving one bag toward the open cargo pod door.

"Thank you, that's very kind of you to offer, but my boss would be very unhappy with me if I didn't weigh everything first. You know how tough he can be." Everyone chuckled and nodded.

I pulled the hand scale from the pocket behind the pilot's seat and put the hook through the weaving of the lightest bag—23 pounds. I asked two men to hold the next bag, put the hook through the top, then grasped the scale with two hands. I moved my legs apart, braced and asked the men to let go—112 pounds. We did the same with the third bag—105 pounds. Forty pounds over. I furrowed my brow, just slightly, and said, "Well, a little over. I know it's important to take this with you, so let's see how we can make this work."

I set the scale on the seat and pulled the fuel dipstick out of the seat back pocket and measured the gas still on board. I had 2 hours of flying time until the tanks ran dry. To fly from Bufeo to my next stop, Molino, required 23 minutes. From Molino to Shell would take another 25 minutes. Forty-eight minutes of flying would consume 12 gallons, so I'd land in Shell with 18 gallons. MAF regulations demanded we land with no less than one hour of fuel aboard—15 gallons—so I had 3 gallons to play with. And two takeoffs, one from Bufeo and the second from Molino, along with the likely headwind would use the rest. I had just enough to finish the flight. Getting out of Molino, weight-wise, would be easier. Bufeo, however, presented a small problem. Three hundred and sixty pounds was the max I could put on board and guarantee a safe take off, especially with the tailwind.

I replaced the right fuel cap and looked to the northeast. The gray was darker. The trees on the hilltop moved a little more. I had to move too. I climbed down, eyeing the passenger. He was smaller than one of our regulars who weighed 150 pounds. I estimated my man that day at a more typical 140 pounds. I chose my next words carefully.

"Good news, we can take almost everything. But with this wind," I made a sweeping motion toward the hill behind me, "we have to be more careful to be sure we don't hit those trees." I pointed in front of me toward the trees in our departure path. All heads turned and regarded the tall green protruding up from the river course and rising above runway level. "We shouldn't do that, should we?" I grinned. They laughed and shook their heads, telling me they got the joke and the message.

"Because you're so skinny," I grinned again, "we only need to leave 20 pounds of cargo behind." I took the scale off my seat, held it in my right hand and waited.

"Okay, Capitán, how about this?" He pulled a smaller bundle from the heaviest bag.

The spring scale indicated 15 pounds. His expression asked if that was close enough. My expression, with scale poised for another load, held firm. He looked at someone in the crowd, shrugged and pulled another bundle from the bag. Seven pounds.

"Let's go," I said, then knelt in the dirt, stuffed the cargo into the pod, closed its door, and helped him into the airplane, next to the still-waiting right-center passenger.

I taxied to the extreme northwest end of the runway and did a slow turn to the right to line up for takeoff. This would be my last look at the approaching weather before I committed myself to flight. The gray looked the same. The trees moved the same, no flying leaves or surprised birds. No rain. The windsock remained as mildly fitful as during landing. Checklists completed, abort points reviewed, wind checked again, I pushed the throttle in. Wheels left dirt at the 70% point. I cleared the trees by more than 50 feet. So far so good. I continued climbing and turned right to 310 degrees on a heading for Molino. As I passed 500 feet above the ground, previously smooth air bumped, not strong yet, but heralding approaching trouble.

I stayed at 4,500 feet for the leg to Molino. My northwest route kept me parallel to the advancing line. Still only mild bumps, but its approach forced serious consideration—land at Molino as scheduled, or skip it and head direct to Shell?

Another dilemma.

On one hand, Jesus valued each person so much that he died to rescue them, regardless of life station. Therefore, every passenger in my plane deserved equal honor and respect, regardless of life station. On the other hand, needs outstripped our capacity. We had to rank every flight request, granting some, declining others.

Absolute caution said, *"Don't risk trouble, get to Shell while you can."* Safe. Certain. Neither complaints nor problems would follow— except for my routine passenger who just wanted to get home. I would apologize, citing safety. He would nod, accept and endure.

But we didn't schedule a stop at Molino just to drop off a routine passenger. We responded to a request to pick up a VIP. A car already waited in Shell to carry Dr. Sotomayor, one of Ecuador's top agricultural scientists, to a conference in Quito. He was scheduled as keynote speaker the next morning. My trusting "routine" passenger gladly accepted our offer of a "combination" seat at a significantly lower price. My decision in the next few minutes would determine if he got a bargain or a hassle.

On that day the situation stalled at debatable. The squall line continued to advance. A half-hour delay would bring risky wind. An hour delay would bring dangerous wind. An hour and a half delay would add pounding rain. If I landed at Molino as planned, my subsequent takeoff would flirt with the beginning of the risky wind window. But if I didn't retrieve him, someone else would the next day—at the cost of bumping some of that day's flights to later days, which would bump those flights to even later days.

I waited until four minutes (eight miles) from Molino where I would normally start descending to reach to correct landing pattern altitude as I arrived over the strip. I looked right, to the north. The dark gray line plodded on as before. Only now its darker color reached higher. More energy. Probably higher winds. I'd have 20 minutes max on the ground. If everything went right, I could unload, load and go in 10. But if the wind got too squirrelly for takeoff, I'd have to wait a couple hours, which would mean overnight.

"Lord," I asked under my breath, "help me to make the right decision." I waited a moment, listening. No inner alarm, just peace. Okay, go for it. I eased the control yoke forward, did not reduce power, and settle into a 500-foot-per-minute cruise descent. That would put me in the pattern in three minutes rather than four, but at Molino, before the descent into the canyon, there was room to slow down.

From pattern altitude, the strip's surface looked good. Dry. No rocks, trees, dogs, pigs, or cows. A tight cluster of people waited at the upper end, off to the side of the turnaround area. Probably my passenger. Another check showed the entire length clear. Molino adults were always good about keeping track of the kids.

I put the main gear wheels onto the flat touch-down area then rolled up the hill, lowering the tail, but keeping enough momentum to reach the turnaround without adding power. At the top, I checked for spacing from the high berm, then swung the tail around to the right. Not quite as good visibility, but this kept the prop blast away from the people.

I hung my helmet on the brace while the engine stopped. Then I turned off the mags, unbuckled my harness, opened the door and hopped to the ground. I shook hands with a couple of men who first walked up but pivoted around to help my "routine" Molino passenger exit. Then I knelt down, opened the pod door and pulled his cargo out.

The scientist, a slender, mustached Latino, arrived and shook my hand. "Good afternoon, Capitán. I'm all ready." He gestured at the two small packs a young man placed at his feet.

The Bufeo passenger had already moved to the right-center seat, making it easy for the scientist to climb into the left-center seat, just behind my own. I helped him buckle in, put his bags into the pod and closed its door. Just before climbing in, I stepped out from under the wing and studied what I could see above the trees of the northern sky. Darker gray, lower. No rain, but upper branches moved more than when we landed.

Engine running fine, checklists done, abort point chosen (surprisingly close on a downhill takeoff), I checked high branches and windsock again. No change. The first part of the takeoff should work fine. Immediately after breaking ground, however, I'd have to turn right to fly up the river canyon until I climbed enough to clear the cliffs on either side. If the wind was building as I expected, turbulence from air spilling over the canyon wall would start just after the right turn.

I exhaled a deep breath slowly. A day running to keep out of the dogs' reach started to catch up. Despite the rush, I asked myself, *The wind looks okay, but are you airworthy, Jim?* Another breath. Deep in. Slowly out. *Yeah, I'm good, but go now or wait until tomorrow. These decisions are why they pay you the really big bucks, pilot boy.* Peace again. I pushed in the throttle, released the brakes and raced downhill.

Abort point. All's good, continue. Fly or run off the end. Estimated liftoff point. Wheels not off the ground, but light. Then flight, wings working. Climbing, still over the airstrip. As the end passed beneath, I banked right to stay inside the canyon. Halfway through, the first bump hit. The lowered right wing blocked the view north, but dimming light told me the bad boys had arrived. I lowered the nose, accelerating to maneuvering speed for good margin above stalling speed, but without endangering the plane's structural integrity. We wouldn't clear the canyon walls as quickly, but it was an acceptable trade-off.

Leveled the wings. Followed the canyon. More bumps. Rain spit, stopped, spit again. Unfriendly ceiling darkened. Looked right, to the north again. Dark gray rain wall just a couple miles away. Rising above the cliff, the plane rocked and bumped more. Not fun, but not terrible. Turned to 295 degrees but kept the shallow climb. Visibility good ahead. Brighter sky ahead. Just had to get out from under the lowering ceiling.

Suddenly, rock-concert loud, firework bright, apple aroma filled my brain. Intense. Mouthwatering. Unexpected as a ballerina at a rock quarry. I spun my head around toward the back seat. The doctor, unconcerned about flight conditions, quietly sliced an apple with a pocketknife. Surprised eyes wide, brows arched by my sudden attention, he offered me a piece.

"Thank you," I said over the engine roar. He nodded and resumed his culinary exercise.

I turned back to the front and lowered the helmet microphone beneath my chin. Slowly, very slowly, I savored each and every small bite of my first apple in a year.

It turned out Dr. Sotomayor had developed an apple tree that flourished in the Andean highlands too high and too warm for other varieties. He visited Molino to research a jungle variety.

Under a Rock

Three years after choosing a pilot's career, I resigned myself to failure.

The good news: aviation challenges abounded. I earned an Instrument Rating. I flew often. The turbocharged Cessna C-210 carried heavy loads fast and high—almost 200 MPH, between 12,000 and 20,000 feet—as I crisscrossed the southwestern US for a Nevada-based mining company.

The bad news: the company's CEO—I'll call him Robert—followed a hidden agenda. Regina and I invested her inheritance in the company. And we purchased the airplane. But as the lies manifested themselves, we smacked into a separation point. The financial hit hurt. The personal betrayal nearly devastated. We packed our two-month-old son and our stuff into a Volkswagen van and escaped the company's remote desert site.

On the way out, suddenly inspired, I stopped at the office. Neither Robert nor the secretary was pleased to see me.

"I want a Quit Claim Deed on the airplane," I said.

When I bought the airplane, I did nearly every wrong thing possible. No pre-purchase inspection. No title search. No vetting the seller who, in this case, was one of Robert's contacts. The first trouble sign appeared when I took the airplane to a shop in San Diego for a 100-hour inspection. The official maintenance log books stated the airplane's engine had received a complete overhaul shortly before we bought it. The shop called. "No way that engine received a major overhaul. We need to talk."

Then, when I asked the FAA (Federal Aviation Administration) about the delay receiving the aircraft's title, they said a Colorado bank had a lien against it. These two situations demanded significant effort to clear up what were obviously cases of misplaced documents. Living and working 50 miles from the nearest paved road, electricity, and telephone greatly complicated resolution.

I waited out Robert's silence. Finally he said, "Okay, we'll draw one up and mail it to you."

"How about if I save you the trouble and write one now?" I said.

Robert blinked. The secretary scowled. I sat down at her desk, slid a sheet into the typewriter and typed the required statements. Then, pulling the page from the machine, I slid it and a pen in front of Robert. He looked at the sheet, looked back at me.

"This airplane deal may turn into a big mess. Save yourself another headache," I said, purposely not reminding him of who paid for it. Didn't want to taunt the cornered weasel. Another moment, then he grabbed the pen and signed. I picked up the corporate seal from the desktop and squeezed it over his signature.

"Thanks," I said and left.

We headed southwest to San Diego where kind friends gave us a landing place to start rebuilding our life. Our family had escaped a bad deal intact, poorer, but wiser.

First tasks—finding a job and a place to live—seemed straightforward. The life rebuild challenge less so. "What do you want us to do, Lord?" We both prayed. And, independently, we received the same answer.

"Jim, get a job, then continue advancing your aviation qualifications," he seemed to say. No why. No plan. No next step. Only admonition. I had no income, no way to care for my family. How was I going to pay for flying? The scariest part? I liked the idea—a lot. With those instructions, we proceeded.

I got a job. We rented a duplex. I worked full-time for nine months, then switched to part-time to enroll in a college course to earn the FAA Airframe and Power Plant licenses. On a whim, because of my interest in electronics, I added an extra class—Introduction to Avionics.

Halfway through the program, I realized we needed more income. At the same time, the avionics instructor received a request from a small avionics manufacturer for a part-time technician. I applied, and the company hired me to do their repair and calibration.

Our customers in the emerging homebuilt and experimental aircraft market preferred to roll their own—even radios. The company met that need by providing airplane electronics in kit form. The client built them, and we provided repair and calibration service. That work presented a unique challenge. Typically, avionics repair centered on restoring a radio to proper working order. We'd spend 90% of the time finding the fault, then 10% making the repair. However, most of the units crossing my bench had never worked in the first place. Made finding the problem more interesting.

Meanwhile, our airplane saga continued producing its own drama. The shop had complied with our earlier, official company instructions—before we escaped—and overhauled the engine. Then they correctly held the airplane until we paid the entire bill.

When we first realized the airplane's engine had not been overhauled as stated in the official log books, I filed a complaint with the San Diego County Prosecutor's Office because we completed the purchase there. The seller, however, was an Arizona dealer. Chances for successful relief looked small.

But shortly after arriving at our generous friend's San Diego home, the prosecutor's office called me—I never learned how they found that phone number. They offered to prosecute the case because they'd been after that Arizona dealer for fraud and could use our complaint to finally catch him. Their handwriting expert examined the airplane's maintenance records and confirmed the dealer had forged the logbook entry. In a plea bargain to avoid jail time, he admitted guilt and paid the entire shop bill.

Suddenly I had the airplane in my hands once again. But not as owner. Even though we paid cash for the airplane, the bank still wanted their money. They were willing to accept payments because the previous owner, an associate of the Arizona dealer, had just stopped servicing the loan. The bank officer sympathized with our plight but could only extend occasional grace periods for late payments. My monthly income hovered around $500. The airplane payments were exactly $449.49. Clearly an untenable situation. But the Lord provided both favor with the bank and cash from unexpected sources. After several precarious months, I contacted the previous owner again. This time he chose to maintain his local business reputation and paid off the loan. Finally, my income supported us.

Regina prayed and then offered to fund my additional flight training from the remaining portion of her inheritance. I completed my Commercial license, then earned my Multi-Engine rating the following year. The year after that, I obtained both my Certified Flight Instructor and Instrument Instructor ratings.

But then my employer moved their operation from San Diego to Grass Valley, California, in the Sierra Nevada foothills. They flattered and worried me at the same time by inviting me to accompany them—flattered because they thought so highly of my work, worried because I loved San Diego and had neither plan nor desire to ever move. Besides, with the airplane now truly ours I entertained a vision of starting an air service to serve the church. Initially, I declined the offer.

One evening Regina and I discussed my vision vs my job. She wasn't against the vision, just my trying to make it happen in my own strength. Frustrated, I stepped outside into the cool night air and sat on the front doorstep, picking up my Bible on the way out. Opened it at random. Started reading Isaiah, chapter 53. Continued through 54. Then as I read chapter 55, God seemed to reach down and pry a big rock off me, suggesting I consider what I read. "My thoughts are above your thoughts," he said to Isaiah. "My ways are above your ways," he added. And suddenly I could see it. No overarching plan, no detailed agenda, just a challenge to trust him that our next step was moving with my job. He would take care of the air service vision in his own way and time.

THE WRONG QUESTION

I arrived at the hangar first that morning, a glow already spreading over the eastern jungle. The steel door boomed as it scraped across the tile floor and I entered the dark lobby. I flipped the switch. Fluorescents blinked twice then sprang to life. Rats scurried for cover, signaling the humans' turn to rule. Chicha's sweet, almost-rotten smell rolled in from waiting cargo.

I passed rows of benches, went behind the counter and turned on the two-way radio to warm it up before starting the morning contact. My notes from last night remained in place. Like a puzzle ring, the plan's pieces intermeshed. But if the wrong one fell out, the whole day could fall apart. At least the weather looked good— so far.

It was my turn as Flight Coordinator—an art/science balancing act we rotated every four weeks. In that position, I had to track each plane's cumulative fuel, seats, space and weight as pilots dropped off and picked up passengers, their baggage, and cargo at multiple places across the jungle. I could promise only what subsequent takeoffs allowed. I also had to factor in pilot qualifications, the required one-hour fuel reserve, and while using a couple dozen rate-plans, cover the cost of the entire flight. And emergencies. And weather.

At 7:00 a.m., I keyed the microphone. "Good morning," I broadcast, "this is Alas de Socorro in Shell. The weather here is clear, with light wind. God willing, we'll complete all your flights today. Remember, when I call your station, give me your weather report first, then emergency requests, and then routine traffic requests for Shell or other stations. After the first roll call, I'll come back to each station in order for your other traffic."

Other traffic consisted of new flight requests, questions about scheduled flights, questions for us in Shell, or requests to talk to another village. I, as Flight Coordinator, handled the roll call and subsequent flight requests. After me, the dispatcher would take over the radio and moderate the non-flight questions and inter-village traffic.

"Arajuno from Shell," I called.

"Shell from Arajuno. Good morning, Capitán. The weather is clear, but we had rain last night. No emergencies. We have traffic with Conombo."

"Roger, Arajuno, copy traffic with Conombo. Thank you." I noted the weather in shorthand next to the Arajuno's space on the contact form. "Achuentza from Shell."

"Shell from Achuentza. The weather is clear now, but we had fog earlier. The strip is muddy from the rain last night. We have traffic."

"Thank you, Achuentza. Atshuar from Shell."

"Shell from Atshuar..." The contact ritual continued through the list. Then I restarted at the top.

"Achuentza from Shell, go ahead with your request," I called.

"Shell from Achuentza. Is our flight coming today?"

"Achuentza from Shell, yes, we're doing your flight today. Please confirm how many people want to fly from Achuentza to Shell."

"We have two people from Achuentza for Shell. And 100 pounds of cargo," he answered.

"Okay, Achuentza, I understand 100 pounds of cargo and two people are flying from Achuentza to Shell. Please confirm."

"That's correct, Capitán. Two people and 100 pounds of cargo."

"Thank you, Achuentza. Your flight will arrive mid-afternoon."

I fielded the remaining flight requests, then picked up my notes and backed away from the radio. "Okay, Pancho, it's all yours," I said as he slid into the operator's seat. I hunted down each pilot flying that day, presented their assignments then went to my plane.

\#

Seven hours later, as I shut down the engine on Achuentza's grass strip, heavy, wet heat poured into the cockpit. The long day hung on me like muddy boots. I smelled like a locker room. But this was the last landing of a used-up day.

"Good afternoon," I said to the gathered crowd, then repeated as I shook each man's hand. We didn't get to this village often and their smiles gave me new energy. I checked my notes then said, "Okay, where are the two people going with me today?" Two men stepped from the group. One's hair was cut short in the newer style, but the other still wore his in a single long braid. Each wore old shorts and tattered T-shirts. One had flip-flops, the other no shoes at all. They didn't look like they'd traveled out of the village much.

"And your baggage?" I asked. They pointed to a pile of sacks and baskets growing at my feet. A 12-foot blowgun leaned against it.

"Thank you for showing me this first," I said, lifting it up. Blowguns had to be loaded before anything else. I spoke to the two passengers from the previous strip who were still strapped in.

"Sorry to bother you, but you have to get out of the airplane for just a moment." They nodded, undid their belts, stepped down and backed off a few feet into wing's shade. I picked up the blowgun, held it horizontally, then threaded it between the door's front edge and the doorpost just above the hinge. It would have skewered anyone still in the airplane. Once inside, I laid it on the floor in the narrow gap between the seats and secured it with two straps tied to cargo rings.

Their cargo created a substantial mound. With two people from the previous strip and these two men, I wasn't sure I could carry everything. I not only had to contend with the maximum allowable takeoff weight of the airplane, but this strip had an additional limit because of its short length and the trees not far from the end of the runway. Indigenous people of the Amazon were generally smaller than North Americans or Europeans. That meant we could carry more of them out of the same airstrip. I always asked my passengers their weight—the question insulted only North Americans and Western Europeans—then made my own estimate. People who'd flown with us before had some idea, but new-timers didn't. The first two men totaled 320 pounds, but the two new guys were smaller, about 150 pounds each. That gave me a total people weight of 620 pounds. So, doing the math, I had the empty airplane at 1,910 pounds, plus 35 gallons of fuel at 210 pounds, plus me at 160 pounds, plus those four guys, plus the 40 pounds of cargo already on board. That totaled 2,940 pounds.

The book said if the strip was dry and the grass short with no wind, I could take off at a maximum aircraft weight of 3,000 pounds. That left 60 pounds for new cargo.

"Of all this," I asked the two new men, waving my hand over the pile, "what's your personal luggage?"

They pulled a bushel-sized basket and two sacks out. I reached into the airplane and pulled out a foot-long scale with a ring on one end and a hook on the other. Holding the ring, I used the hook to hoist each of the three bundles in turn. Fifty pounds. And the blowgun I'd already loaded was another five pounds. Fifty-five pounds total new cargo. I set their luggage next to the pod door and looked back at the pile, now only slightly smaller. They looked at me. I looked at them.

"I can only take another five pounds. What's most important?" I asked.

A small chorus offered choices in the 20–30-pound range, each with its compelling story. I weighed a T-shirt-wrapped lump tied with vine. Yep, five pounds. I put it with the luggage.

"Okay, that's it." I knelt on the ground and stowed each piece of baggage in the pod, then stood and directed the passengers to their seats. I helped everyone buckle their safety harness and gave the safety briefing: how to unbuckle the harness (do so only when the plane was stopped), how to operate the doors (do so only when I said so), the location of the fire extinguisher, first aid kit and sick sacks, and our flight time to Shell was 45 minutes.

I closed the doors and said goodbye. The people backed away to the edge of the strip, but reluctantly, as if they were expecting something. "God bless you," I called, then turned and climbed up into the pilot's seat. I fastened my harness and reached for the ignition key but felt a tap on my shoulder. I turned to the man sitting behind me.

"Capitán," he asked. "What about them?"

"What about who?" I asked.

"Them," he said, pointing toward the crowd, a normal village airstrip gathering. I didn't see anyone too close or waving.

"I don't understand."

"They have to go too," he said.

"Who has to go?" I asked.

"Them." He pointed again, tapping the window for emphasis. "His wives and mine. And the kids, too."

I looked at him a long moment. Finally, I said, "There's no room."

"But they have to go," he insisted.

I unfastened my harness, opened the door and hopped to the ground. I turned to look back up at him and asked, "Who are they?" He called out, and four women carrying bundles and trailed by kids stepped from the group.

"So...you want them to go with us now?" I asked.

"Yes," he answered. The entire group leaned toward us, quiet, attentive.

"But there's no room," I said again. Our small aluminum box was full, even with me standing on the ground. That had to be obvious. I was missing something...

Then I remembered the voice. "I talked to you this morning on the radio."

"Yes, Capitán."

"And I asked you how many people were going. You said two."

"Yes, Capitán, my cousin and me."

"And here I am," I stated evenly, succeeding only partially to keep the edge off my voice. In this culture, yelling at, or berating him would be a far worse sin than bedding the wrong person. "What more can I do?" I asked in my most reasonable tone. "You said two people and I have two seats available."

"But they have to go," he persisted.

"Why didn't you tell me about them this morning? We could have scheduled another flight."

"You didn't ask," he countered.

"Yes, I did. I asked you how many people were going, and you said 'two.'"

"And here we are, my cousin and me." He indicated the man crammed into the back seat, now starting to sweat in our equatorial sunbaked, non-moving airplane.

"Yes, you said two people, not"—I paused and turned to the cluster of now fully engaged villagers and counted—"four adults and five children."

"That's right, Capitán, you asked how many people were going. I said two and here we are," he repeated, genuinely bewildered.

"But, with you two, there are 11 passengers," I said.

"Yes, Capitán, that's right, 11 passengers," he agreed.

"But I asked you how many people were going, and you said two."

"Yes, Capitán, that's right, two people," he agreed again.

I was still missing something important, but we had to take off soon or I'd spend the night in the jungle. I looked at the trees at the end of the strip, looked at them, then back at the trees. After another moment's silence, I turned to them and lied—technically. "Now I understand. You want all of these," I waved my arm to include the two families, "to accompany you on this flight."

"Yes, Capitán," he nodded.

"That's very important. It's always better to have your family with you when you'll be away from home for a long time."

"Yes, Capitán," he nodded.

"I miss being with my wife when I have to go away. She cooks for me like most wives do, but I like spending time with her. Do you miss your wife when you're not at home?"

"Yes, Capitán."

"And my children get lonesome when I'm away. Do your children miss you when you're away?"

"Yes, Capitán."

"Mine are always so glad to see me when I return home. They run up and jump on me and laugh and ask all kinds of questions about my trip. They all talk at once and tell me what they did while I was gone. Do your children do that?"

"Yes, Capitán."

We stood for a moment looking at his kids. Then I said, "Our families are very special, aren't they?"

"Yes, they are, Capitán."

"God's given us a great responsibility to take care of them, hasn't He?"

"Yes, Capitán."

"After all, they face many dangers and a man's job is to protect his family. And sometimes that's hard."

He nodded assent.

"When you walk the trails, you have a machete ready— especially for the snakes, don't you?"

"Yes, Capitán," he nodded again.

I looked at the ground, shuffled my feet a bit, looked up again and smiled. "When my son was very little like yours here," I pointed with my chin and pursed lips, as they do, at a toddler holding the edge of his mother's skirt, "fire fascinated him," I said, thinking of ours. "I had a hard time keeping him away from it."

He smiled and looked at his boy.

"And my daughter," I continued, now pointing my chin at a canoe pulled up onto the mud along the river running parallel to the strip, "loved the water. She'd try to step out of a boat anytime we went anywhere."

We both chuckled, smiled.

"I've always wondered, how do you keep them from tipping over?" I asked, indicating the canoe again. "Seriously, I've been in them. They tip all the time. How do you keep them from just turning upside down?"

He smiled again then said, "It's easy. You put heavy things in the bottom, not too high. And make everyone sit and stay still."

"But I've seen men standing in them..." I protested.

His grin got bigger. "That's because we know how to do it."

"Okay, true enough..." I conceded. "Sounds like my airplane."

"Like your airplane?" he asked quizzically.

"Yes, they're just like canoes. I have to be very careful where I put cargo." I held my hand at chest height, fingers extended, palm down like an airplane flying. "If I put it too far back, the airplane gets very unstable and I can't control it." I flipped my hand over, pointed my fingers down and motioned down to the ground. I returned my hand to the supposed straight and level position and continued, "But if the weight is too far forward, I can't lift the nose. And if I pack in too much weight, I can't get the plane off the ground at all." I held up my left hand, fingers pointed up like trees at the end of a runway, then ran my right hand like an airplane into them. "That's very bad if that happens. Many die."

Still sitting in the right seat, he looked out the front to the trees at the end of the runway, then back at the other passengers in the airplane. Then he stared down at me, mouth agape, eyes wide. I looked at my hands still tangled like an airplane in trees. Finally, he asked, "So you have to be careful not to load too much into your airplane, don't you?"

"Yes, I have to be very careful," I agreed.

He nodded slowly, looking at the two families still clustered in the wing's shade. Then spoke in Shuar to his cousin seated behind him. They conversed a moment, nodding, then he spoke to the families. The women shrugged their shoulders, gathered in the children and moved back to the small crowd. "Okay, Capitán, we're ready to go," he said.

I climbed back up into my seat, replaced my helmet and started the engine. As we accelerated down the runway, he fixed his eyes on the trees before us, keeping them there as we cleared their tops by the requisite minimum 50 feet.

That day I learned old-time Shuar culture did not assume women had souls, therefore they weren't fully "people" as men were. If I'd asked how many passengers wanted to fly, he would have said 11, but I asked how many people. He'd answered my wrong question with his true answer.

CRASH AT NUMBAIMI

The phone rang midway through lunch. I shrugged *"Sorry"* to Regina and my girls, stood and answered. Lucas, our dispatcher, said a local Ecuadoran commercial operator crashed in the village of Numbaimi. They needed help. "Gotta go, ladies. Emergency." I grabbed the remaining half sandwich from my plate and headed across the street.

In the hangar, Luis, the Pista Doctor assigned to us, stood next to the radio. Lucas lowered the microphone and said, "No more news, Capitán Diego. Weather is good. Capitán Carlos is on the ground in Charapacocha but hasn't called ready for takeoff yet. And Numbaimi isn't answering on the radio since their first call."

"Thanks, Lucas. Zero-Four is ready for my next flight. The doctor and I can go in that," I said. Then, "Oh, we'll have to cancel that trip for today. Can you let the passengers know?"

Lucas nodded, then turned back to the radio. I looked at Doctor Luis.

"I'm ready," he said, holding up his bag.

I wrote a new flight plan and handed it to Panchito for delivery. I preflighted the airplane before lunch but did another walk-around as Dr. Luis strapped himself into the copilot's seat. When I called the tower for permission to taxi, telling them I'd filed a flight plan for Numbaimi, they asked if I knew about the accident.

"Shell Tower, from Alas Zero-Four. That's affirmative. I have the Pista Doctor aboard," I answered.

"Alas Zero-Four, Shell. I'll inform DAC [Department of Civil Aviation]. Cleared to taxi to the run-up area. Call ready for takeoff," the tower operator said.

Emergency flights demand extra attention to combat extra

adrenaline. Finally ready, I called the tower for takeoff clearance. In a few moments, we were in the air for the 40-minute flight to Numbaimi. I called Lucas with our standard post-takeoff report. He acknowledged my numbers, then told me Brian (Capitán Carlos) had taken off from Charapacocha (five minutes from Numbaimi) with a full load. He couldn't bring anyone back but would land in Numbaimi anyway. I continued because I had the doctor on board as well as room for anyone injured who needed quick transport to the hospital. Crashing into trees generally yielded bad results, so I anticipated at least one patient. I hoped everyone else could sit.

We leveled at 5,500 feet then settled on course 137 degrees direct to Numbaimi. This course, now an aerial highway in my mental moving map, followed the Pastaza River generally southeast. Every 10 miles or so (five minutes' flying time) a village appeared—Copataza, Mashient, Numbaimi, Charapacocha. Reminded me of freeway exits.

Ten minutes from Numbaimi I eased the nose over into a high-speed cruise descent. Minutes could mean lives.

Then Brian called from the ground at Numbaimi. "Zero-Four from Zero-Seven."

"Go ahead, Brian," I answered.

"They're both dead—Bernard and Juan. No passengers. The only cargo is a beef. Where are you now?"

"Copy that. I'll relay the word to Shell. We're just passing Mashient. Should be there in five minutes. And I've got the Pista Doc with me. Over."

I turned to the doctor. We didn't take time to get him a headset, so I made a thumbs-down sign, then said over the engine noise, "They're both dead." His face fell.

We sat silent. Then I realized our mission had changed from aiding the living to removing the dead. I turned to him again and said, "We have to bring the bodies back to Shell." He sighed, nodded, then looked away.

I called, "Shell from Zero-Four." Lucas had heard my

conversation with Brian, but Brian and I had lapsed into English. Better to ensure clarity when delivering such bad news.

"Zero-Four from Shell. Proceed," Lucas responded.

"Lucas, Capitán Carlos reports that both pilots are dead. The doctor and I will bring their bodies back to Shell. Over."

A lapse, then Lucas answered. "Zero-Four from Shell. Capitán, I understand both pilots died. Please confirm. Over."

"Affirmative, Lucas. Please advise DAC and any family members that might be in the hangar. We're landing at Numbaimi now. Over."

We landed, parked next to Brian's plane, and stepped out. Brian met us, shook hands with the doctor, and said in Spanish, "The wreck is about a kilometer that way," pointing toward the departure end of the runway. "These guys," he motioned to a half-dozen village men standing around us, "can show you."

I turned to the group and said (still in Spanish), "The doctor and I will fly the bodies back to Shell if you can help bring them to the plane. Capitán Carlos' plane is full." The men agreed to help. Brain's passengers looked up, relieved. Brian nodded, glad for an answer to the dilemma he faced.

We each carried a meat tarp in the pod of our planes, so I borrowed Brian's, grabbed mine and returned to the group. They led the doctor and me along a well-used path running parallel to the runway. I was glad for the chance to walk. Our constant hassle to meet needs normally kept us within a dozen feet of our plane. Despite the reason for walking, the hike itself offered a respite.

Small, puffy white clouds decorated deep-blue sky. Fresh east breeze carried humid, earthy jungle smells, some decay, some mud, but also flower scent and far-away aromas—the ethereal kind that cling to perfect days meant for making grand plans and perfect flights. But on that day irony prevailed, confirming that sometimes appearances deceive.

Whining bugs followed, dining on us while ignoring local residents. We tromped, single file, along a path meandering through bright, sunny fields of shoulder-high grass, then under dark, leafy-green caverns, then between tall, closely packed, vine-draped trees. We crossed ground cut by small rivulets, traversed low patchy brush scattered across bare, muddy dirt and occasional dry, hard patches. Fifteen minutes later, deep among the trees, we turned left off the path. We pushed another 50 feet through more underbrush, then stopped.

Invisible from the path, we came into a gap between tall trunks and confronted the wreck. A denizen of the sky snatched from the air, thrown down, now lay a broken, dead bird. The single-engine, high-wing Dornier 27 lay on its right side. The top of the cockpit rested against the tree trunk. Its wheels pointed out at us. The right wing was broken off and twisted behind the wreckage. The left wing, still attached, pointed straight up like a drowning hand's last wave. Its tip leaned in against the tree.

The fuselage looked mostly intact. Luis and I moved closer. Though others had checked their fate, we moved carefully—just in case. The left cockpit door, the pilot's door, lay open, forward against the engine cowling. We looked down into the cockpit. Both pilots, still strapped into their seats, leaned back and down toward the airplane's right side, now resting on the forest floor. No breath. No sound. Empty husks, devoid of soul and spirit.

The doctor moved to unbuckle them, but I motioned for him to wait. I wanted to see the cockpit as it was, just in case we had to cut them out. The doorframes were only mildly deformed when the wings' main carry-through spar bent. The seat rails looked straight, the seats themselves intact, even the safety harness anchors remained in place. The instrument panel, its top following the engine cowling curve, looked intact on either side of its stout center post. The unbroken windscreen was still in place. The panel itself was mostly flat except for two slight depressions, one in front of each pilot position. All the instruments remained mounted in their panel cutouts. The three-lever throttle quadrant mounted on a small pylon jutting out from the panel face appeared intact. Three sticks rising from the cockpit floor—two joysticks, one for each pilot position and flap handle between them—retained normal shape and position. The cockpit area was hardly damaged. So, what killed them?

Then I remembered the village men and the doctor waited on me. "Okay," I said in Spanish, "let's get them out."

We unbuckled Bernard, the aircraft and company owner, first. He'd been in the pilot's seat on the left when the airplane sat on its wheels but now lay on top of Juan in the copilot's seat. I was acquainted with Bernard—a German who moved to Ecuador to run his aviation company—and guessed his weight at 250 pounds. Pulling him up out of the cockpit required our combined effort. Once we lifted him clear of the aircraft, we set him gently onto one of the tarps. Then we pulled Juan's 190-pound frame from farther down the hole of the sideways cockpit. Luis started a more detailed exam of their bodies while I returned to the cockpit. And then I saw it.

The Dornier's cabin was about the same size as our C-185's—room for two pilot seats, then four smaller passenger seats set in two rows. And as we did with our planes, Bernard and Juan had removed the middle and rear seats to make room for cargo—four quarters of newly slaughtered beef. A big one, well over 1,000 pounds, I guessed. Sitting there. In the cargo area. No net. No straps. Two pieces of half-inch cotton clothesline X-ed across the pile but now cast aside in four burst pieces.

Witnesses told us the airplane didn't clear the trees but snagged their tops, then fell down into the forest. I leaned out of the cockpit and surveyed the broken branches on the ground. Then I followed the scrape marks on the trunk up to broken upper branches. While not a trained accident investigator—DAC might provide one—the sequence of events seemed clear.

After takeoff, the plane ran into dense foliage that caught and stopped it. It probably teetered for a moment, both pilots startled, but alive. Then it slowly tipped and slid down the trunk, hitting the ground nose low. It probably didn't free fall but impacted at, I guessed, 5 to 10 Gs. The cheap clothesline didn't even slow the half-ton of beef. It smashed the two men into the panel with the equivalent weight of 5,000 to 10,000 pounds. Then after the plane stopped at the base of the tree, the tail came down to horizontal and the beef fell back into its original location. Bernard and Juan didn't have to die. The crash was survivable. The cargo killed them.

I turned and walked back to Luis. He'd just finished confirming, officially, that the two men were indeed dead. As we started wrapping the tarps around the bodies, the village men cut several lengths of vine from the trees. They wrapped the bundles, then made a support harness for each. Other men cut two 10-foot poles and inserted one through each harness. Two men lifted each bundle by the pole ends and the two other men put their arms under the middle, clasping each other's wrists to form a center support. Luis and I did the same for the other body.

The march back proved hotter, buggier, and less idyllic. The bundle containing Bernard's body swayed with each pole bearer's step over bush and down slippery creekside. Each pass of the rubberized tarp bundle scraped our forearms as Luis and I gripped each other's wrists and tried to carry our share of the weight. Half walking and half stumbling with a sideways twist increased the challenge. Sometimes one or the other of us had to let go to avoid three-inch thorns or navigate a creek crossing. The short hike in morphed into a long trek out.

Made me wonder what Bernard, whom we carried, or Juan in the other bundle, had thought about that morning. *Did they have any premonition they'd slept in their own beds for the last time, given their last hug, tasted their last breakfast, seen their last dawn, were making their last flight? Probably not*, I thought. Life's momentous moments often caught us by surprise. I silently asked his swaying body, *"Did you ever consider life on the divine side? Ever reconcile your life with God?"* His public life suggested not.

I said aloud to the men with us, "When these two woke up this morning, they expected to be home tonight for dinner. They didn't plan to die, but now we carry their bodies. What about you? If God called you today and said it was your turn to die, would you be ready to meet Him?"

Some didn't respond. A couple others stopped their conversation, looked at me, nodded slightly. I started to say more but stopped. Both of them got that far away, pensive look. Hopefully, they were hearing the Holy Spirit joining the conversation in their heads. More words from me would probably only muddy the waters.

We finally set the bundles on the ground next to the plane. I pulled my canteen from the cockpit and poured water onto the forearms of the two guys supporting the center of Juan's bundle, then the doctor's and my own. The scrapes remained, but we washed off sweat and mud.

I removed and stowed the center and aft seats, then fastened the cargo net and large Herc straps. *Just like hauling a beef,* I thought. If these men had done what I was doing, they'd probably be alive. I'd be helping them into seats as passengers rather than securing their bodies like cargo.

We loaded each bundled man into the cabin and I completed the tie-down process. I thanked our helpers, then Luis and I boarded. Forty minutes later we landed in Shell. Our hangar helpers and some DAC officials worked together to keep the growing crowd off the ramp as I taxied up and shut down the engine. Juan's father was the first to meet us. Weeping, he helped unload his son's body. As I watched blood seep from a hole in the tarp and cover the father's hands and arms, I realized that even though the two men who died hadn't known Jesus, they were precious to people here. I wondered, *How would their loved ones cope with this sudden tragedy? Would it draw them closer to Jesus or drive them further away?*

Many hands moved both bodies from the airplane to a pickup truck. With a final thunk, the driver closed the tailgate and drove to the hospital. Dr. Luis accompanied them to complete the official paperwork. The press of onlookers, friends, and family melted away, leaving me alone with a bloody airplane. Panchito moved the airplane to our wash area, but I was no longer airworthy. I spoke with the flight coordinator and walked back across the street, thankful for each step taking me closer to my wife and kids.

#

The rest of the story soon revealed itself. Juan and Bernard landed in Numbaimi to pick up a beef. Village men said that particular beef was one of the largest they'd ever butchered—the four quarters alone totaled nearly 1,200 pounds. Juan said it was too heavy, but Bernard ordered it loaded. Juan protested. Bernard insisted, then also agreed to carry the hooves, head, and hide—an additional 150 pounds. The two men argued, shouted, almost came to blows. Juan said he would not fly the airplane loaded that way. Bernard said, "Fine! I'll fly it!"

At this point, the Dornier 27, with its 270-horsepower engine, weighed 4,530 pounds—450 pounds over its maximum allowable gross weight and 1,380 pounds heavier than our 285 horsepower Cessna C-185 would be for the same takeoff.

Bernard's personal short-field takeoff procedure always kept the accelerating airplane on the ground until the very end of the runway. Then at the last moment, he'd pop on full flaps and pitch up sharply to balloon over any obstacles. MAF takeoff procedure, on the other hand, required that we adjust our takeoff weight until we could complete our ground roll and become airborne within 70% of the available runway length. And this assumed we'd already determined that our climb angle after lifting off would allow us to clear obstacles by at least 50 feet.

Witnesses said Bernard stayed on the ground until six feet from the end of the runway. He applied flaps, pitched up, and jumped vertically 100 feet. Then, having traded all his excess airspeed for altitude, flew into treetops 20 feet higher.

For many days after the accident, condolences for our loss poured in. The common knowledge said a MAF plane had crashed. In a village 80 miles to the south, the people mourned for three days until they learned the truth. In another village down the river from the crash site, people said to us, "Now we understand why you don't always take our cargo. We used to think it was just because you didn't want to. Now, every time we hear one of your planes fly over, we pray for you."

The 3-D, full-color images in my brain and dreams reminded me my life didn't belong to me, but to God. My serving him didn't also grant me the right to trifle with it. My life depended upon his grace, but he also expected me to use the brains he gave me to care for it.

Made me thankful for two things: our supporters' prayers that kept me walking close to God's grace, and MAF's strict safety rules that acted like stout guard rails on jungle aviation's twisty road.

NEVER SAY NEVER

Grass Valley sits comfortably amidst the Sierra Nevada foothills—broad valley to the west, towering mountains to the east. We bought an old farmhouse with a barn three times bigger on an acre and a half of land. We had maples, a fruit orchard, grape vines, two cross-fenced pastures, and a stand of 100-foot pine trees with long, straight, branchless trunks for the first 80 feet.

A month after we moved in, I stood with Regina watching sunlight filter through pine tops down onto our land. I thought of the Tahoe National Forest a few miles up the mountain. The stunning views down the road. The absence of city traffic. Town was only two miles away but could've been 20 for the little it impacted us. I felt at home, in a place I could put down roots and grow. I pictured the improvements we'd make to the property. We knocked out a wall the night we moved in. Already thinking of expanding the back south-facing wall for solar heating. The barn would morph into shop and artist studio. Maybe we'd finish and rent out the top floor. And why not a horse or two in the pasture? Eventually, the kids would inherit the house. But in the ensuing years, we would turn it into a modest mansion.

I turned to Regina and said, "Honey, burn the boxes."

"What?" she asked, eyebrow raised.

"Yeah, burn the boxes. We don't need them anymore. This is home. We're never moving," I declared.

"Never?"

"Nope, never," I confirmed.

She nodded, neither agreeing nor disagreeing.

While I did note her ambivalence, I failed to notice another's reaction. God in heaven was running the universe, spinning galaxies, answering prayers, renewing hearts and minds. But my statement caught his attention. He gave an angel charge to tend a misbehaving galaxy and leaned over to open a trapdoor in heaven's floor. The hinge creaked, and he looked down at me confidently

*proclaiming my future as fact. He mused, "Never? Now that's interesting ..."
He smiled and closed the door. "Never," he repeated to himself, shaking his head
and chuckling as he walked away.*

*I continued fixing airplane radios and moved into our new homestead. At
the same time, I began freelance flight instruction at the local airport (Nevada
County Airpark) in friends' C-150 and C-172. Then, when a new flight club
formed around a Grumman AA-1B Trainer and AA-5B Tiger, the members
asked me to be their instructor as well. I balanced both jobs for a year.*

*One day after an instruction flight, I walked across the small parking lot
behind the FBO (Fixed Base Operation), talking with my student. Suddenly I
heard someone say, "You're going to buy and run this FBO." I stopped mid-
stride. Looked in every direction. No one there. My student continued walking.
Stopped. Turned back, puzzled. "Anything wrong?" he asked.*

*"No, nothing ..." I replied, still searching for pranksters hiding behind cars.
Found none. So, who spoke? And what a thought. Preposterous. Impossible. Yet
it also piqued my interest. I'd been the FBO's customer for months. I knew I
could offer better service. But I had no money, even if it were for sale. Still ...*

*A few weeks later the owners put the FBO up for sale. Regina and I jumped
in. We took out a second mortgage on our house. Using that as a seed, I assembled
a small team of investors who purchased the business. Regina and I served as
managing partners.*

*I learned: About business—Regina became a better accountant than the pros
I hired. About management—if I took care of my people, they'd take care of
me. About politics—the perils of becoming unequally yoked.*

*The flying proved fabulous. Hard to believe I actually got paid to spend all
day in and around airplanes. I taught a lot of people to fly. Seeing the sudden
spark of passion flare in their eyes when they conquered a difficult maneuver,
when they realized they could fly, fueled many days. Helping people reach their
destinations stoked my need to serve. Seeing and hearing them marvel at the
beauty of God's creation seen from flight's unique perspective fed my inner artist,
made me feel each flight was a song composed or a painting brushed.*

*The flight school grew. We expanded our air taxi service, successfully
navigating a major regulation change to earn a single- and multi-engine Part 135
Air Taxi Certificate—made more daunting by our assigned FAA Inspector
who deemed the "letter of the law" to be insufficient.*

I hired pilots to instruct and to fly charter. Most worked out well. One shone. Joe Leonhardt, a retired Air Force fighter jock, who moved into the Chief Pilot role. He proved worth more than his weight in gold in professionalism and customer service. He became a role model I imitated every way I could.

Satisfied I'd finally planted the essential taproot, I settled into a challenging, but very good life. Safe. Secure. Set.

CITY IN THE SKY

Our annual MAF Ecuador Staff Family conference took place right after Christmas. The Mangayacu church camp sat just high enough to be mosquito free, yet only 30-minutes' drive from Shell. Great location. But after our week retreat finished, everybody turned left onto the highway to head back to Shell. Regina, the kids and I, however, turned right and headed up into the Andes Mountains. Four and a half hours later, we drove into Ecuador's capital city, starting a six-month fill-in while our Quito pilot family left for furlough.

Suddenly dropped into the midst of a 500-year-old city of 1.5 million people, my work changed dramatically. It became as much about keeping our entire fleet in the air with current permissions, fuel, and parts as it was about flying a particular mission myself. I exchanged navigating between mud holes for finding my way amidst the warren of downtown offices. I manipulated yoke and throttle less, computer keyboard and mouse more. I traveled by air less, and taxi more.

Rubbing shoulders with imperious Air France captains and Ecuadorian Civil Aviation officials in carpeted hallways demanded a different working uniform. I traded jeans and hiking boots for pressed trousers, shined shoes, pilot's shirt with epaulets, navy blue tie, a leather jacket and briefcase.

Unanticipated consequences surprised me—chaotic traffic, diesel fumes, crowds, noise, robbery risk, and disagreement between streets and maps. But they soon faded to background annoyances. Physiological effects of frequent, large altitude changes took longer to bring under control. On any given flight day, I might go from airport elevation of 9,250 feet, up to 18,000 feet, down to sea level, back up to 17,000 feet and then finish at 9,250 feet again. For the first two or three months, I stayed close to bathrooms (not easy while actually in the air) and slept only fitfully. I called Neal Bachman, my predecessor. Doctors advised him, he said, to take megavitamin doses and drink plenty of water. A week of that regime alleviated both problems.

Mastering a Spanish more complex than the jungle variety presented my biggest trial. In the jungle, a ten-year-old's level sufficed where most either spoke Spanish as their second language or were content with its simpler forms. Quito life instantly reduced my communication ability to a three-year-old level. Church became a chore to be endured, social life a test of how long I could smile and nod. Aviation remained my only respite, the one life area I felt like an adult.

Five months into our six-month temporary assignment, Neal transferred to a non-aviation ministry with a local church in Quito. That vacated the position of Quito Base Manager, which Gene asked me to fill. Our move became permanent.

Initially, the Quito base flew two trip profiles with one turbocharged C-206: Air ambulance to bring serious Amazon Jungle patients to Quito, and medical support flights in the northwestern Coastal Jungle. Within a year the work expanded.

I came to MAF from the world of commercial air charter aviation—technically known as FAR Part 135 Air Taxi. Flying in the clouds using a government-authorized instrument flight system was a given. Ecuador had a smaller, though adequate, system, but our MAF focus was on jungle flying. We flew IFR (Instrument Flight Rules) between Quito and Shell only as a last option. However, once in Quito, I began flying IFR regularly. While I couldn't fly in all weather, using the authorized system greatly expanded the times I could fly. That encouraged the rest of our pilots to take fuller advantage of the system which, in turn, provided our clients better service.

Within a few months we realized we had enough demand to offer scheduled service for a fixed price per seat between Quito and Shell. We flew one round trip—Quito-Shell-Quito—on Monday, Wednesday, and Friday. Mission workers, family members, even NGO clients could ride to either city within an hour rather than endure the four-to-five-hour ordeal over the road. The shuttle, useful during normal times, became indispensable when strikes or landslides closed the road for days or weeks.

Shell sits on a sharp 30-by-10-mile plateau marking the boundary between Andes Mountains and Amazon Jungle. At 3,400 feet elevation, the town perches above jungle to the east but shrinks below mountains to the west. The Pastaza River gushes from its mountain gorge restraint 150 feet below the Shell airport. Once free, it spreads out in a wide, twisted braid of channels creating a thousand gravel bars and dozens of green islets on its way toward the Atlantic.

When I flew to Quito, I took off from Shell's Runway-30 climbing straight out, northwest toward the pass leading me into the belly of the Andes. In five miles I entered the gorge. Three more miles, I passed the electronic intersection, TOPO, and turned slightly left, to the west. Kept climbing. Fifteen miles south of that path, the 17,000-foot snow-covered volcano, Altar, pierced the sky. Closer, jungled foothills mounted successive ridges to the lofty peaks. From the closest cliffs, waterfalls cascaded hundreds of feet, long silver arrows racing to hidden rivers below, without name, on no map, known only to their Creator.

Climbed more. The river cutting deep into the canyon reached 6,000 feet elevation in the next 30 miles. But the closest ridges pointing toward me rose more quickly, reaching for 7,000, 8,000, 9,000, 10,000 feet. Power loss in the gorge would be bad. The road offered no help—tight against sheer cliffs on the north and hanging over sheer drops on the south. We scouted a half dozen flat places, all on cliffs just above the river, and kept them firmly in mind. I thought again about landing on one. Break the airplane for sure but offered the best chance to save the people. Surviving a forced landing anyplace else on that route lay in the province of miracles.

Kept climbing. Passed over Baños, a mountain resort town clinging to the very base of an active, 16,500-foot volcano. Tungurahua remained quiet for nearly a century but then began erupting again sporadically in 2000. On the days it spewed, I flew wide on the upwind side of its dense column of smoke and ash. Volcanic debris is not aircraft friendly.

I had good weather, so started my turn north cutting the corner low over a 10,000-foot ridge. If wet jungle air blowing up the canyon hit this ridge, it would rise with the terrain, cool, and produce a cap of cloud folded over the top. As the air descended the downwind side, it would warm and shred as the cloud evaporated—a river of cloud, always forming, always flowing, always shredding.

As I turned north, I escaped the gorge and entered Ecuador's central Andean valley. The good weather let me level off at 12,500 feet. Bad weather would have compelled me to climb to 18,000 feet and fly IFR. Mountains, some perpetually snow-capped like 22,000-foot Chimborazo on my left, or the 18,000-foot volcano Cotopaxi ahead on the right, still rose above me. But they lay far enough away to allow a sense of expanse, of open freedom.

What we call civilization appeared, jungle giving way to roads, fields, and towns. The *Pan Americana*, Ecuador's principal north-south highway, ran through the valley. It also contained most of Ecuador's major cities and farming country. When the Incas conquered this valley, only 70 years before the Spanish Conquistadors arrived, they replaced local people groups with other conquered groups from far away. The descendants of the shuffled societies came to be known collectively as Quichuas. Productive farmers, their myriad of bordered plots and field covered the 9,000-foot valley floor and spread up every available slope reaching a thousand feet above me. I imagined a farmer behind his oxen team looking down upon the top of my wings, much like I observed condors in the jungle.

This is earthquake country and the mountains' beauty belies

their treacherous hearts. They have swallowed entire towns amidst their violent thrashing, lain quiet, then swallowed rebuilt towns again. The Incas spoke of the volcanoes as quarreling demon lords unmindful of humanity's thin veneer about their feet.

My route followed the Pan Americana, past the city of Ambato, and over the city of Latacunga. More farms and roads. More greenhouses—acres of plastic-covered buildings glowing red, yellow, pink, green, orange, every color of Ecuador's burgeoning flower trade. Then after 50 miles, the valley narrowed again, and the ground rose below me. A pass formed between the giant Cotopaxi Volcano on my right, and the more diminutive volcano pair, Illinizas, on my left. A 12,000-foot-high ridge ran between the two gateposts. As I crossed it at 12,500 feet, I passed over a remnant of the early US space program.

Before communications satellites proliferated, 1960 and 70's technology required that specialized sites be located all around the globe to maintain constant contact with orbiting Mercury, Gemini, and Apollo spacecraft. On this ridge, locally known as "Mini Track," I looked straight down into its upward-pointing dish antenna. It reminded me I shared at least a visceral connection with one of aviation's more glamorous sides.

The ridge, with its highway snaking through man-planted pine forest, passed quickly behind me. The valley floor dropped again to 10,000 feet, but immediately on the right rose the 14,500-foot volcano, Rumiñahui. A massive explosion blew out its side in ages past, forming the massive cliffs that claimed Freddy's life.

Farm field quilting opened, making space for the cities of Machachi and Aloag. To the west, on my left, Aloag hosted the entrance to the heavily traveled, but treacherous road winding up over the western Andes then down to the coast. To the right, another blown out volcano, Pasochoa, guarded Aloag's eastern flank.

I flew over more hedge-rowed fields. Suddenly a city appeared. A big city, squeezed 40 miles north into a narrow valley only four miles wide that clung to the eastern slopes of the 16,000-foot volcano, Pichincha. Roofs, miles of roofs. In the south, flat, gray cement roofs covered one- and two-story houses. Those gave way to the red tile roofs marking the old city. Then I came to the newer, more prosperous northern sector with multi-story offices, apartments, and wider streets. To the east stood the tall towers of condos on the ridge between Quito and the Pifo valley. Beyond that, the eastern Andes rose to escort the 19,000-foot snow-covered volcanoes Antisana and Cayambe.

I spotted the international airport ahead, the biggest, straightest open space in the sea of tightly packed buildings and narrow streets. I talked to Quito approach control. They sent me directly toward the runway, then transferred me to the control tower. The operator cleared me to land straight in, so I flew over the bullring then touched down on Runway 35.

The next day I flew in the opposite direction to the northwest Coastal Jungle, which offered the greatest variety of terrain and flight conditions of any route in the country. After fueling, loading cargo, presenting the flight plan, then loading passengers, I radioed for a clearance if I needed an instrument departure, then radioed again for permission to taxi. Getting to the departure end of Runway 35 was a short but potentially hazardous roll from our ramp. Our nearly two-ton Turbo C-206 was definitely the little gal on the airport. During high-traffic times, we joined the line on the taxiway, keeping up with the Boeing or Airbus ahead. The trick was to hang back far enough so when the big-engined beast added power to turn onto the runway, we didn't get blown over—literally. At the same time, I had to move fast enough to keep ahead of whatever taxied behind me.

When my turn finally came, the control tower authorized me into takeoff position but had me hold in place. I lined up over the centerline and stared down nearly two miles of pavement—just enough for the heavier jets, but nearly a cross-country flight for us. Some jungle strips were that close, needing only five minutes from start up to shut down, but a whole day's hard walk overland.

The tower operator cleared me for takeoff, I pushed the

throttle fully in and waited a moment for the turbocharger to spool up. Even though the engine oil temperature was warm, the first takeoff of the day at this altitude always required a moment more for the engine to wake up. As the manifold pressure and RPMs settled into place, I released the brakes.

At that altitude, even with turbocharging, I needed almost 1,500' to get airborne and a total of 2,800 feet to gain 50 feet of altitude. That left another 7,400 feet of runway beneath me as I climbed north. The 15,600' volcano, Pichincha, remained on my left. I wouldn't be topping it on this flight but continued straight until its skirts lowered enough for me to cross over. At the town of Calacali, I finally had room and turned left to a northwest heading passing on the north side of Pichincha.

As I continued on the northwest heading, we crossed the equator—a common occurrence flying out of the Quito base. When we first installed GPS in the Quito airplane, one of our pilots programmed the locations of several airstrips we frequently flew to. I happened to draw the very next flight and was using the traditional VOR navigation system but also monitoring the route the GPS presented to see how they compared. At the point where we routinely turned right to head north toward the destination airstrip, the GPS indicated a left turn.

Maybe there's a small discrepancy between how the two systems define this point, I thought. Because I was flying according to instrument rules, I followed the VOR and turned right as normal. But the GPS showed the course as farther and farther to the left. Not a good sign.

Later I learned the helpful pilot forgot that even though most of our airstrips were south of the equator, a few—like the one I headed to that day—lay north of the equator. A minus sign required for the unit's programming had to be changed to a plus sign. Reminded me that for all the overarching perspectives flying offered, it remained incredibly dependent upon getting all the details correct, every time.

The lowest terrain beneath me was over 9,000' elevation, but the weather was clear, so I only had to climb to 12,500 feet. Some days clouds in this pass required me to fly IFR to pass through. That meant donning oxygen masks, climbing to 16,000' and picking up the airway (electronic highway in the sky). Fortunately, the instrument route, though higher, was almost identical to the visual route, so the normal trip time of 45 minutes was increased by only five minutes.

But this route from modern mountain metropolis to isolated jungle village had two weather choke points—clouds bunching up in the mountain pass I just flew through, and low stratus layers covering the Coastal Jungle. Every flight could involve instrument flight. Both pilot and aircraft had to be certified and current.

The terrain began dropping in long, finger-like ridges streaming from the 15–20-thousand-foot Andean peaks down toward the Coastal Jungle and the sea. I stayed in a valley between two of them, the Pichincha Volcano still on my left and the Maquipucuna Biological Reserve on my right. Its sheer cliff faces pointed arrow-like along my route. Five minutes later I passed the Mindo Cloud Forest Reserve.

Another four minutes and I reached Pacto/PACTO, both a town below and the name of an electronic aerial intersection. The valley floors were now down to 5,000' and the mountain extensions broadening, merging into the lower Coastal Jungle. I had to start descending soon to arrive at the correct altitude for landing, but clouds butted up against the foothills and spread all the way to the western and northern horizons. I had to time the descent to reach ROKAX—another ATC (Air Traffic Control) electronic intersection—at 6,000 feet, or above the cloud tops, whichever was higher.

When I arrived at ROKAX, the white blanket still lay far below, so I called ATC. They authorized an instrument descent through the stratus layer. I turned north, lowered the nose, watched the airspeed build in the smooth air, and kept the descent rate to 500 feet per minute to be nice to my passengers' eardrums. If I did it correctly, a glance at my passengers would reveal them content in their own worlds, maybe even bored.

I had those moments of just holding course and descent rate to again enjoy my world, my space as a sky creature. On top of the clouds, brilliant white carpet beneath, deep blue expanse above, land-side cares remote at best, their existence a non-factor to the denizens of the air. The cloud tops began taking on distinct form, slow undulations like the sea's turning swells. Closer and closer, never stopping, we approached the floor. Wispy cloud tendrils reached up, tickling the plane's wheels, then wings, then enveloping us in light gray. No bumps in coastal stratus. A thin, soft layer that I hoped had a smooth, definite bottom. We passed through the temporary sky floor and entered earth space, still well above the hills and their trees, dark, rolling mottled green below, smooth gray above, clear in between.

Passengers, catching sight of their world, took notice. Closed books. Spoke a few words to each other, then returned to contemplate the growing detail below. They knew their work approached, so game faces were in order.

One of our medical mission clients, Dr. Cal Wilson, worked with the Chachi Indians in Esmeraldas province. Getting his team to their work site required a 10-to-12-hour drive to and through the city of Esmeraldas on the Pacific coast, then a four-to-six-hour canoe trip to reach their clinic on the Onzole River. But we flew them to a strip called Limones on the coast near the city of Valdez in an hour. From there they still had a three-to-five-hour canoe trip, but the time savings allowed them to arrive on site, ready to work, rather than waiting until the following day.

One problem serving Dr. Cal and his team became apparent—coordinating their estimated arrival time at the airstrip with our landing to retrieve them. We considered installing a radio at the clinic, but the most likely delays occurred on the river journey between the village and the airstrip. Water levels changing unpredictably could easily add an hour or two to their trip time. Initially, we flew along the river, trying to locate them en route to Limones. We found them once or twice, waggling wings to respond to their waves, but the scheme still required long waits.

Finally, I equipped them with a battery powered shortwave radio that functioned in a wooden dugout canoe. I used a version of our standard jungle village unit made by Stoner Radio. Two-thirds briefcase size, the sealed unit contained a two-channel, five-watt, two-way radio and its batteries. The setup wouldn't survive dropping into the river but could cope with splash, spray, and mist. I selected a six-foot, tunable vertical whip antenna clamped to the canoe's side, then coupled that with a 12-foot "ground" wire that trailed the canoe in the water.

On their return day, they radioed a progress report along the river and I scheduled their pickup flight. However, success depended upon the canoe radio operator using a simple antenna tuning procedure to compensate for different conditions. The operator turned the radio on, moved a switch to the "Tune" position, adjusted a sliding button on the antenna plus or minus a quarter inch or so to get a maximum meter reading, moved the switch to the "Operate" position and started talking—a 15-second task. Unfortunately, while the canoe operator expertly navigated the river labyrinth and skillfully captained the canoe and its motor, he possessed less electro-mechanical aptitude. His life experience did not include adjustments smaller than plus or minus six inches, which was also the full mechanical range of the antenna slide. Results were not always optimal.

Seeing the Big Pumpkin

When I moved to the Quito Base Manager role, I discovered traditions colliding with ministry needs. For example, we scheduled flights Monday through Saturday but remained on-call only for emergency flights Sundays. That worked for all our regular users but one—HCJB.

HCJB started as an international radio ministry in the mid-1930s. In the ensuing decades, it grew to also include two hospitals, a village water system ministry and village health promotion. They also established a research clinic at Zapallo Grande— Spanish for *Big Pumpkin*—that focused on finding a treatment for Onchocerciasis, or River Blindness. This infection spreads by fly bites and causes total, irreversible blindness in millions of people worldwide.

Initially, reaching Zapallo Grande from Quito required a 12-to-18-hour drive that positioned the doctors for an additional four to six-hour canoe trip on the Cayapas to reach the village—if the river cooperated. But when MAF set up the Quito base, the trip time was reduced to 45 minutes total. Besides greatly increasing the team's productive time on site, it also opened the door to collaboration with international medical researchers.

Part of their research involved analyzing blood samples drawn from affected patients. However, Zapallo was too remote to staff and equip a lab able to process those samples. Once flights were available, however, the HCJB team and MAF found a solution. When the doctors and technicians were in the village, they radioed us when ready to collect patient blood samples. If the weather looked good, we approved the collection. Forty-five minutes later, we arrived with ice-filled coolers. We packed the samples and flew back to Quito. A waiting car delivered the coolers to the lab. Our six-day schedule allowed for sample collection during the week but presented a problem for actually staffing the clinic.

The HCJB medical work relied heavily on national doctors and technicians. Many were loaned part-time from Ecuadorian hospitals for the research project—with one caveat. They had to be back in Quito and on duty at their regular jobs Monday morning. That dramatically limited who could participate in the research. So, I asked our Quito team to consider offering HCJB Sunday non-emergency flights to and from Zapallo. I reasoned that the HCJB work was bona fide ministry the same as a pastor, worship leader or bus driver bringing folks to church. And if we were all in the ministry, we should be able to serve them without trampling over anyone's Sabbath rest concerns. The team agreed, so we developed a plan. Fly them to Zapallo Grande on Thursday and bring them back to Quito on Sunday. HCJB negotiated with the Ecuadorian hospitals and won approval that also allowed for the occasional weather glitch, dramatically improving their staffing levels.

Flying to Zapallo, I had only two passengers aboard, but we were heavy with clinic supplies and special equipment. Our regulations authorized landings at full gross weight, but the strip could get soft, making taxiing and subsequent takeoffs challenging.

The strip sits down at 300 feet elevation within a warren of jungle-covered hills. When flown at low altitudes, the area becomes a twisted, bumpy maze. If low clouds pressed down, getting lost while hunting for the strip presented a real danger—until GPS. The satellite signals offered tremendous confidence that the strip was "over there" exactly.

Winding through the labyrinth, the Cayapas River encircled the village and its airstrip almost completely in a long, tight ox-bow. Villagers delighted telling us of big fish caught on the airstrip when flooded by a rising river. Fortunately, reports for several days included little rain and normal water levels. Forty-two minutes after takeoff from Quito, we arrived overhead.

Because of the heavy airplane, I flew a low pass first to double check the surface. Normally I chose the steeper approach over a hill and landed to the northeast. That allowed us to touch down on the strip, roll a short distance and go around if something wasn't right. It was also the direction we took off. But a stiff breeze dictated a landing to the southwest. That placed my landing abort point one-quarter mile out from the end of the strip. Past that I was committed to touching the ground someplace.

I passed 500 feet over the strip, checking the entire length. No pigs, kids, dogs or logs marred its surface. I could even see occasional patches of dry dirt along the footpath running its entire length. The fast-growing grass was moderately high but okay.

As I passed the end of the strip, I made a climbing left turn back up to pattern altitude, then flew the rectangular pattern to set up for landing—upwind, crosswind, and downwind. Then I lined up with the runway centerline and kept my aim spot motionless in the windscreen. Wind held steady. Airplane was set up. No runway incursions. A quarter mile out, just over 100 feet above ground, everything looked good. I continued, flew low over the roof of the house built there despite our objections, touched wheels to sod, braked, and came to a complete stop halfway down the 1,700-foot runway.

I prepared to turn around and taxi back to the unloading area where a small group waited to greet the doctors and carry the cargo to the clinic. Taxiing a heavy 206 on a soft strip required a delicate balance of power, brakes and nose wheel steering. Too timid and the plane would either bog down and stop, or else move but not turn. Too aggressive and the plane would tear up the surface, creating a rut that would affect later takeoffs and landings and also offer an erosion point.

I was in the middle of the strip, so looked left and right. Left looked drier. In fact, I could see a few of the bare dirt patches I'd spotted from aloft. I increased power to start the plane moving through the soft turf, then reduced it to keep the speed down once we started moving. I headed left to put my left main wheel on a big dry spot in preparation for turning right to head back in the opposite direction.

As I reached the spot to start my turn back, I looked right to be sure no one had wandered into the area. Three hundred horsepower swinging a 6-foot, 70-pound 3-bladed knife would quickly mince anyone in its path. The area looked clear, so I continued moving. While I was still looking right, the airplane dipped slightly left. *Must be a low spot hidden in the grass*, I thought. I'd need extra power to climb out. Still looking where I wanted to go, I tightened my grip on the throttle. I just started pushing the heel of my right hand against the knob but stopped and pulled the power back. Something didn't feel right. The plane still tilted left. I turned my head left to look out the left window and could see neither trees nor people. I saw only grass. Grass? *How deep is this low spot?* I wondered. I looked down at the left main landing gear. The leg disappeared into the grass, obscuring the wheel completely. Then I looked up and out along the left wing. The tip, normally more than six feet off the ground, now touched the grass.

I pulled the power back to idle then shut the airplane down completely. Unstrapping and hanging my helmet, I asked my passengers to exit also. As we climbed out the pilot's door on the left, we had to duck low and head aft to come out from under the wing. When the passengers were well clear of the plane, I returned under the wing, got down on all fours and crawled to the landing gear. The flat leg curved out and down as normal but disappeared not only into the grass but into the ground as well. I pulled grass away and saw the top of the wheel below ground level in a dark hole.

I reached inside the airplane, turned on the power and radioed Pancho, our dispatcher back in Shell on the other side of the country still waiting for my on-the-ground call.

"Shell, Shell, Shell from One-Zero."

"One-Zero, from Shell. Go ahead, Capitán," Pancho answered.

"We're on the ground in Zapallo, but a wheel fell into a hole. Everyone is okay. I'll investigate and call back," I explained.

I shut everything down again, then stood next to the plane. My passengers had work to do, so we put the welcoming committee to work carrying their cargo to the clinic.

Next, I had to get the airplane off the runway so any help I might need could land. With the wheel in a hole, towing or pushing the airplane was impossible. Then I realized something about the gathering crowd. Zapallo Grande mixed two distinct people groups in good enough harmony to live together for 400 years—indigenous Chachi Indians forced into the jungle by the Spanish Conquistadors, along with Coastal Blacks, descendants of survivors from a slave shipwreck off the Ecuadorian coast.

The Chachi are short. The Coastal Blacks stood tall. I called to Eliseo, a muscular Coastal Black who served as the airstrip coordinator and also a community leader. I explained an idea. He listened carefully, nodded, said, "One moment, Capitán." He spoke to the crowd, then strode off into the village. Fifteen minutes later he returned with a dozen more men, some Chachi, some Coastal Blacks. He gathered another dozen from the crowd then motioned to me.

I addressed the group in my eastern Ecuadorian Spanish. Eliseo translated into a mix of coastal Spanish and Chachi. I lined the Chachis along either side of the fuselage, then grouped the Blacks under each wing. Next, I showed each man how to place his hands along rivet rows where skin attached to ribs or bulkheads. I gave the signal, and all lifted simultaneously. The entire airplane rose three feet vertically. Then the whole group carried the airplane sideways a dozen feet, circled to point it back toward the loading area, and gently set it down. I attached the tow bar to the nose gear and four men pushed on each wing strut. Together we rolled it to the loading area and pointed it back down the runway.

A walk around revealed no damage to the landing gear, fuselage, pod, wing or propeller. However, the outer third of the left horizontal stabilizer and elevator were bent upwards more than 10 degrees. Clearly not airworthy. Not surprising, but still a bummer. This, our newest Turbo C-206, had been deemed operational by Civil Aviation's bureaucracy only a few months earlier. Equally apparent, I needed help.

I powered up the radio again, called Shell, and talked with Dave, our maintenance director. After hearing my story, he asked a series of questions requiring detailed answers. We signed off the radio. I opened the emergency tool kit stowed aboard and removed inspection covers on the stabilizer and elevator skins. Shining my flashlight inside, I checked every place Dave requested. I counted ribs, which ones sustained damage, the condition of the spars, the measured location of any bends, breaks or popped rivets. Confirming I'd answered every question, I radioed Shell again and passed the information to Dave.

"Okay, copy that. I'll plot this data and check the manuals. Call me back in 15 minutes," he said.

I turned the radio off again, checked my watch, then strode down the runway toward the hole. This would certainly qualify as an incident, if not an accident, which would, in turn, give birth to a succession of paperwork and interviews. That meant a series of exact measurements, so I started a sketch. The still-visible wheel tracks in the grass showed where I'd first touched down and each time I'd applied the brakes, straight down the center of the runway. I passed the airstrip's 50% marker and paced off 52 feet more to the end of my landing roll, a total of 921 feet from the runway threshold. I noted those on the drawing then resumed counting paces. The tire tracks veered left where I'd started to position the airplane for a complete turn back to the right. One hundred thirty-eight feet from the marker, the left main gear track stopped at the hole.

A sun-dried, bare dirt footpath passed inches from the hole— the spot I'd aimed for as the safest place to put the wheel. I got down on all fours again and probed the hole. This was no mere soft mud spot—my reach found no bottom. I shone my flashlight into the hole. It dropped away four or five feet into a cavern. A six-inch thick, grassy sod plug lay atop a small mound on the floor directly below the hole. The cavern itself seemed to run at a 45 degrees angle across the strip. Time almost up, I rose and walked in the direction the cavern ran to the far side of the runway. A sinking soft spot lay concealed in the grass at the runway's edge.

On the radio, Dave said Brian and Danny were gathering materials and tools to attempt an airworthy field repair that would allow me to ferry my airplane back for permanent repair. They estimated taking off in the C-180 within 30 minutes. Flying from Shell, crossing the Andes Mountains directly to the Coastal Jungle in a normally aspirated C-180 was not foolhardy. But it did stretch the airplane's capabilities—even if the weather cooperated.

Eliseo brought a large white sheet I'd requested earlier. I stretched it out flat over the hole, then laid thick branches along two edges to hold it in place. The marker would be visible from the air as well as on the ground. The C-180 would probably land shorter than I did in the C-206, but if not, they could still roll by the hole safely.

I returned to the airplane, pulled out the MAF Aviation Operations Manual we always carried on board and turned to the sample Incident Form. On a separate piece of paper, I answered the questions: runway measurements, weather conditions at the time of landing, hours accumulated on the airplane, hours I'd been awake, my activities for the previous 48 hours, any medications I was taking, any unusual stress factors, damage to the airplane, etc. I drew a picture of the main gear tire hanging through the cavern's ceiling.

Two hours later I heard the C-180 before I saw it. I radioed with the latest weather info and the marker location. They circled the field, approached from the same direction I did, then landed, stopping well short of the hole.

Brian and Danny were both licensed mechanics as well as professional pilots. While I knew how to do a lot of the airframe work, my secondary specialty was avionics, so I became their helper. Besides tools, rivets and other hardware, they brought specially fashioned pieces of .050" aluminum to reinforce the two bent spars once we straightened them. Battery powered drills and Cherry rivet guns allowed us to attach the braces rendering both stabilizer and elevator strong enough for flight loads. Strategic application of duct tape streamlined the installation. By midafternoon, the plane was ready to fly.

Brian and Danny reviewed their work with Dave via radio. I, the moderately knowledgeable observer and soon-to-be test pilot, helped confirm their diagnosis and treatment. All agreed I could do a one-time ferry flight—without passengers or cargo—from Zapallo Grande to Quito.

With the hole still marked, I taxied to the far end of the runway and took off in our usual departure direction. The airplane performed normally, but I circled the strip a couple times. No vibration or control anomalies. I continued a climb toward ROKAX, obtained a clearance and continued climbing into the low stratus layer. But I didn't break out on top of the clouds as I expected. Still, in the soup, I asked Esmeraldas tower for the latest weather reports. A TAME (Ecuadorian state airline) B-727 had passed the airway between Quito and Esmeraldas a half hour earlier. They reported a solid cloud layer below them at 10,000 feet without cumulus buildups. The tower operator read me the latest Quito report—broken ceiling (50-90% sky coverage) at 12,000 feet. Good visibility underneath. No cumulus clouds observed.

I'd be in the clouds until just before ROKAX, fly in visual conditions for a few miles, then enter clouds again as I descended into Quito—a common weather situation for the route. The field repair had, so far, made no discernible difference in the aircraft's performance. But I didn't want to bounce in turbulence or try to evade ice in what amounted to an experimental aircraft. I wondered, *Should I return to Zapallo or continue on to Quito?*

As I debated, I broke out of the cloud tops and saw all the way to the skirts of the Pichincha Volcano. Stratus clouds had indeed plugged the pass but looked like they topped out at 15 or 16,000 feet. No cumulus towered above the layer. I could reach PACTO and beyond in good visual conditions. Once there I'd have to shoot the ILS (Instrument Landing System—a high precision procedure) approach through another thick stratus layer. I called Esmeraldas again, asking for an Instrument clearance into Quito.

I'd temporarily switched the audio off our private shortwave frequency in order to concentrate on talking to ATC. But, as I switched it back on, I heard Brian talking with Pancho.

"Shell from Zero-Three. Affirmative. Tell Gene and David we're returning to Zapallo because of an instrument failure. We'll stay overnight and try to return tomorrow. Ask them to let our wives know we're not coming home tonight. I'll call you again landing in Zapallo."

"Zero-Three from Shell. Roger, Capitán. I'll tell them. Standing by for your call. Shell out."

"Zero-Three from One-Zero," I called. "What's up?"

Brian answered, "Our attitude gyro just turned belly up. The vacuum pump still works, so the gyro itself must've failed. Don't like the idea of two hours' partial-panel IFR this late in the day, at high altitude. We're going back to Zapallo for the night. Hope to have VFR weather tomorrow. How's Ten doing? Over."

"Ten's flying just fine. Good work you two. Also, good call on going back. No cumulus en route, but I'm going to have to shoot the ILS to get back into Quito. Looks like lots of clouds in the pass. Don't think you could do it VFR. Anything I can do for you guys? Over."

"Nothing now," he answered. "But, can you be on the radio first thing in the morning for a Quito report? Over."

"That's affirmative," I replied. "I'm scheduled on frequency at 7:00 but can give you an earlier report if you want."

"Contact time is fine. Talk to you then. Gotta call Pancho now. We're back at Zapallo. Over."

"Okay, copy that. Thanks for coming to help. Sorry you're stuck there now. At least you've got a place to sleep. Over."

"Roger. Shell, Shell, Shell. Zero-Three landing Zapallo," he said, switching back to Spanish.

"Zero-Three from Shell. Copy you landing at Zapallo," Pancho responded.

"Affirmative, Pancho. I'll call you on the ground," Brian said.

I continued on, receiving radar vectors to shoot the ILS instrument approach to the Quito airport. Smooth air in the cloud, no ice. On final, I broke out of the clouds around 12,000 feet to excellent visibility underneath, finished the approach and landed.

The following morning dawned clear of clouds from the coast to the Amazon. Brian and Danny refueled from our cache in Zapallo, took off and landed at Shell before lunch. I ferried the damaged C-206 to Shell where Dave and the maintenance crew had removed the horizontal stabilizer and elevator from Zero-Nine, the regular Quito base C-206 temporarily in the Shell hangar for maintenance. By mid-afternoon, I returned to Quito with a repaired aircraft.

The Zapallo Grande strip fix took longer. When Brian and Danny returned for their unanticipated overnight, they checked out the hole. "It's huge!" Brian reported later. He climbed in, and while standing on the floor, his head was entirely below the runway surface. A local resident also hopped in and walked "a long way" downhill, well past the airstrip edge, then back uphill toward the source that turned out to be a large soft spot along the opposite airstrip edge. After others—doctors, technicians, curious villagers—checked it out, they concluded that during the airstrip construction someone had filled a large hole with logs instead of rocks as instructed. The logs rotted, creating a hole that filled with water which, in turn, enlarged the hole, which then allowed more water to flow and so on. In only five years, underground erosion created the cavern. A dry-appearing spot on the surface was, in fact, the thinnest portion of the cavern roof. For some time, it sustained the weight of people walking across it. But a heavy C-206 wheel broke through.

Eliseo mustered a work team. They attached two bamboo

poles to a wide section of log. Two workers would thump it down on the ground while listening. A solid sound indicated solid ground. A mushy sound signaled a soft spot. A hollow sound revealed a hole just below the surface. Then they dug open all holes and soft spots, and filled them with rock, gravel and finally dirt. Twelve days later we reopened the strip.

FLYING RACHEL

The stall horn warbled like electronic gargle. The airspeed needle pulsed around 50 knots as the airplane settled into the descent. My feet came alive, tapping alternate rudder pedals to level the wings. Using ailerons at such a slow speed only raised the risk of a stall from induced drag. Not a good idea so close to river, rock, and tree.

Final approach to this river sandbar (dubbed "Palm Beach") hadn't improved in 36 years if we believed the old movies. Probably harder now. MAF planes grew heavier and faster than their 1950's progenitors, so I was maneuvering a three-quarter-ton pickup truck where a VW Bug used to fly. And this particular beach had been large enough to land on only for a few months straddling 1955 and 56. Never before nor since.

But why approach at all? We never landed, though we could've—once. Besides incurring grave management displeasure, the available runway area was too short and rocky for modern aircraft. Even if some authoritative miracle occurred allowing us to pilot a MAF plane again, the landing aircraft would become a playhouse for local kids until the next high water carried away its remains.

Nate Saint's last landing place drew us anyway. Wooing spirit and imagination, it attracted our inner-pilot-selves like a mystical magnet. A light schedule combined with a passenger-free plane set the stage. We'd all done it at least once.

Normally, to land at the nearby village of Toñompade, we'd fly at 2,200' through a gap in the hills just wide enough to let the Curaray River pass. Then we'd angle left to follow the broadening valley for a minute. As we reached the village, we'd make a half turn right to position the airstrip on our left side. But in the gap, responding to loud, but unspoken delving into a hidden heart chamber, we curved to the right following Nate's path instead.

What was he thinking when he stayed close to the ridge on the right to have a straight shot at the beach? He must have watched the same trees flashing by closer and closer off the right wingtip while juggling the throttle to stay on glide path. Out of the corner of his eye, below to the left, he would have seen the same black shadow racing along brown river growing larger and larger, dashing up to meet his wheels just where the gravel rises from the water.

I did the same. The touchdown point grew bigger in the windscreen. I passed below the treetops on the banks. I could almost hear the sound of big tires rolling on sand and stone. Was he sweating? I reached my abort point, pushed in the throttle, and climbed away to my next assignment. Legal. Safe. Still alive.

But Nate Saint had continued down and landed for the last time. During those moments when he braked, stopping the yellow Piper in a spray of sand, he had no idea how many lives his skill would touch. While he completed proper shutdown tasks, his four companions waiting on the beach could not imagine how many thousands would soon know all their names, nor could they guess the price for that fame.

Nate Saint, Jim Elliot, Ed McCully, Peter Fleming, and Roger Youderian built a tree house and camped on the beach. They wanted to contact members of a tribe known to outsiders as "Aucas," but who called themselves Waorani. Unfortunately, the five men did not fully understand the tribe's perspective.

After generations of abuse from without, the Waorani called all foreigners "cowodi" (outsiders) with the same passion we'd speak of enemies. The old saying, "Shoot first and ask questions later!" proved too verbose. They shortened it to "spear first." They had no interest in questions or their answers.

Within their clans, twisted tempers took expressions of revenge to demonic levels. An angry man would as likely spear grandma as kick a dog. By the time he was five years old, a boy memorized the names of his family's enemies. His job as a man was to kill them all. If a man's child got sick, everyone knew it was because an enemy had put a curse on them. A witch doctor could tell him who. Dad and friends then hunted and killed the perpetrator of the curse. What if he wasn't home when the vigilantes arrived? No problem, anyone close to him would do— man, woman, child. The new victim's family then hunted and exacted revenge on the killers, which generated return revenge, etc. The Waorani had set themselves on an effective course to extinction.

On 8 January 1956, after apparently friendly Waorani visited the beach a couple of times, they attacked. A party of six men and three women speared all five missionaries to death. Still enraged, they then hacked the airplane apart with machetes.

In the world's eyes, of course, the five men acted impulsively, if not stupidly. While they assured each other they would not repeat the mistakes of five missionaries killed in Bolivia the previous decade, they planned secretly, consulting neither leaders nor friends. They ignored history, dismissed local knowledge, and barely considered the great cultural divide they dared to cross. A needless waste of lives, some said. A preventable tragedy. Thoughtless and irresponsible.

But God knew differently. He knew their hearts' motivation extended far beyond human wisdom, even their own. On one hand, they possessed neither understanding of the risks, nor foreknowledge of their fate. On the other hand, they submitted themselves to the King's plan—obedience their part, outcomes his.

Two-and-a-half years later, three women and a girl—Rachel (Nate Saint's sister), Betty (Jim Elliot's widow), Dayuma (a Waorani refugee from intra-tribal warfare), and Valerie (Jim and Betty's four-year-old daughter)—survived initial contact with the tribe. During the nearly two months the women lived in the jungle, they began the long process of convincing the Waorani that all "cowodi" were not cannibals. The women became a catalyst for a Waorani epiphany—discovering "forgiveness," a subject for which they had neither word nor concept.

In 1961, Catherine Peeke of Wycliffe Bible Translators began working in the Waorani village of Tiwaeno. Rosi Jung joined her in 1969. First, they learned the Waorani language. Then they developed a writing system. After that, they began the long process of Scripture translation. Pat Kelley, also of Wycliffe, started a literacy program among the tribe members in 1971 so that when the Word was ready to be read, they would be ready to read it. Finally, 36 years after Nate's first landing, the Waorani translation of the entire New Testament was dedicated on June 13, 1992, in the small church at Shell, Pastaza, Ecuador.

The spirit of the occasion could be best described in Revelation 5:6."... and with Your blood, You purchased men for God from every tribe and language and people and nation ...." More than 300 people from nine countries and five tribes within Ecuador attended the presentation conducted in both Spanish and Waorani. The master of ceremonies was the son of Minkayi, one of the men who killed the five missionaries. Three more of the attackers—Dyumi, Geketa, and Kimo—also came, as did Dayuma, several translation helpers, and many representatives from the various Waorani villages. Nate's sister Rachel was there as well as his three children—Steve, Kathy, and Phil.

When the three killers met Nate's children, they said, "Please tell your children that we're sorry that we killed their grandfather. We didn't know what we were doing. Please ask them to forgive us."

A special moment in the ceremonies came when David Underwood, Wycliffe's Ecuador Field Director, presented a special token of their appreciation to David Bochman, MAF Program Manager in Ecuador. Mr. Underwood expressed, on behalf of the entire Wycliffe team, their deepest appreciation for the hundreds of flights MAF had conducted to help make the translation work possible. "Without those flights," he said, "the translators could not have traveled from their work center to the villages; the helpers could not have come out for their meetings; supplies and medicines could not have been flown in. None of it would have happened."

Three days after the dedication, I approached Toñompade again, this time neatly sandwiched between gray clouds above and sharp jungle hills below. A dark, tropical downpour sat squarely over my destination, obscuring village and strip. I backed off a few miles upriver, reduced power and flew loitering ovals in a wider part of the valley. Ten minutes. Fifteen minutes. The storm refused to budge despite approaching sunset, dwindling fuel supply, and my earnest desire. But, as I circled with diminishing probability of landing, I realized that God had closed another circle.

What Nate and his friends started with a chancy landing nearly four decades before was now completed. The jungle might hide the Waorani from the world, but beast though it might be, it did not, could not hide them from God. He knew exactly where they lived and his Word was coming to them. In the meantime, I made a final turn and headed southwest back to Shell.

Betty's and Valerie's lives moved onto other paths and ministry, but Rachel chose to live in Toñompade and continued ministering to the Waorani. She lived in a small single-floor, multi-roomed, multi-technology home—metal roofing, indoor plumbing, some wiring, but split bamboo walls, battery electricity, and spotty water supply. She worked on various translation projects but focused her main efforts on "lifestyle evangelism" and advocacy. She also maintained an apartment in Quito, shuttling back and forth between the two locations using a combination of car or bus between Quito and Shell, and then flying with us to her jungle home.

The road trip between Quito and Shell taxed everyone even if everything went right—no landslides, no bridge washouts, and no strikes. A private car could make the trip in just under five hours, while larger vehicles needed six or more. The last 30 miles of road, the only connection between Baños and Shell, wound down the side of the Pastaza River canyon, unpaved, rutted, potholed, muddy or rocky, often single lane, clinging to cliff side on the north and hanging hundreds of feet over the gorge on the south. Buses plunged over the side or rockslides buried vehicles every year, sometimes more often. The route, in fact, presented enough challenge to inspire the local production of T-shirts saying, "I survived the Shell Road!"

Not long after my assignment to the Quito base, Rachel's church in Texas made a bold financial decision. "Rachel," they said, "ground travel from the capital down to MAF's base in the jungle is too hard on you. You're in your late 70s and shouldn't have to put up with that ordeal. We're going to cover the cost of direct flights for you between Quito and Toñompade."

Rachel had become large and less flexible, so I developed a plane-loading configuration just for her. I'm short, so my seat anchored well forward, then I positioned the seat behind me most of the way back. Next, I made room to receive her normal 200–400 pounds of cargo—provisions for her stay in the jungle, items purchased for Toñompade residents, tools, maintenance supplies, medicines, her own luggage, and the silver bag.

The normal flight route went south from Quito, over Latacunga, almost to the Tungurahua Volcano, then east abeam Ambato down the Pastaza River canyon, over Shell, then northeast to Toñompade. Took 1.5 to 1.8 hours, depending upon weather. Sometimes I flew IFR between Quito and Ambato, or Ambato and Shell. A few times, bad weather out in the jungle required I shoot the instrument approach in Shell where we'd wait for Toñompade to open again.

Occasionally, events converged to allow a more direct route. If Rachel arrived early enough, and if I could get the cargo loaded quickly enough, and if the weather over the Andes Mountains around the 19,000-foot Antisana Volcano was good enough, we flew direct in visual conditions. Takeoff to touchdown took only 45 minutes.

Following the direct route, in particular, was like jumping from one planet to another. In Quito, after preparing the airplane amidst roaring jet engines and blaring traffic, I crossed acres of smooth pavement, savoring crisp mountain air, but was still under supervision of high fences, security cameras and guards. Then, garbed in fine trousers, shined shoes, pressed shirt, and tie, I strolled into carpeted offices, mixing with international airline captains to present my flight plan to uniformed civil aviation officials.

Still, in the slick, high-tech world, I accelerated on miles of smooth concrete and took off sandwiched between airliners. I climbed over jammed city boulevards and multistory buildings. Both the tower and Quito Approach control established immediate radar contact with my airplane, skillfully vectoring me around conflicting traffic.

Then, I left the world of the ground-bound behind and entered mine. I soared over trackless Andes peaks, ridges and draws. Looked down upon a thousand unknown meadows and up at giant, snow-encased volcano peaks. Topping the divide, I saw Amazon Jungle stretching east to Peru and beyond. Then I started a descent that passed over eastern foothill cliffs, tumbling waterfalls and rocky rivers merging with primordial forest. Condors soared below me. Clouds, already forming, flanked me. Here, between earth and sky, I found it easy to immerse myself in His presence.

Then I flew low over the green canopy, entered Toñompade's pattern, hemmed in by the ridges, checked wind and strip, and landed. Gravel and grass-laced mud sprayed as my landing gear touched, rolled, slid, rolled again and stopped with only a little skew. I turned and taxied, backstopping again in front of the path leading to Rachel's house.

I opened the window and then the door. Hot. Muggy. Soaked jungle atmosphere barged in, vanquishing any high-altitude air left in the cabin. Immediately I sweat everywhere. Tie? Whose dumb idea was that? I tugged the knot, sliding it loose. I hopped down from my pilot perch, shined shoes splatting into tropical goo. Then I stepped back to help Rachel step down, carefully, slowly, deliberately putting her foot first on the landing gear step then the other onto her home turf.

The kids gathered. Moms followed. Some dads. Rachel spoke with them. I unloaded the pod, trying not to kneel. Bags and boxes emerged. Rachel distributed some to new owners, others to kids eager to carry them to her door.

My shirt back soaked through. My chin and nose dripped. The bugs circled. The chiggers advanced through the grass, intent on reaching my ankles. When I walked on grass jungle strips every day for a couple weeks, I developed the same immunity to their bites as the local residents. But while living in Quito, the critters gave me a couple hundred bites every encounter.

Finally, pod empty, mud scraped from tires, I was ready to go. And then Rachel brought out the silver bag. She unzipped its top, pushed aside the insulated sides and brought out an iced soda and a cool ham sandwich—ambrosia! I sat sideways on my seat, legs and muddy shoes dangling over the edge.

"I must take care of my pilots." She grinned. She turned and hiked carefully up the narrow path away from the airstrip. I finished my treat, swung into the cockpit, closed the door, and flew back to Quito.

Seeds in Rain

One October morning my boss's boss, Gene, invited me to coffee. He told me that MAF asked Dave Bochman, my boss, to take over the leadership of MAF's program in Moscow, Russia, by mid-December. Then, he asked me to fill Dave's role as Ecuador Program Manager. I'd move from caring for two staff families and two national employees in one city to overseeing 14 families, 10 employees, and two national apprentices spread across the entire country.

A few weeks later, while preparing for the change, the phone rang again. I glowered like it acted out as an unruly child. No joy. Theatrical sigh. My management of a flight program seemed to have devolved into a tangle of spreadsheets and admonitions to cut spending even more. Budget deadlines waited for no man.

Ah yes, flight operation. That was still true. This could be a call for an emergency flight. I reached across a mound of stapled reports and open three-ring binders topped by keyboard to the phone pushed back, perched over the desk's edge.

"Good afternoon, Alas de Socorro," I answered in Spanish.

"Hi, Jim. How's it going today?" Tim Anderson, a missionary also stationed in Quito, asked.

"Good, but busy. Budget time. You know how that goes."

"Sure do. Listen, I'm calling to ask a favor. I need a flight out to the jungle."

That got my attention. Tim had a successful city ministry. We'd occasionally talked about him visiting the jungle where we flew most often, but he and his wife, Debbie, were just now getting back to normal after a bout of severe hepatitis. "Okay, tell me what you need," I asked while reaching for pad and pencil.

"A friend of mine, a major supporter actually, is coming to Ecuador next week. He and his wife and daughter want to see the jungle, especially an Indian village. It's all he talks about. Can you help?"

"Well ... " I paused, searching for the right answer while wearing two hats. One displayed Aerial Service Provider whose answer was always "*¡Si, se puede!*", Spanish equivalent of "We can do it!" The other looked for a way to counsel a friend about reality.

He sensed my hesitation. "These folks really help our work ... "

Another pause. "Okay, let me see what I can do. What days are you thinking of?" We talked details, but I stopped short of commitment. Clearly, this request meant a lot to Tim. He led a large, multifaceted ministry reaching many. His work merited support. But his request presented a problem that wasn't his fault.

An unwritten, rarely spoken, but fiercely guarded agreement rested at the center of our good relationship with the indigenous people we served. We flew only known or invited people into jungle villages. Tim's request would be like me knocking on his door escorting a gaggle of foreign tourists there to video his quaint lifestyle. Couldn't do that. Jungle folks trusted us.

Despite my skepticism I prayed, then listed a half dozen villages. Radio inquiries revealed four willing to receive visitors. I called Tim to confirm the choice of willing villages along with our usual jungle visitor briefing. Subsequent days produced further restrictions to the visitors' schedule, leaving us with only a single date for the trip.

Tim and guests arrived on time for our early morning takeoff from Quito. He introduced me to Doug (a middle-aged New York Mercedes Benz dealer) and Connie, and their daughter, Mary. Easy going, neither boisterous nor stiff, they seem pleasant, even gracious on first contact. We boarded the aircraft and, after receiving clearance from Ground Control, taxied to the active runway behind an Air France jet.

Our departure point, convenient to my passengers and me, did create an additional complication. Normally we launched to interior destinations from Shell, our base on the edge of the Amazon Jungle. Leaving from Quito added 45 minutes to each end of the trip. That reduced our flexibility for a quick look-see and scoot back if the weather turned bad. The extra time required to get from the Andes Mountains to the jungle meant we'd have fewer options to meet changing conditions.

We launched, climbing south to 12,500' for the first leg out of Quito. Had to get that high to clear Mini-Track. Once over the blocking ridge, the valley opened again around Latacunga. Then, as we passed abeam the city of Ambato and neared the volcano Tungurahua, we turned left to head east down into the jungle via the Baños Pass. That route would take us along the Pastaza River and directly over Shell. The morning reports indicated variable, but operable, weather in the jungle. As we descended lower and neared Shell, however, radio calls to update the weather indicated all four of our options were closed or marginal. An emergency flight request would justify extra push to get in, and out. But, the worst outcome for not completing this flight would be disappointment. I didn't want to strand my passengers, so I chose the conservative route. We could return to Quito or wait in Shell for better weather. Frustrating, but a typical jungle day.

I was about to divert to Shell when I realized a large area on the south side of the Pastaza River was clear. My earlier choices were all on the north side. Then I remembered Kusutka. And the man who owed me a favor.

So, Daniel, I thought, *can I just drop out of the sky into your home?* Twenty-five minutes later we circled Kusutka. As I finished the landing roll-out and turned the plane to taxi back to the village plaza, Pancho called on the radio.

"Zero-Nine, Zero-Nine, this is Shell. Do you copy?" he asked.

"Shell, this is Zero-Nine, go ahead," I responded.

"Zero-Nine, from Shell. Capitán, Charapacocha called for an emergency flight. Snakebite. You're the only plane in the area. Can you get him?"

So much for plans, I thought, then radioed, "Shell, from Zero-Nine. That's affirmative. Tell them I'll be there in 20 minutes. Please ask them to have the patient and companion ready to go."

"Zero-Nine from Shell. Okay, Capitán. Will do. Thank you."

As the surprised villagers made their way to the unexpected airplane, I explained to Tim and his three guests about the change. "I know you planned only a half-hour visit, but this is a life-and-death matter. I have to do what I can. But don't worry, these folks are very friendly. I'll explain why we're here, then take care of the emergency. From here it's 20 minutes to pick up the patient, then 45 minutes to Shell. Figure 15 minutes to refuel and file my flight plan, then 25 minutes to get here again. I'll be back in two hours tops. Don't worry, these are very friendly folks," I said in my most assuring voice.

Tim grinned, ready for adventure. The New Yorkers grinned, but wide eyes and short, quick nods betrayed their "What have we gotten ourselves into?" concern. I opened the door and hopped out. Fortunately, Daniel stood among the cluster. I asked him for the favor of a tour. He hesitated only a moment, then agreed. His quick assent relieved me, gave me confidence to also let him know I was leaving. Now. No problem, he said. He was happy to take care of guests dropping out of the sky. Five minutes later I was in the air heading southeast to Charapacocha.

The patient needed help—lots. When I reached him, two hours had passed since the bite. The patient and companion were ready, so we loaded and headed to Shell in less than 10 minutes. In the air again, the weather looked troublesome. I could get into Shell—shoot the instrument approach if necessary—but the system that shut down the north jungle no longer sat still. It was moving south.

I made a visual landing at Shell. But as we moved the patient to the ambulance, rain started, clouds lowered, and the airport shut down. Neither me nor my New York passengers, now stuck in an Amazon Jungle, ex-headhunter village, were going anywhere.

I hung by the radio for an hour, bothering Pancho, bothering any village radio operator who happened to be on the air, asking for reports and best guesses. Kusutka's radio was not among them because, I later learned, their radio had been out of service for a week. Hard rain continued in Shell. Hard rain continued in the jungle. I worked on Program Manager tasks around the hangar, my main obligations still safe on my desk in Quito. Someone offered and I accepted lunch. Conversation-drowning rain against metal roof filled hours. Radio remained silent.

To retrieve my passengers from Kusutka and return to Quito on that same day, I had to leave Shell by 4:00 p.m. to remain within legal daylight limits. If I was still in Shell at that time, I'd also have to decide whether to return to Quito by myself—operable weather along that route—and come back the next day, or else stay in Shell that night and pick them up the next morning, weather permitting.

At 3:20 the ceiling lifted over Shell, but the jungle remained closed. I preflighted the plane, just in case. At 3:40 north jungle stations started calling in reports of improving weather. That signaled a good trend but didn't show when the south jungle would improve. At 4:00 reports sounded good enough to take a look, so I launched. The weather southeast along the route to Kusutka remained marginal. I flew under clearing, almost blue skies above me, but over a solid cloud layer below. I had no way to tell if it extended all the way to the ground or not but continued. I expected I'd have to turn around when my calculations said I was over Kusutka. Ten minutes out, still solid cloud below. Five minutes out, the same. I considered turning back, but no reason to quit early. If I couldn't get them, there was no rush. Then, time up.

There, below me, a hole in the clouds framed the airstrip directly beneath it. I slowed the airplane to 80 knots, added 20 degrees of flaps and started a careful descent. At that reduced speed, I could make complete circles smaller than the hole. That would allow me to stay out of the clouds—dangerous and illegal in that location at that altitude. I entered the hole to discern the visibility under the clouds. If I could see far enough, I could continue to a landing. If not, I could climb back up on top and return to Shell. A turn or two would tell me what I needed to know.

I reached the cloud layer and entered the gray, circular canyon. Tops rose above me. The bottom rose to meet me, its distinct edge predicting a thin, defined layer. Good sign. Another half circle and I could see space between the ceiling and the treetops. A little lower I could see several miles. Excellent. I was good to go lower. I descended to pattern altitude to inspect the strip. Would it be dry enough to use? Water still ran off the sides, but no large pools sat on the runway itself. I made a low pass in the same "terrain" configuration—80 knots and 20 degrees flaps. Slow enough to maneuver in tight places, as well as allow time to inspect things outside. That configuration also kept the airplane well ahead of the power curve, enabling me to climb immediately any time I pushed in the throttle.

Kusutka, at 1,640 feet long, was huge, one of the best airstrips in the jungle. But I flew the entire length anyway, keeping the wheels one foot above the ground. With that view, I confirmed no standing water remained, no debris, no new ruts, no creatures. The entire surface glistened like dark chocolate. Dark dirt said mud. Mud meant slippery, which meant I might have a problem stopping before the end of runway. But I was alone, so the plane was light. I could land very slowly—about 50 knots if the wind remained calm—so I should be able to stop in time. The only other challenge would be, like a car with bald tires on ice, keeping the plane going straight.

I climbed, circled left for the landing pattern, made another approach and touched down. Light taps on the brakes verified slippery, but I was able to keep the wheels from sliding, finally stopping a little farther down the strip than normal. Then came the dance of rudder, brakes and nose wheel steering to get the plane turned around to taxi back to the village plaza. I preferred to remain in place and let the passengers walk the extra few feet.

But their likely state of mind prompted me to make the extra effort even if it meant carving up the runway surface more than absolutely necessary.

These were New Yorkers, after all. Godly folks, but definitely not accustomed to mud, bugs, snakes, and dark, smoky, thatched-roof huts. And that was before my delay fed their fears of abandonment in the untamed wilds of the Amazon Jungle—with headhunters. I already pictured wide-eyed, sweaty, mud-streaked faces ghostly pale from dread, or beet-red from stress. I imagined them staggering, slipping, almost falling, trying to run toward the plane, gasping, maybe even crying. I knew our reunion, five hours since I'd left them, was not going to be pretty.

I rolled, slipped, and slid back down the runway, finally reaching the plaza. A look around showed no one. Odd. I shut down, completed the after-landing checklist, then hopped out. Mud covered the sides of the fuselage and horizontal stabilizer. The cargo pod under the belly was completely encased—not surprising. Still no one. They couldn't have missed my arrival since the low pass prior to landing demonstrated the C-206's robust ability to transform gasoline into noise.

I considered walking into the village but then heard laughing. Laughing? A mix of gringo and indigenous laughs sprinkled out from between the huts closest to the airstrip. Then a small gaggle of kids squirted onto the path, running ahead of strolling adults. Strolling? A chattering cluster of village men surrounded Tim and Doug. A separate gaggle of women enclosed Connie and Mary. All of them ambled, more intent on conversation than their rescuing airplane. Multiple, animated cross talks in Shuar, Spanish and English danced between them. The only indication they knew of my presence was their gradual movement toward the runway, their five-hour overdue departure apparently an afterthought.

Grins. Big grins. Handshaking. Arm clasping. Mud on shoes only. My four passengers, almost reluctant to leave, finally presenting themselves. Goodbyes and sound bites of "Amazing!" and "You won't believe it." bounced among hand waves. New

Yorkers with amazed eyes, Tim with fulfilled eyes. Didn't make sense, but to reap benefit from the weather break, we had to leave now. I engaged my professional pilot game face and left questions until later. No cargo, so no need to clean the pod door. I seated the couple in the middle row behind me, daughter Mary in the third row because she weighed the least, then asked Tim to crawl across the front row to the copilot seat on the right. Door closed, engine running, I started the slip-slide turn process again, pointing the prop blast away from the farewell crowd, and taxied to the takeoff end of the runway. The guests waved all through the turn, calling farewells and "God bless you!" despite engine noise. Tim sat quiet, reflective.

I did one more muddy turn at runway end, completed checklists, radioed Pancho in Shell and took off. Above Kusutka we climbed up through the same cloud hole. On top of the layer, I turned northwest to fly over Shell. From there we'd head west up the Baños Pass out of the jungle and into the Andes Mountains. I set up a cruise climb to 15,000 feet in order to fly by instrument rules. When we reached 12,000 feet, I'd have to put oxygen masks on everyone, so as soon as I finished configuring the airplane, and talking to Pancho and to Air Traffic Control, I turned to my passengers.

"I'm sorry you had to wait so long," I apologized. "The weather closed the whole ..."

"No problem," the family chorused.

"God had an amazing plan," Doug said.

"It's the most amazing experience of my life! I'm so glad we came," Connie exclaimed.

"That was awesome!" Mary hollered from the aft seats.

Tim broke his silence. "You won't believe what God did." He chuckled then added, "I wouldn't believe myself if I hadn't been there." He paused, then looked right at me. "Remember how we've talked about my visiting the jungle someday?"

"Yes," I answered.

"Well, I'll be coming back. Often." Then he told me. Hard rain interrupted their tour about an hour after I left them. Visiting foreigners provided the year's biggest entertainment for Kusutka, so when Daniel sheltered the visitors beneath a large thatched roof without walls, nearly all Kusutka's 130 residents followed. Then it rained harder. After watching the rain, watching each other, watching torrents cascade off trees, a very bored man said to Tim in Spanish, "Aren't you some kind of preacher?"

"Yes," Tim answered.

"Well, talk to us," the man insisted.

They met, listening to Tim for almost four hours. He talked to them about God the Creator, about the Fall, about the Law, and about Christ as Redeemer. Suddenly, while Tim spoke, a man started speaking in a loud voice. Tim stopped, but the man continued. Then another started. And another. Soon several spoke. Most loud, not to each other, but as if proclaiming something to the whole group. Tim had little experience hearing Shuar speakers, but these people seemed to be speaking in a different language. And, as much as he could tell, no two were alike.

Tim remembered a similar account recorded in the Bible (Acts 10:44–46). So, accustomed to dealing with inspired crowds, he regained their attention and explained what was happening. Then he asked if anyone there wanted to surrender the headship of their lives and follow Jesus as their Lord. Several responded by voice or raised hands. Some jumped up. Apparent chaos quickly revealed itself as new, enthusiastic peace. Tim prayed with those desiring a new start, a new life. Daniel, who met Jesus when God rescued his son, joined them, renewing his commitment to serve his redeemer. In a moment Kusutka's Christian population went from one to many.

Tim paused as I handed out oxygen masks. "They asked me to move there," he said. "When I told them I couldn't, they asked me to come back every week. I don't think I can fit that in, but certainly, I'll come once a month." He put on his mask and settled back into thought.

Then he leaned forward, turned to me as he slid his mask to one side. "That was a divine delay. God's used it to sink Kusutka into my heart. Even if I can't do anything else, I feel like we planted a seed." He slid the mask into place and settled into his seat once more.

I checked the flow to everyone's mask, then climbed through 12,000 feet and leveled off at 15,000 feet as we flew through the Baños Pass. A few minutes after making the turn at Ambato, the clouds opened and we continued under late-afternoon skies. We crossed Mini Track again and descended to land 30 minutes before official sunset.

Then the surprise. Tim's seed sprouted. Sooner than expected. Stronger than imagined.

Three brothers, Rueben, Arturo, and Daniel encountered Jesus during that first meeting. Excited, they told their father (one of the few not present for Tim's message) he should also follow Jesus. But, he said he'd watch them for a few years and then decide.

Arturo, the youngest, said, "Dad, you're a leader in the community. You should be leading, not us. If you accept salvation from Jesus, it will be the key to unlocking the whole village."

His dad dismissed the idea. But that night he dreamt that Arturo spoke truth. The next day he chose to turn the management of his life over to Jesus. Within a few weeks, more than 80 Kusutka residents made the same decision.

Tim honored his promise and visited Kusutka at least once a month, preaching, counseling and training new leaders. A year later he left Ecuador for a year of obligatory home ministry to raise support in the US. Some mission observers predicted that the Kusutka church would wither without Tim's constant input.

Not long after Tim's departure, a Kusutka church leader radioed us, saying, "We were reading in the Gospel of Matthew where the disciples were told to 'Go and preach the Gospel.' In our morning prayer meetings, we asked ourselves just who, exactly, was being commanded to do that. We finally decided it was us. We're supposed to go."

Radio conditions were poor that day, so he paused and asked if we copied all that. We did, so he continued. "We've been sending music and evangelistic teams of three or four people to the villages around us. We've been to all of them within 3 to 10-hours' walk. Now we'd like to go further, but it takes so much time and is harder for some of us."

He paused again to be sure we heard. Then he continued with a request. "We know you're very busy doing many flights. But we're wondering ..." Despite the poor radio connection, I could almost hear him swallow. "Is there any chance, any way at all, you could fly us to some of the more distant villages that have airstrips?"

Maintaining a professional radio voice, I said, "That's affirmative. We can do that. When you're ready, give us specific requests during the morning radio contact. If possible, try to give us a week's notice." After we finished the radio contact, those who'd heard his request did the happy dance.

Rather than wither as predicted, the sprouting Kusutka church grew and reached out in ways unprecedented for people who grew up with headhunting parents.

They established one of the jungle's first Christian High Schools in Kusutka, sending more than a dozen graduates to serve as full-time teachers in other jungle villages. Then they started four new elementary schools that serve 400 students. After that they inaugurated two seminary extension programs serving 45 students, placing one in Kusutka itself and the other atop towering cliffs on the north bank of the Pastaza River in Kumai.

Along the way, they initiated many community development projects—building 10 schools and as many churches, clean water works, bridges, a system of medical and dental caravans flying into villages. They also established five pharmacies in villages without airstrips. Additionally, they helped villages acquire chainsaws and generators.

The team grew to fielding a staff of 12 Ecuadorian and expat missionaries working in the jungle to support a host of Shuar pastors and evangelists.

And, most uncharacteristically of all, they sent the first Shuar foreign missionary for a two-year term working with an unreached jungle people group in Honduras. Despite the rain, the seeds sprouted.

FIGHTING FIRE

Our airport also hosted a firefighting base. The USFS (US Forest Service) and the CDF (California Division of Forestry) shared a facility at the east end of the field. Every year during fire season the two agencies based aircraft there—two Grumman S2F tankers, and two spotters, or Air Attack (in firefighting terminology) planes. The CDF used an ex-military, normally aspirated Cessna O-2 while the USFS used the civilian version, a turbocharged Cessna C-337. The CDF owned their O-2 and hired a pilot for it. The USFS, on the other hand, contracted out to a civilian supplier for the C-337 and its pilot.

For our last two seasons involved in the FBO, I also flew as the contract pilot for the USFS airplane. Second only to MAF work, flying for the USFS was the most fun I ever had in an airplane. It had all the advantages of combat flying—the excitement of sudden alerts, different missions, working for a worthy cause—with none of the disadvantages—shooting at people, people shooting at me, blowing up and breaking things.

When on duty, I had to be present at the base, not nearby at the other end of the field. So, with the base director's permission, I installed a landline telephone in the ready room at a small table I set up as a desk. While waiting for a fire, I took care of business.

I arrived at our FBO early to do a management walk-around and collect my in-basket. Then I drove to the Air Attack base and preflighted the airplane, including a run-up that brought the oil temperatures for both engines into the green arc. We had to be ready to fly by 9:00 a.m. and, if dispatched, be in the air within five minutes. We usually lifted off in less than two. The larger tankers had to be in the air within 15 minutes but usually made it in five.

My front-seat passenger was usually the Fire Boss, Pete Forbes, the guy in charge of directing the tankers on a fire. The C-337 made a perfect platform. The two forward seats were well ahead of the wing leading edge, giving superb visibility both up and down, even in turns. The two engines in-line on the fuselage rather than the conventional arrangement placing an engine on each wing, dramatically reduced control problems in the event of an engine failure. It also eliminated the view-blocking engine cowlings on the wing. The airplane provided good short field performance for a twin. And the turbocharged engines yielded significantly more power at the high altitudes required over the Tahoe National Forest.

The contractor modified the aircraft interior to meet USFS requirements by removing the last row of seats. In their place, they secured a special pallet containing the USFS radios. Cables from the pallet passed through a large tube running along the floor up the center of the cabin between the remaining four seats. They connected via more conduit to two special audio panels and control heads mounted for the pilot and copilot seats. Their communication networking offered amazing capability. Via its system of repeaters, I could fly in a deep Sierra Nevada canyon in Northern California and talk with another USFS station in Bakersfield hundreds of miles to the south.

I had three jobs. First, I was Pete's chauffeur. Upon alert, I got him into the air and headed toward the fire ASAP. I set max continuous power, then chose attitude and airspeed for a high-speed cruise climb consistent with terrain avoidance. Once on scene, I reduced power to max loitering—about 45% in the Sky Master—and started a wide, right-hand orbit around the fire to give Pete the best view possible. He conferred with the ground commanders, assessed the aerial view, then called in the tankers. We continued right-hand orbits 1,000 feet above the fire. As the tankers arrived, they entered left-hand orbits 500 feet above the fire. Pete would then assign each tanker its specific drop—partial load, full load, along an extended line, all at once, whatever the situation required.

Second, I acted as his receptionist by monitoring as many as six different radio inputs—Regional Air Traffic Control, local airport frequencies, the Common Traffic Advisory Frequency, the tanker frequency, ground unit frequencies, the USFS Dispatcher, and others. I dealt with aviation communication directly and answered the USFS channels he assigned to me. I either took a message, asked them to stand by, or switched them over to Pete's audio.

Third, I watched for spot fires. Making right-hand turns—sometimes for hours—at loitering speed (even with flaps partially deployed) limited my view over the nose to mountains and air traffic. But, my view out the lower edge of the left-hand pilot's window proved surprisingly good. As each orbit transitioned from downwind to crosswind, I searched ahead of the main fire line for spot fires started by windborne embers. They revealed themselves with thin wispy ribbons of light smoke snaking surreptitiously upward, sometimes a mile downwind.

We also flew lightning fire watch. When thunderstorms formed over the mountains in late afternoon, fire lookouts stood their posts all night, if necessary, watching for lightning strikes. The lookout marked his tower's windows with a grease pencil for every strike. In the morning he used his instruments to determine the heading from the tower to the approximate strike location. The dispatch office triangulated the reports from multiple towers to determine the strikes' locations.

In the morning, the dispatcher sent Pete and me, and sometimes an additional observer, to overfly the possible strikes. We'd look for any sign of fire, usually the telltale thin ribbon of smoke not yet visible farther away. If we found a fire, Pete informed the dispatcher, who then called out the appropriate ground unit. I pulled the throttles and props back to loitering power and orbited the site until the ground units arrived in the vicinity. Then Pete directed them as they hiked in to put out the fire.

Their Last Picture

Dark, angry clouds merged with hillside treetops. Hard rain beat on the hangar's metal roof. A full flight schedule awaited us, but we kept airplanes inside the hangar. We waited an hour, listened to a special, second, morning radio contact. No change. We weren't going anywhere soon.

I flew from Quito to Shell for my last base inspection before heading to the US for furlough. As Ecuador Program Manager, my visits ranged from one to five days and usually included some flying as well. Not that day. We still hoped for a break, so didn't start a project we couldn't put down. I always had more paperwork. But Danny Osterhus and Job Orellana remained uncommitted. Then I said, "We've got those decals Gene brought back from the States. You two want to start mounting them on the airplanes?"

They looked at each other, considered, then said, "Yeah, we could do that." Danny was a mechanical genius and artist. Job cared about our public face. They retrieved the package from our dehumidified parts room. I went to the pilot's ready room, found a vacant desk and took the first document off the stack.

A couple hours later, I rose to do a circuit of "management by walk-about." The hard rain reinforced everyone's focus on their task at hand. I went from desk to bench, mostly unnoticed. Then I came to Danny and Job. They'd just finished installing letters on another airplane. Running horizontally along the engine cowling, it read, "Alas de Socorro 10" (the other airplanes were labeled with their appropriate numbers). They did a masterful job—straight lines, even spacing, good positioning. It looked great. All the planes looked great. I asked them to wait there while I retrieved my camera.

"I want a picture to show Gene that we finally installed the decals," I said. Danny and Job grinned as they posed for the shot.

A couple days later I flew back to Quito. Then after another week, Regina, the girls, and I took the airline to California, starting our five-month stint at home. We chose Fall rather than the more popular summer furloughs so Regina could complete another college semester.

We spent the first weeks camping in a sister-in-law's Pasadena living room. We enrolled the girls in school and commuted every day while hunting for an apartment in San Dimas, close to Regina's college. We eventually found a second-story, two-bedroom apartment next to a large park. The utilities and phone were installed on Friday and we moved in on Saturday. Busy weekend, but I had to remember to communicate our new phone number first thing Monday morning.

Sunday night, late, Regina and the girls in bed, I stood in the dark at our bedroom door, ready to crawl in myself. But I felt strongly compelled to fire up the computer and check email once more. What was that all about? It was Sunday night. What could be so important that it couldn't wait until Monday morning? My hand gripped the knob. I started to turn it. But no, I had to check.

I returned to the dark living room, found the computer on the table, opened the lid, turned on the power, waited for it to boot. *This is stupid,* I thought to myself. I was about to close the lid when the boot-up finished. The glowing screen threw the only light, a pale yellow, into the dark room. Okay, might as well check. I opened cc-Mail, started the dial-up procedure and listened to the sing-song tones. It connected and a string of message headers poured in, all with subject lines saying some form of "Bad News."

As I moved to open the first, the rare Southern California drizzle outside morphed into hard rain. I double-clicked a message from Dave McCleery, my assistant program manager. Everything changed. "Everyone" had been trying to reach me all day with terrible news. At 6:20 that Sunday morning, Ecuador time (same as Eastern Standard Time), one of our planes crashed, killing Danny, Job, and Job's brother Walter Orellana. They were searching for an aircraft missing since the previous day.

A C-206 flown by a commercial operator disappeared on a flight from Quito to Shell. Speculation said it crashed in the Baños Pass, but bad weather prevented anyone from looking. The next day, Saturday, weather improved enough for Henry to fly one of our planes from Quito to Shell. Conditions in the pass didn't permit visual flight, but he flew the official instrument airway and approach into Shell. While above the pass at 15,000 feet, he heard an emergency beacon on the international frequency, 121.5 MHz and reported its position. The Army promised to send a helicopter the moment the weather cleared.

Meanwhile, Job worried about the missing pilot, a longtime friend, and proposed searching the pass. Danny offered to fly. Dave, in his role as manager, rejected the idea. He said both Job and Danny were too emotionally involved to be safe. Besides, the crash site was now known, eliminating any need for searching. The Army's helicopter was the only thing that could help any survivors. Dave told them again to not fly a search.

Job didn't sleep but paced most of Saturday night. Sunday morning, pre-dawn light revealed cloudless sky, so he left home to meet Danny at the hangar. They preflighted a C-185, deciding Danny should fly while Job acted as observer. Job drove to the other end of the airport to present the flight plan at Civil Aviation. On the way, he recruited his brother, Walter, to act as an additional observer.

Back in our hangar, the three men climbed into the plane and taxied to the run-up area. The tower told them they'd be number two for departure right after the Army helicopter preparing to fly up the pass. After a delay the tower said the helicopter had starting problems, so they were cleared to depart. They lifted off just after 6:00 a.m., climbing straight out to the west, up the Baños Pass.

The Baños Pass, sometimes called the Pastaza River Gorge, runs about thirty miles down the eastern slopes of the Andes from the mountain town of Baños at the upper end, opening and spreading out into the Amazon Jungle at Shell. The pass is flanked on both sides by steep inclines and cliffs as well as many smaller tributary streams. Each of these streams forms its own canyon running perpendicular to the Pastaza.

A pilot flying the pass sees the central gorge winding between the tips of ridges pointing in, finger-like, from either side toward the center. Sometimes, thick clouds in the pass preclude visual flight completely, leaving the much higher instrument route as the only option. Merely reduced visibility, however, allows safe passage if the pilot follows proper procedures. Where gaps between fingers on either side of the gorge line up, they form an open space wide enough for a single-engine Cessna to turn around, especially if he configures his airplane for terrain flying and slows to the appropriate speed. Our procedure was to first look through the pass. If we saw clearly to the next open space, we flew that far. After that, we looked ahead to the next open space. If we saw that one clearly, we continued. If not, we turned around and went back the way we came. Always keeping the "back door open" gave us a safe out.

Pilots working for the commercial operators didn't always follow that procedure but rather preferred to fly straight down at cruise speed, brushing between ridge top and cloud base. The pilot Danny and Job hoped to find alive did exactly that, running out of room and striking a perpendicular ridge just below its crest.

Our guys flew up the gorge, quickly finding the beacon's signal. In a few minutes, they located the most likely side-canyon to search. Meanwhile, the Army's helicopter took off and headed toward them.

Danny turned left (south) to fly up the side draw, slowing and configuring the airplane for terrain flight. He continued on that heading, apparently spotting the wreckage on the ridge to their left (east). They passed it, turned 180 degrees to the left to fly parallel to the ridge (north). As they approached the accident site, just a hundred feet or so above the ridge top, Danny reduced his speed even more. They flew very slowly past the site. Suddenly the airplane snapped left, rolled inverted, continued all the way around in time to dive straight into the mountainside. All three died instantly.

God must have designed shock for our protection so we can do what must be done. Instead of getting into bed, I awakened Regina. Explained, asked for help. She phoned and secured airline reservations for early the next morning. I packed. At 5:00 a.m. we drove through driving rain to Ontario (California) International Airport. By 11:00 p.m. Monday night, I was back in Quito. From the terminal, I immediately boarded a van, rode all night and reached Shell by 4:30 a.m. Tuesday morning in time for the funeral that afternoon.

Over 1,000 people participated in the massive service, held in the small evangelical Shell church, *Luz de Evangélico*. Mourners packed every seat and standing space inside the sanctuary. The church placed a large canopy over the parking lot, creating another seating area that filled and overflowed, blocking the sidewalk and highway.

Three closed caskets sat on the platform, each displaying a family picture at its foot. They sat in a sea of flowers flooding the front of the church knee-deep—arrangements, bunches, and loose blossoms.

The entire service was ardently evangelistic and full of hope. It's one thing to know all the right things that are supposed to be said, but an entirely different matter to see that hope alive and thriving, rare beauty in the midst of grieving.

We MAF pilots carried Dan's casket. Pilots from the Shell-based commercial operators carried Job's. Policemen carried Walter's because he was the Teniente Politico (a cross between mayor and police chief in small Ecuadorian towns).

We loaded each casket into a van or pickup truck and drove to Shell's main plaza. The Provincial Governor and other government officials spoke. Then we loaded the caskets back into three vans and made a procession to Puyo. I was in the van with

Dan and couldn't see the end of the kilometer-long line of cars, trucks, and buses following us the entire distance to the cemetery. Hundreds of people packed so close, no one could move, pressed together so tightly we took a long time to carry the caskets from the vans to the grave all three would share.

By day's end, I was numb, exhausted, remote, detached. I didn't sleep well, often half waking, not clearly discerning dream from truth, nightmare from reality.

The official investigation started the next day. Rolland, our Safety Manager from MAF's US headquarters, arrived on a different flight, but we rode from Quito to Shell in the same van. He assembled our entire staff, wives, hangar helpers, maintenance techs, pilots, everybody, even Danny's parents.

We sat in a circle in the HCJB guest house's large living and dining room. I looked around the circle and felt splintered. I was there in several roles—Danny and Job's boss, their friend, their families' friend, a brother in Christ, a professional aviator and a few more I couldn't identify. Rolland asked questions. We answered. And we talked. Goods. Bads. Posthumous kudos. Dormant concerns now finding expression. The talking helped, grieved, and angered me all at the same time.

It helped me to know how deeply they were loved and how passionately they loved their families, their friends, and the people they served. They lived lives worth imitating. The daughter of one of our national workers said after the funeral, "Danny was ready to die. I'm not. What do I do?" Dan, Job, and Walter were faithful to finish the course set before them and left a legacy worth copying.

It grieved me because their deaths were pointless. Job and Danny were experienced, skilled pilots, Walter a community leader. All three men had wonderful wives and young children. All three loved Jesus. They spent their last moments on earth setting aside their own comfort and safety, trying to help someone in need. But better help was en route, only minutes away.

It angered me because, as I listened to the chain of events and concerns not fully connected until then, I saw how human nature had defeated both Christian community and MAF's good safety systems.

Danny flew the airplane. The flight plan listed him as Pilot in Command (PIC), and as was our standard procedure for the C-185, they removed the right-hand control yoke. He was perhaps the most naturally gifted aviator I ever met, able to eke out an airplane's very last drops of performance. He was particularly good at slow flight, able to consistently control the airplane as it flew on the very edge of stalling. Unfortunately, Danny's judgment took longer to develop than his skill. In his MAF career, Danny had a few incidents and two accidents. After each event, he received remedial training and then flew under extra supervision. During those embarrassing, stressful times, he cooperated with his mentors and accepted correction humbly. His evaluations reported excellent skill, as always, and a maturing judgment process.

As the program manager, I relied on the official procedures our professional flight evaluators followed to keep me informed of all our pilots'—including mine—ability to operate safely in the narrow niche our environment demanded. They all agreed Danny met or exceeded our standards and I concurred. Danny's affable, ready-to-help nature endeared him to everyone.

But during our debrief session, some staff members, including wives, said things like, "Danny was an accident waiting to happen," or "He took too many chances," or "He was reckless, I knew it was just a matter of time before something really bad happened."

I was shocked. What signs had I missed? Evaluators pronounced him fit. Friends judged him rash. How could such disparity hide so long in our small Christian community? The enemy, taking advantage of human nature, had indeed defeated us. What hindered his friends from talking to me, to somebody? What motivated Danny and Job to blow past a direct command to not fly?

I believe that, after Danny turned to fly parallel to the ridge, he slowed below our normal terrain speed of 80 knots to maximize viewing time. Job and Walter looked to their right (east), but at that hour, on that day, the rising sun had just crossed the horizon in a cloudless sky. The airplane they sought was just below the crest of the ridge nearest them, in deep shadow. Danny slowed even more. The stall warning horn probably sounded intermittently. Then, as Job or Walter reported seeing something, Danny turned to look as well. With Job and Walter blocking the view, he would have to push up to see over their heads. Without thinking, he pushed against the left rudder pedal. The combination of high power and high angle of attack demands a lot of right rudder input to maintain coordinated flight. The sudden shift of rudder over to the left induced a cross-control stall. The airplane entered a spin to the left, striking the ground before completing a full turn. Don't know if that's what really happened, but it's what I saw in dreams for months afterward.

For a long time, we talked about recovering from the accident. And we did... and we didn't. The three families healed, went on, grew in new ways, but they would never be the same. As a ministry, we didn't recover either. We healed, but never returned to who and what we were. But just as in any war, the battles didn't stop because we lost comrades. The fight went on. The needs in the jungle went on—patients to help, teachers to schools, preachers to services, and missionaries to the lost.

I don't know which surprised me more after resuming furlough in the US: that I thought I saw Danny on the street just in front of me, or that, for a short but eternally long moment, it seemed normal and right that I should. That hole will always remain, as will the expectation that it's about to be filled. Ironically, the picture I took of them grinning, displaying their work on the airplane, reminds that I will, indeed, see them again.

Needy Circle

Dark blue sky above, white puffs below. I flew above a layer of cotton-ball clouds that extended to the horizon. Just below them, jostling jungle hilltops reached up, almost touching. Those sharp peaks are the last ripples of the Cutucu Mountains, which my amateur geologist eyes saw, in turn, as the last eastern wave of the Andes Mountains before all flattens into the Amazon Jungle.

Careful to maintain an exact heading of 179 degrees, I slowed the airplane to 80 knots and set 20 degrees of flaps. Peering through the gaps between the clouds, I saw the air below remained as clear as above. Same over the entire region. Checking heading once more, I wiggled down between the clouds. Should see the Cusuimi River once I got under the layer. Until then, heading and time were all I had to locate the strip.

Underneath I had barely room to fly between cloud base and hilltop. There, close to the earth, everything happened quickly. Tucked in close to clouds above, I sped over ridge and gully below. Dodged hills poking up too high but kept track of heading. Down so close to terrain, what little height I had, offered little big-picture perspective. Like in a mythical magician's maze, I could've easily lost my way. My only option then would be to climb up between the clouds, fly back north until I got an exact fix on a known location, then return to a southerly heading and try again. I had neither time nor fuel for that option. And not picking up those passengers that day would've impacted the group's translation work in Makuma. Not life and death, but important.

We faced that risk-benefit question, solving its equation anew many times a day. Was landing at a marginal strip worth the risk? What about pushing on in questionable weather? When a combination of equipment and skill allowed us to conduct an operation, did that also mean we should? Depended why we were trying. Picking up passengers for in-town shopping warranted little risk. Evacuating a snakebite victim justified maximum push. That day's flight supported extra effort.

Suddenly to the right I spotted the river. The area's enormous rainfall produced many impressive rivers in just a few miles. Easy to pick the wrong one. Fortunately, in that case, the jumble of tight hills quickly bunched them together, reducing the possible candidates. Double-checked the chart. Yep, should be there. Double-checked the river's unique color. Yep, that was the correct river.

I shifted my primary heading reference from the compass to the river. That would bend my course a bit left, to the east, then sharply back to the west—all in the next four minutes. As long as I kept the river in sight, I'd find the strip.

Kept my scan going. Didn't fixate on one thing. Looked ahead to clear the next peak. Looked up to stay clear of clouds. Looked down at the river to stay on course. Looked at the panel clock to anticipate arrival. Repeat: Ahead. Up. Down. Panel for airspeed. Again: Ahead. Up. Down. Panel for vertical speed. Once more: Ahead. Up. Down. Panel for engine gauges. And again. And again. And again. Keeping the beat, my eyes moved in regular rhythm. My inner ear and kinesthetic sense felt airplane motion. My hands and feet guided airplane motion, both response and pro-action. That intimate dance of man-machine meld required experience, intuition and clear thinking, simultaneously stressful and joyful.

I cleared another peak. There! In front of me, the Shuar village of Cusuimi crouched in a bowl, tightly shielded between two ridges. Like guardians, they hid it from bright sky, cutting it off from time and world. The small cluster of thatched roofs sat deep between tall trees at the base of the ridge. The lighter grass strip marked the single open scratch in the dense, dark jungle covering hill and canyon.

I crossed over the airstrip and dipped my left wing for a better view. No kids. No cows. No pigs. No puddles. Not too dark. Shouldn't be too soft for landing. The ridge granted no room to the left, so I made a big, backward "S." First I turned right, away from the strip and slowed to 60 knots (70 mph). The lower airspeed allowed me to maneuver safely within the smaller area.

I continued turning right a full 270 degrees to get into position for the other half of the "S," a left, descending circle. The airstrip was on my left again as I dipped into the bowl, slowed to 52 knots and set the flaps to 40 degrees. No square pattern. The bowl was too tight. Just a constant descending circle to touchdown. I controlled airspeed with pitch, trimming out as much pressure as I could. Adjusted glide path with power. A little low, pushed the throttle in slightly. A little high, pulled some out. Each power change affected the airspeed, so my scan shuttled between looking outside at the touchdown point and looking inside at the airspeed indicator. Too fast, back pressure on the control yoke. Too slow, pushed forward slightly. Another delicate juggle, throttle in and out, yoke forward and back. When done right it yielded a satisfying song. Done wrong yielded only disappointing results.

I crossed the runway threshold at river's edge, pulled power back and raised the nose. The combination almost stopped the descent and also slowed the airplane. The wheels dropped onto soft muddy weeds with a cushioned jolt. The tires started rolling. I stepped hard on the brakes to dump all the speed I could early in the rollout. Then I released them as the wheels slid, throwing up twin geysers of muddy grass globs. Pressed again as the wheels rolled, let off as they slid. Takes longer to say than do. I stopped near the middle of the strip, then added power again to taxi uphill to where I should meet my passengers.

I shut down the engine and the propeller shuddered, then bump-bumped to a stop. Sudden quiet—except for tiny, silvery pings of cooling engine exhaust and descending notes of gyros winding down—enveloped the cockpit. I sat a moment feeling suddenly cold, shivering despite the heat. While legal, that approach definitely increased adrenaline flow. I felt like I'd just run a race. A couple of deep breaths slowed my breathing. I wrote landing time on the flight sheet, reviewed shut-down checklist, pulled helmet off, unbuckled the harness, took one more deep breath, opened the door and hopped out.

Time works differently in the belly of the jungle-beast. A moment before, I commanded a twentieth-century magic machine. Standing beside it, boots in mud, packed trees towering 100 feet, I could be in any time—now, 1,000 years back, 1,000 years ahead. My time remained undistinguishable, defined only by what I brought with me. I looked over to a small area cleared from the undergrowth brave enough to grow a few feet from its forest shelter. Trees darkened the path to the village, revealing nothing beyond a few feet.

At first, I didn't see them. But there they waited. Quiet. No demands. No questions. As I approached, the middle-aged couple stood. I greeted them in Spanish, but they didn't answer, only gave slight smiles. In the less-visited portions of the jungle, many did not speak it and I knew only a few words in Shuar.

They smiled, eyes and teeth shining against the shadows, eager to spend their week as they did every month. I wondered, *While they're gone, who cared for the kids? Who tended the garden? Did someone hunt for him too?* Yet they stood there, ignoring the cost, content in the sunshine with a life we deemed hardship and poverty.

"Wen 'yah-hay," I called out, believing I said something in Shuar like, "*I have come.*"

In the old days—for hundreds of years until the 1950s and 60s—the Shuar (also known as Jivaro to the outside world) lived in semi-nomadic groups of nine or less—dad, mom, kids, and married daughter with her new husband for their first year. But revenge cycles tortured their lives for those centuries. The father of a sick child asked the witch doctor only one question, "Who put this curse on my son?" The witch doctor performed his rituals and named the guilty party.

Then dad and friends stalked and killed their new enemy—or anyone near and dear they could find. The survivors, of course, exacted a blood price from the assailants, expanding the vengeance circle. Killers tried to prolong their own lives by acquiring and holding onto soul power. A man had many options to gain soul power, but he accumulated the most by taking and shrinking an enemy's head. The fiercest displayed their trophies hanging from door-side poles, or sometimes their belts.

So naturally, anyone approaching a dwelling unannounced was assumed an enemy. Residents preemptively counter-attacked with spears, not questions. To avoid perils of mistaken identity, visitors called out loudly while still some distance from the house. Those in the house called out in return, confirming peaceful contact.

"Wen 'yah-mek," the man in front of me responded, meaning *"you have come."* He said no more but picked up a half-bushel-sized basket covered with banana leaves tied in place with vines. She grasped a small burlap bag. They were old enough to remember their parents shrinking enemies' heads, but their eyes glowed with their purpose today. Once a month we flew like bees to flowers, collecting the small team of Shuar language helpers by ones, twos, and threes from the villages. They left hunting, gardens, home, and family to labor together for a week in Makuma with Gospel Missionary Union (now Avant Ministries) translators. They completed the Shuar New Testament a few years earlier, and now they continued with the Old Testament translation.

Even holding a Shuar New Testament in hand, some saw only a book, a good book, perhaps, yet just one among many. But I wondered what stories the production of that volume hid. How many thousand man-hours did the translating teams invest? How many days did they live away from home? How many sleepless nights did they wrestle with barely pronounceable words? How many times did we pilots throw 3,000-plus pounds of aluminum at slippery mud airstrips? How many mechanics worked all night busting knuckles on recalcitrant aircraft engines? How many technicians burned fingers repairing village or airplane radios? How many electricians waded into the river to keep the small hydro plant producing power for the translator's workshop? How many wives tended hot stoves in the jungle sauna, or nursed sick children while the work went on?

Over the years, some of them surrendered their lives to pave the way. Others carried on in sharp hardship. Most persevered, unknown, unimagined, names never inscribed on plaques or honored at banquets. Fortunately, their Redeemer knew each and every one—fully. And God, working through their unseen labor, so transformed the culture that even unbelievers lived free of the revenge cycle. "For he makes his sun rise on the evil and the good, and sends his rain on the just and on the unjust" (Mat 5:45 ESV).

I knelt in the mud to load their cargo into the pod, then laughed. They were the smart ones. They wrestled translating esoteric life principles accurately across four languages separated by continents and centuries. I, the technical wizard from the sky, just drove the taxi. They made this flight every month because the Holy Spirit compelled them to translate his Word. The same Spirit compelled me to fly. I'd be miserable if I didn't—adrenaline and mud notwithstanding. Likewise, they needed to translate as much as they required water and air. They'd shrivel otherwise. The only way they could meet their need to answer God's call to translate was if I met mine to fly. As the wet mud soaked through my jeans and cooled my knees, I realized I actually enjoyed the privilege of serving them. Who would've thought Jesus could be so creative with a machine?

The Greased Chute

Between FBO instruction, charter flying, and USFS Air Attack work, I spent a lot of time in the air. I loved every minute, feeling I was indeed where I belonged. Unfortunately, a tiny voice deep inside continually spoke, calling me to something else. My flying depended largely upon running a successful business. And business bored me. Yet I remained enthusiastic about giving good service. That's an essential component of a good business, but not the foundation. Successful businesses required a strategy designating profit as the primary goal. Income had to exceed expense for the business to survive. Nothing wrong with that. I saw it as necessary to a healthy economy. But the realization grew that profit did not motivate my soul. Others could focus on profit—I chose service.

My call to service quickly clarified itself as a call to ministry. I started a prayer meeting in my office every morning. Sometimes alone, sometimes with eight or nine others. Didn't matter. And I started praying for God to show me how to "go into ministry." At that time in my walk with the Lord, the word "ministry" meant one of two things: either serving as the pastor of a church or else working as a traveling evangelist. Missionaries were people who did that sort of thing in other countries.

And that was the rub. I knew pastors, some were good friends. And that showed me I did not have the gifts a pastor needed. I didn't mind public speaking, kind of liked it, actually. It was the rest of the lifestyle I was not equipped for. So, my prayers sounded like this: "I'll do anything you want, Lord, anything at all. But just so we have one thing straight, I won't be a pastor. That's not even on the table."

I prayed that way almost every morning for two years and remained mystified why I received no answer. Can't say what opened the blinds, but one Sunday morning I suddenly realized how wrong I was. I realized committing to walk with the Creator of the universe left no room for negotiation. No 70/30, 80/40, or even 90/10 splits. Just his way or the highway. That epiphany changed my prayer to: "Lord, I'll do anything you want, anything at all, even be a pastor (PLEASE don't!)."

A week and a half later, an aviation business associate, Scott Granger, flew into our airport. He represented the West Coast Cessna distributor, so we usually talked about our FBO becoming an official Cessna Dealer rather than just a Cessna Pilot Center. We chatted and then Scott stopped and said, "You know, Jim, I never mentioned it before, but I'm also a volunteer rep for an organization called MAF—Mission Aviation Fellowship."

"Really?" I answered. "I met some guys while doing my aviation maintenance training in San Diego who were getting ready for that. Sounds like a cool outfit."

"Yeah, they are," he agreed as he passed his MAF card over to me. I fingered through my card file, found his Cessna card, then dropped his MAF card behind it. We resumed Cessna business talk. An hour later he got into his airplane and flew back to Oakland. I returned to my work and forgot about his card— almost.

For the next couple weeks, our business slowed. Unanticipated events forced students to cancel lessons. Charter customer plans changed. Benign weather ruled the Sierra Nevadas, sparing us thunderstorms and lightning strikes. Campers, loggers, and motorists exercised extra caution. The only hint of flame came from the small coil of smoke rising from my card file. Scott's MAF card seemed to glow like a fiery coal, brighter and hotter each day.

Suddenly I had time free of compelling crises. I spent hours prayer-walking the large ramp while on Air Attack duty. Slowly, ever so slowly, a radical idea sprouted. Tiny at first, I easily dismissed it. Become a missionary pilot? Sounds like a good story. How about a Western? But it grew bigger, stronger, solidifying in sync with the heat from Scott's card. I made some phone calls.

The Wycliffe recruiter's first question: "How old are you?"

"37," I answered.

"You're too old. Our cutoff to start training is 27. Sorry, but thanks for your interest in Wycliffe," the recruiter politely ended our conversation.

I was relieved. Decided I could let that silly idea go. The idea hung around like a stupid song stuck in my head. Then it seemed less silly. And then it got even stronger. This is no good, I thought. Better call MAF too. They'll confirm what I already know and I can be done with this.

My first question to Ernie Doerksen, the MAF recruiter: "What's your maximum age for joining as a pilot?"

"Depends. We're more interested in your experience, your skill, and of course, your calling," he answered.

Uh-oh, I thought, This is not going in a good direction. After a lot more ramp-pacing-prayer, I became convinced we should apply to MAF. Now converted to the radical notion of missionary service, I foresaw only one minor problem. How was I going to tell Regina I wanted to give up our home, our beautiful surroundings, our place in the church, our friends, our place in the community? We were living a dream. How could I ask her to dump it so I could fly? I considered the indirect approach, something like: "Honey, the next time you're at the supermarket could you pick up some mosquito netting and a couple machetes?" While initially appealing, further reflection dissuaded me and I chose the direct approach.

Just home from the airport, I walked up to her, put my hands on her shoulders, looked straight into her eyes and said non-stop lest I lose my courage, "Honey, I think God's calling us to join MAF so we can move to the middle of the jungle where I can fly airplanes for Jesus ..."

She stared at me wide-eyed for a moment, then started crying, tears running down both cheeks. Surprised at her reaction, I thought, This is going to be harder than I imagined.

Turned out she was crying for joy. When we first met the guys at the A&P school in San Diego who were preparing for MAF service, she felt it was exactly what we should do—I loved Jesus and liked to fly. What's not to like about this combination, she thought.

However, I informed her—very clearly, she recalls—that "My ministry was to the United States. We weren't leaving the country under any circumstances."

Five years later, when we ran the FBO in Grass Valley and I prayed about a calling to ministry, she asked MAF to send literature to me—anonymously. I opened the envelope, said, "Hey, I remember those guys in San Diego getting ready for MAF. Sounds like a great ministry!" then tossed it into the round file.

Two years later, seven years after the first contact, she suddenly realized her dream—the dead one I was clueless about—the dream she'd permanently shelved, suddenly, miraculously sprang to life before her eyes. Her reaction served as a powerful confirmation to me. Less than two years later we were on our way to Spanish language school in Costa Rica—the mission world equivalent to instant. Made me feel God had opened a door, then kicked us through to a greased chute on the other side.

Starry Night

Was I getting old? No. Must be my imagination. On the other
hand, I couldn't deny the reality of the request. A youth leader
from the US was bringing a team from Azusa Pacific University
to Ecuador for a two-week mission trip. But, unlike many such
trips, this group was coming to work—hard. They wanted flights
for 15 students, their baggage, food, and tools out to the Waorani
village of Damointaro. There they would provide the grunt-labor
for major airstrip repair. Then, after three days, we would fly all
their stuff to Quiwado, another Waorani village eight miles down
the Tiweno River, while they made the same trip overland. We
could land five passengers in Damointaro, but only take off with
three. A short hike seemed an ideal way to provide an additional
cultural experience and to save money.

On its own, outsiders choosing to hike that route presented a
challenge sufficiently daunting to catch my attention. Only eight
miles, as the condor flies, separated the two airstrips. Healthy
young adults could cover that distance easily in a couple hours.
But the actual path measured over 12 miles. And that crossed
muddy, boggy ground, choked with centuries of fallen trees, brush
and, oh yeah, the innumerable creeks that fed the river. But what
grabbed my attention like a cold slap, was the group's leader. One
of my son's classmates, wild, mischievous Danny Rhon, was
returning to the jungle as the responsible adult, guiding the group
as they adventured in the Amazon Jungle. Reality's plumb line
tilted a few degrees.

But Dan pushed, creating his own new reality. After graduating
from the mission high school in Quito, he returned to the US and
completed a year of community college. From there he enlisted in

the US Marine Corps, excelling in one of their toughest specialties. From there he returned to civilian life to earn a degree at Azusa Pacific University. He brought the team to Ecuador a few days after graduation. And he was scheduled later that summer to return to the military—US Army this time—to pursue graduate study in physical therapy and commissioning as an officer.

I met Dan on our ramp as he herded his charges to their planes. Hard to believe the man standing before me was the same guy. Taller, stronger, he sported the same smile, the same mischievous glint in his eye. But now he walked and talked like a grown-up. Office duty already laid claim to my day, so we spoke only a moment, then they were gone.

We did a couple supply flights to Damointaro. Then the morning they set off on the trail, we ferried their equipment over to Quiwado. We covered the distance in four minutes. They arrived eight hours later, barely before dark, muddy, spent, but triumphant. After three more days, on a Thursday, we returned to pick them up. The other pilots retrieved most of the students and their gear. I flew in the Atshuar territory farther southeast all day. But I returned to Shell from Montalvo with enough time left in the day to fly the 36 minutes out to Quiwado, load Dan, the remaining three students and make it back to Shell before sunset. Great weather combined with almost no cargo promised a quick turnaround in the jungle.

In pre-GPS days I used a couple methods to find Quiwado. Easiest was flying a half hour northeast, 066 degrees, to Toñompade—difficult to miss because of its unique location where the Curaray River valley shrank to a canyon then broadened out again. Once over Toñompade, I'd turn right to 108 degrees and fly seven more minutes. The other option was to fly over Damointaro and either follow the Tiwaeno downriver or take a heading and fly another four minutes. I also learned to identify a unique junction where the canyons of a smaller river and the Tiwaeno joined to create a finger pointing right at the airstrip. It proved surprisingly easy to spot from either side, even under low ceilings. But that day, I followed the GPS directly to it.

The strip itself offered a pleasant respite from the usual slippery Waorani mud strips, perhaps because it sat a little higher above the water. The community maintained the 1,300-by-50-foot runway well. They kept the grass short and cleared underbrush from the edges. They even kept the trees in the approaches under control. Reminded me of a golf course fairway. However, Quiwado was an almost-one-way strip. We could land in either direction—the abort point landing to the west was after touchdown but landing to the east we reached the abort point on short final. Takeoff was definitely one way. We always departed to the west because the east end, nearest the village proper, sat a half dozen feet above the rest of the strip. And it was weight limited for takeoff—200 pounds under gross for the C-206.

I landed about 5:00 p.m. Dan and his three students stood in the small plaza ready to go, their few remaining bags in hand. They all smiled and almost clung to their hosts sending them off. Clearly they had bonded, but equally clear was their unspoken desire for a hot shower. The cargo loaded quickly, most going in the pod. The passengers, all adept air travelers now, boarded and strapped in briskly. More waves, goodbyes in Spanish or, for the more adventurous, attempted Waorani phrases. I noted 17:20—5:20 p.m. in non-pilot speak. Still plenty of time before sunset. A good ending for a good day—for me, several successful flights; for them, life-altering perspective changes.

I completed the pre-start checklist, yelled "Libre!" out my open window (Spanish equivalent of "Clear!"). Turned on the master switch, then turned the ignition key to start. Silence. No propeller turning. No groaning of the starter motor even trying to turn. No clicking of the starter contactor trying to engage. Just silence. Everyone outside continued looking, waiting for spinning blades and authoritative ka-chugging of 520 cubic inches lighting off. Everyone inside stopped talking. Their raised-eyebrow stares bored into my back. I repeated the checklist. Yelled out the window again. Silence.

Not willing to give up—yet—I asked Dan and students to stay buckled in while I called Shell on the radio. At least I had battery power. We talked symptoms. We talked things to check. I let the passengers out of the plane but asked them to stay close. I removed the cowling, checked wires, connections, tapped the two contactors. (The starter contactor sent high-current power to the starter motor. The battery contactor connected the airplane's entire electrical system to the battery.) Hoped to find something loose or stuck. Found neither.

On the radio again, we reviewed symptoms. My best guess for the culprit pointed at the starter contactor. For about one-tenth of a second, I considered removing the cable leading to the starter motor from the contactor terminal and holding it on the battery side of the contactor.

Pros: the starter motor would spin and the engine would start. We could fly home to hot showers and, for me at least, my own family and bed.

Cons: a non-pilot would have to operate the controls inside the airplane, or else hold the connection during start. The outside person would then have to: One, find a non-dangerous place to secure the loose end of the starter motor cable. Two, replace the cowling despite the spinning wheel of death six inches from the cowl's forward fasteners. Three, reenter the aircraft and secure the door. All in roaring wind blast.

Fortunately, the one-tenth second passed without further consideration and we discussed other options. No other aircraft were close enough to get any of us back to Shell before sunset. Truth was, Dan, KC, Jake, Katie, and I were stuck there for the night. Eyes revealed the trauma of anticipated hot showers lost, but no voices complained. Instead, they smiled, saying, "What's one more night?" But then came a realization. Most of the luggage left on the previous flight. Still no complaints. We explained the predicament to our surprised hosts. No problem, they said. Sleep in the schoolhouse. Among the remaining cargo, we found exactly enough sleeping bags and mosquito netting for everyone—

without any awkward combinations.

The local folks brought us a pot of cooked rice and another pot of yucca soup. But how should we eat it? In the quick twilight, a couple of us gathered banana leaves and cut them into bowls and spoons. Then KC discovered that the hard lumps in the bottom of her knapsack were, in fact, a couple cans of tuna. Ambrosia! Between that and the remaining bottles of water, we feasted, albeit with slightly singed fingers.

Too early for sleep, we wandered outside. The airstrip provided an open view east and west from zenith nearly all the way to horizon. Trees on the south of the airstrip and to the north of the village restricted the view somewhat. But by walking over to the large open plaza at the east end of the runway we found a great vantage point.

Complete dark enveloped us, but with flashlights off, our eyes adapted quickly. The dark became luminous when, with no man-made light interfering, starlight drenched us from several thousand points. The Milky Way shone a brilliant band crossing the night sky from east to west 20 to 30 degrees above the southern horizon, a thousand diamonds set in the seeming mist of a myriad more stars.

Against that backdrop, Mars rose deep red in the east. Over the next days, its path along the ecliptic would take it through the constellation of Scorpius, passing close to the brilliant red, supergiant star Antares. Toward the south, just high enough to clear most of the tree line along the runway, hung the Southern Cross. Its two most brilliant stars, Acrux and Mimosa, defining its bottom and trailing points. Together, they acted as heralds of the two equally brilliant stars, Alpha and Beta Centauri, following 10 degrees behind. The sky felt black but luminous and three dimensional.

And then, the old hunger awoke. Those stars, the closest to Earth besides the Sun, seemed touchable—almost. Could I reach out far enough? If not with my hand, what about my spirit? "Lord," I asked again, "will they remain forever out of reach?"

And for the thousandth time I also felt his assurance that, while connection might not happen soon, I would not have to wait forever. If not on this side of the veil, then for sure on the other. I pushed down that longing again. Not roughly, lest I exasperate hope, but firmly with an assurance that the One who promised was also faithful to deliver. Even so, I considered sleeping outside to bask all night under stars. But mosquito thoughts prevailed.

After delaying too long, the five of us returned to the schoolhouse. We hung nets from the rafters, then tucked them under the sleeping bags. Mosquitos not only flew in through unscreened windows but also came up through the gaps between floorboards. Nastily clever critters themselves, they could carry malaria. And that parasite, some immunologists said, was the epitome of malevolence perfectly designed by pure evil to evade detection while ravaging its host's body.

Sleep came quickly despite night jungle activities. Morning's first light woke us, but no hurry. I was first up in time for the morning contact. Walked through dewy grass to the airplane. Mist rose in streamers from between the taller trees. Already dawn's coolness started its retreat from the coming sun, promising another hot, sauna day.

I unlocked and opened the door, leaned inside the cockpit, then turned the master switch on. The turn coordinator gyro started spooling up. I flipped the avionics master up and radio lights snapped on. I turned them all off except the Codan HF radio. Even though it was a completely solid-state unit, I gave it a moment stabilize, then switched channels to the village frequency. I put the receiver audio on the overhead speaker and listened to Alan, the flight coordinator, finish up his conversation with Bufeo. I picked up the handheld microphone, keyed the PTT switch and called, "Shell from Alas One-Two."

"Proceed, Capitán Diego," he responded, also in Spanish.

"Good morning, Alan. Any word yet on the plan to help us?" I asked. "Over."

"Yes. Capitán Daniel *[Rogers, not Dan Rhon my passenger]* is gathering parts and tools. He's planning to depart in about 30 minutes. I've asked him to drop off two passengers at Toñompade on his way to you. He'll be in Quiwado in less than two hours. Over."

"Okay, we'll stand by for his arrival. Thanks. Alas One-Two out." I turned off the switches. The gyro tone dropped as it spooled down. Leaning back from the cockpit, I stood up straight and closed the door. Better to shut the cabin, I decided. Might be hot, but it would keep the bugs out. Cooling off, on the other hand, would have to wait until we got to altitude.

An hour and a half later, Dan arrived. We opened the cowling again, repeated a couple checks, finally deciding our original diagnosis was correct. We replaced the starter motor contactor, refastened cables, and double-checked all bolts were tight. Then the smoke test. After making sure the cowling pieces were well clear, I returned to the cockpit, sat in the pilot's seat and cranked the motor, but left the fuel off. The propeller turned with its usual energy. Dan and I replaced the cowling, then I called the passengers over. While we loaded, Dan returned to his plane and sat in the cockpit waiting.

I repeated all the checklists and yelled clear. Quiwado's residents watched. The engine roared to life. Smiles all around. Dan started his plane, then took off, leaving the runway clear for me. A moment later I pushed the throttle in and followed him down the grass strip. Forty minutes later we landed in Shell, glad the experience was over. But some moving of the Lord's Spirit, invisible at the time, carried forward. Within a year or so, Dan and KC married, as did Jake and Katie.

VIEWPOINTS

I, too, was once a flat-lander stuck in two dimensions. Didn't matter if I lived in the mountains. I was glued to Earth's undulating surface, meticulously following its ups and downs. That restraint did grant a type of security. I need concern myself only with the challenges of moving left or right, forward or back. Vertical decisions faded to choosing stairs or elevator.

But as I earned my wings, I realized I'd also become an interloper into three-dimensional space, a ground-pounder granted provisional access at my own risk. Suddenly, up and down questions greatly complicated life. The sky might look free, clear air for thousands of miles, only birds and clouds for companions. But, in fact, it demanded scores of answers.

How did I find my destination? No signs pointed the way, no roads led anywhere. In fact, how did I know where I was now? No monument marked my spot. Chosen goals remained unreachable if I didn't know my starting point.

What about boundaries? How did I stay away from where I was unwanted? Major air terminals disdained the uninvited. Military Operation Areas, where warriors practice their sharp art, detested intruders. Like busy freeways, both periled the unwary trespasser.

And when cloud filled, or night hid the land below, how did I know what I flew over? Mountains? Desert? Ocean? Swamp? What if I unexpectedly returned to flat-land? How would I know what awaited me?

Fortunately, flying high above all obstacles required only the simplest navigation. Ancient mariners called it "dead reckoning." I determined the heading to my destination, then used a compass to fly that course. Measured the distance, then divided it by my speed to learn how long the trip would take. I started the clock upon departure then, when the time was up, arrived. Unless...

The wind pushed me off course, affected my speed, or both. In that case, I picked intermediate checkpoints. They'd show how far off course I was, or if I was early or late. So, no worries, I knew I'd get there. Unless...

Everything beneath me looked the same—rolling hills, blank desert, endless jungle, undulating ocean. In that case, I went out of my way. I picked a place near my destination I knew I could find. Went there, then took a new, shorter course to my target. And flying high made it easier to find. I'd just arrive a little late. Unless...

An angry ceiling pushed me down low. There, where I looked up at hilltops and counted individual leaves below, everything happened fast, twisting, turning, following river and creek, dales between and dips beneath low ridges that pointed in all directions at once, exhausting me trying to keep track of where I might be, where my destination once lay and, while I was at it, trying to not run into anything harder than air. On such days, I made life-and-death decisions for patients, passengers and myself based on ancient practice and my discernment of subtle terrain features.

That life could, of course, invoke paralyzing stress and multiply dreadful error. Especially if, like a butterfly pinned to display board, it remained fastened to two-dimensional thinking. But God allowed me to discover the unique perspective of the pilot's seat.

From that vantage point, my natural eyes saw beyond trees and hilltop, replaced imagination of what might be with knowledge of what was. I applied for a residence visa after my very first flight. Only a few years later, God granted me entrance into another land, a different world hidden in plain view upon the same planet. Of course, that country had its own stringent admittance requirements.

I had to bring functioning hands, feet, eyes, ears, and brain, then mesh them with an ungainly prosthetic called an airplane. I'd never soar on my own wings nor navigate by magnetic sensors grown within my nervous system, but using that mechanical contrivance I could fly with the inhabitants of that country, the subjects of that kingdom.

Each control, every instrument performed specific tasks and offered specific information. Confusing? At first. But once I learned to synthesize their messages, my brain started seeing and thinking in three dimensions. Just as speaking my first language no longer required conscious analysis of myriad grammar rules, so too did the amalgam of their readings paint a complete, dynamic picture of my situation. What biological abilities and senses my body lacked, that machine provided. Whatever guidance that machine needed, I delivered. Apart we both remained grounded. Together we flew.

I learned to move around three axes. If I pulled or pushed on the control yoke, the nose would pitch up or down. If I turned it right or left, the wings would bank right or left. If I stepped on the right or left pedal, the nose would yaw in the same direction I pushed. Interesting flat-land crossovers allowed me to push in the throttle to release 300 horsepower, while twisting the propeller control acted like a car's transmission. That allowed me to leave the Earth and return. But actually going to a specific place at a set time required finer control.

Sitting in the pilot's seat with controls in hand, I faced a plethora of gauges. With them I could not only fly safely inside clouds, I could determine my position anywhere on the planet within plus or minus 30 feet. They enabled me to fly anywhere I wanted, thus granting me equal sky rights with a two-ounce swallow or 25-pound condor.

And, as a properly documented sky resident, I could, like my fellow citizens, revel in freedom and ignore ground creature constraints. Maybe that's why I liked to fly direct. Take off, clear the obstacles, then turn to the heading. Hold that course through climb, cruise, and descent, brooking neither deviation nor detour. Such straight routes let me laugh at mountains, dismiss big waters, ignore deserts and canyons. They confirmed my emancipation from two-dimensional earth. They affirmed my citizenship in three-dimensional sky. The pilot's unique perspective rewired my brain. It replaced street and highway grids with a mental moving map that revealed the true lay of the land and plotted straight lines between departure and destination. Frustrating on the ground, but priceless in the sky.

So, for one morning's flight to the Waorani village of Damointaro, I turned to the direct heading—074 degrees—and climbed to 5,500 feet. Even at that altitude, much of the Waorani territory in Ecuador's Amazon Jungle appeared flat. But deep twisting river valleys cut its gentle rolls. They appear suddenly—either when flying overhead or seen on-end—then disappear moments later as if they never existed. Those brief glimpses revealed convoluted canyons hemming in jumbles of small hills and ridges. Their deepest floors hosted serpentine rivers fed by webs of creeks and rivulets.

Secluded in the bottom, thatched roofs clung to small open spaces wedged between forest and water, marking the villages of men. The twisted labyrinths defined their lives granting them neither experience nor concept of straight. Made me glad for the special perspective I enjoyed.

As the strip appeared off the nose, I turned slightly right to fly perpendicular to the runway and entered a crosswind leg. That positioned me to see the entire runway surface out my left window. The wind came from the west, on my right, so I planned a left turn for downwind leg through a notch between a hill on the left and the canyon wall on the right. The strip disappeared as I flew through the notch, then reappeared. I continued downwind a bit longer than in a normal pattern because the notch forced that leg so close to the runway. Finally, I made a left 180-degree turn combining base leg and entry to final approach leg in one maneuver. That put me farther from the runway threshold than normal but presented the only option for landing in this direction. It also allowed me to direct my flight path through another notch on the opposite side of the hill.

The previous night's rain left the narrow, undulating grass strip still soft. I touched down three airplane-lengths from the approach end, then braked hard, released the brakes, braked hard, released, braked again, repeating the pulsing to prevent skidding the tires in the slippery grass and mud. I finally stopped the plane about 70% of the way down the strip, then turned and taxied back to the waiting crowd.

That day my passengers were Wycliffe's Ecuador Director, David Underwood; their literacy specialist, Pat Kelly; and two assistants. The four came to honor graduates and discuss the program's future. After plane-side greetings and the typical mail and cargo distribution, the entire crowd atypically left the strip with my passengers and headed to the schoolhouse. I was left alone, standing in the grass under the wing—not a normal pilot condition on a village airstrip.

But in this case, being alone was neither unwelcome nor unplanned. I came prepared. My passengers estimated their activities would run about an hour. So, lunch and a thick wad of paperwork waited in my bag stowed in the aft cargo area. I opened the cargo doors wide, untied the bag and started to climb into my temporary office seat. I purposely parked the airplane with the sun shining in the front rather than the back. Gave me shade, fresh air, room to spread out, and—most importantly—no distractions.

A tap on the shoulder stopped me. I turned to face a Waorani man almost my height. I guessed he was 60 to 70 years old—not by stance, wrinkles, or gray, for he stood straight, well-muscled, with chopped black hair thicker than mine—but by long, empty earlobes left over from the old style of wearing large discs in the piercing, and splayed toes that had never known shoes. He was from the generation of warrior who could kill three men in seconds, chase down a wild boar, and climb 60 feet up a smooth trunk to retrieve a stupefied monkey fallen from higher branches when hit with a drugged dart.

He wore a gray long-sleeved shirt, a snaggletoothed grin and absolutely nothing else. Still grinning, he spoke Waorani to me and kept on talking, greeting, questing, I couldn't tell, but the tone was friendly, inclusive.

I answered in Spanish. He continued in Waorani. After a couple quick exchanges, I realized I knew more of his language than he knew of Spanish. I got his name, "Cawena." He didn't get mine, or at least didn't repeat it. Still leaning into the cabin to assume my perch, I indicated I had to work. He cheerfully ignored.

Decision time: Continue with my plan for my work, or take this as a divine opportunity to build a relationship? Then I recognized a technically acceptable compromise. My plan included a walk to inspect the airstrip. Torrential rain and relentless jungle fought to erase the works of men. Only vigilance alerted us to when and where we should fight back with cutting, filling, and clearing. I chose to do it right then. I was sure when he realized we couldn't communicate, he'd get bored and leave.

I pulled on my MAF baseball cap, moved away from the airplane and started walking down the center of the strip. In my mind's eye, I superimposed the ideal runway form onto the vegetation before me. Was the surface free of ruts, holes, and debris? Was the grass too tall? I also scanned left and right to spot bushes encroaching onto the runway surface or growing too tall along the strip edges.

As I looked down its length, I realized I was forcing a straight, flat, alien presence onto Cawena's tangled realm. This strip connected our two worlds, an interface between his confused warren and my orderly space. Did he understand the incongruity, the vast difference? I learned long before that primitive living conditions are not synonymous with primitive thinking. The jungle folks displayed keen intellect and perception. In this case, I knew he didn't comprehend my sky but had to admit I'd be lost in his forest. Yep, two different worlds.

We kept walking, me checking, Cawena talking. Suddenly something rose up within me, truly wanting to understand him.

Not a word made sense, but his intent was clear—communicate. I stopped walking and gave him full attention. He continued narrating the tale, intent that I at least get the gist.

I'd already exhausted my minuscule Waorani vocabulary to no effect—"hello," "goodbye (three forms depending on the leaving group's size)," and "yes/I like it." So, I pulled out my last trick and recited the names of other Waorani village airstrips. As I spoke their names, I could see them laid out on my mental map, no need to consult the paper version.

"Toñompade," I said.

Cawena stopped his monolog. His toothy grin changed to knowing smile. He pivoted on one heel to face northwest toward Toñompade, invisible, six miles away, in another canyon, along a different river. He extended his right arm horizontally, straight out in front of him. Then keeping his bicep level, he raised his forearm first vertical, then straight out, then back to vertical. He repeated the motion several times, correctly indicating the straight-line direction to that village.

Intrigued, I slowly named another, "Dayuno."

He turned to face the correct direction—almost due north—and repeated the motion toward the village 12 miles and three river canyons away.

"Nemonpade," I tried.

He turned northeast-by-east and repeated the arm motion.

"Tiwaeno," I tested.

Again he turned, motioning southwest-by-west to the village 10 miles away.

"Tzapino?" I questioned with increasing incredulity.

Once more. Northeast, nine miles away.

Jungle-covered, river-infested geography precludes straight paths. The trail to a destination one mile north might leave in any direction at all, then twist to cover 10 miles before arriving—if a trail existed. Except along the river, no vista beyond 20 or 30 feet presented itself. Anyone living there would know the trails intimately but have no access to the overall picture.

I knew most of the Waorani who regularly flew with us. Cawena was not one of them. I, on the other hand, lived in the sky for years, spent hours building my mental moving map. How could Cawena know? Did he possess a special kind of sight that let him see beyond what confronted him on the trail? Could he see order where I saw only chaos? Reminded me of a proverb that says, "In all your ways acknowledge Him, and He will make your paths straight." Many parts of my life looked like spaghetti spilled on the floor. But, every time I committed my way to Jesus, he overlaid his template upon my mess and led me straight to the best destination. Made me realize God's geometry was different from mine.

Its difference surprised me again eight weeks later. For many months I felt we were approaching the end of our Ecuador time—another year or year and a half, I thought. However, Regina and I realized our family needed priority attention—soon. So, we asked MAF leadership for time back in the US. They graciously granted our request, allowing us an entire month to regroup, renew, and refresh.

Leaving proved both easier and more difficult than I anticipated. Easier, because I had trained my replacement, Dave McCleery. He took over my program director's duties mid-stride with hardly a bump. But harder, because I realized my Sky residency visa was expiring. Giving my family my full attention was clearly the right thing to do and proved well worth the trade. However, I missed the three-dimensional life. Moving from getting paid to fly, to paying to fly presented a daunting hurdle. Eventually, the Lord granted me an aerial tourist visa and the means to use it. I could, once again, visit that alluring high country I once called home.

APPENDIX

CARGO - STUFF

We tried to keep cargo separate by putting it into the pod under the plane or securing it behind the seats. But many loads compelled us to creatively combine people and their stuff. Safety presented the big challenge. Because we treated every life equally—Latino, Indigenous, General, laborer, our wives, and our kids—we put great effort into cargo containment.

When pod and rear cargo areas weren't enough, we removed one or more seats, then folded and added them to the cargo, securing everything to the aircraft floor and inside cabin wall. Passengers might find themselves sitting inside a cargo tunnel, but always had access to one or more cabin doors.

MAF equipped our aircraft with an engineered cargo restraint system including extra cargo tie-down points installed in the airframe, Brownline seat & cargo tracks built into the floor, a tested cargo net, and an array of small and large straps. Correctly secured cargo could withstand a 10G stop. If we hit a cow, then stopped upside down and backward in a ditch, the cargo would stay in place. We received extensive instruction on proper tie-down procedures—encasing the cargo with the net, proper anchor rings, number of tie-down straps, kinds of knots, and where to fasten the three-inch-wide, ratcheting Herc straps. But some cargo required special tie-down procedures:

ROOFING

Village folks constructed their housing from locally available materials—branches, saplings, logs, grass, vines, bamboo, and occasionally rocks. Traditionally they used the ground as a floor and dug holes to anchor vertical members. Some tribes, like the

Waorani, bent the verticals together and bound them at the top producing a bee-hive shaped, curved roof and wall combination. Other tribes such as the Shuar, used thicker, straight verticals poles, then lashed horizontal beams crossways to support triangular roof trusses with overhanging eaves.

But as the outside world encroached into the jungle, building styles changed. When missionary influence and overriding civil law combined to virtually eliminate the revenge killing cycle, fortress-like exterior walls disappeared. Thin, split bamboo interior privacy walls replaced the earlier solid barriers, but most folks left outside walls open to catch a cooling breeze.

Then, as the government began providing teachers, schools appeared in villages. With either government or missionary funding, we flew a contractor into a village. Using chainsaws, the contractor's team felled trees, cut them into long planks, and left them in drying stacks. A year later we'd fly the contractor in again along with boxes of nails, construction fencing, and other hardware. The contractors constructed a schoolhouse and teacher residence from the dried planks, often preserving them with used motor oil. Then came the roofing.

All tribes thatched their roofs with thick, elaborate mats made of palm fronds or long grass. Thatched roofs offered many benefits: Anyone with the skill could make one from free material growing everywhere. They allowed cooking fire smoke and hot air to pass through but kept water out. And the smoke drove out bugs. But thatched roofs had two big drawbacks.

They took many hours to make but lasted only as long as the rest of a traditionally constructed structure—five years at most. The common knowledge saying "Lions are the king of the jungle" ignores reality. Termites rule. In the end, they and their cousins ate everything, wood, grass, and lion carcasses.

So, funding agencies and their contractors turned to corrugated sheet metal as the default roofing material. After constructing a framework of joists and rafters, the contractor could quickly fashion a watertight covering that lasted for years.

Actually getting the roofing sheets out to the village, however, proved challenging.

The 4 x 8-foot (some were 3 x 10 feet) sheets for a single roof made too big a load to carry over 50 or more miles of narrow, twisting, slippery jungle trails. In that section of the Amazon jungle, fickle, pernicious rivers offered few reliable cargo transport options. Flying provided the only viable option. But loading and carrying the sheets was tricky. Handling them required thick gloves and great care. Pointed corners and sharp edges pierced any material pushed against them. They were too wide to lie flat in the cabin and some were too long.

To carry them, we rolled and tied small stacks into 18 to 24-inch diameter tubes. Then we removed the covering from the aft cabin bulkhead exposing the mostly empty tail cone. With the C-185 we removed the copilot's door and on the C-206 we opened the aft cargo door. We fed the sheet metal tube into the cabin. If not needed for a passenger, we removed the copilot seat, otherwise, the tube extended into the now open tail cone. Then we lashed the entire stack to the cabin cargo rings, tied the cargo net over it, and secured the whole package with the large cargo straps. We also fastened a small plywood sheet across the front edge of the tube. A sudden stop could throw the sheet bundle forward like a flying guillotine blade.

COMBUSTIBLES

We carried combustible liquids—avgas, jet fuel, auto gas, diesel, pressurized propane tanks, and occasionally kerosene. For our own use, we maintained two remote avgas (gasoline for airplane engines) caches—one in the Amazon jungle at Makuma, and the other in the coastal jungle at Zapallo Grande. Our regulations required us to land at the fuel cache location with one-hour reserve still in the airplane tanks. So, we fueled from the remote dumps only under unusual circumstances—bad weather or an extra, unplanned, but important flight request. If we moved people from many locations to a single remote site, we positioned extra fuel there beforehand to avoid the extra time and gas burn of returning to Shell to refuel.

To stock each cache, we filled two 55-gallon steel drums, then let them sit an hour to equalize the liquid temperature with ambient air temperature. After double checking both caps tight, we tipped the barrel onto its side with each cap, in turn, held at the lowest point for a few minutes to ensure no leakage. Then we rolled the barrels to the airplane and up a ramp into the cabin. We stood them upright again, then secured them with a cargo net and large ratcheting Herc straps. The load, 660 pounds of fuel and another 50 to 70 pounds of drums used most of the airplane's available capacity. Offloading from a C-185 required removing both pilot seats and the copilot's door. The C-206 was easier since we needed only to open both rear cargo doors.

The trick, however, was to get the barrel off the airplane without damage to barrels, airframe, or people. After positioning in front of the open door, we tipped the barrel on its side. Then we propped two or three strong poles or planks against the door frame. They had to be long enough to contact the ground far enough away from the door to create a ramp. The pilot and a helper pushed the full barrel out the door onto the ramp. Cramming in as many bodies as fit, the receivers hand rolled it down the ramp and over to the cache location in a shed next to the loading ramp.

Storing fuel in drums for long periods required special care to prevent water contamination. Even with tightly sealed caps moisture inside the barrel condensed into the fuel and, because water weighs more than gasoline, sank to the bottom of the barrel. Left too long it rusted the barrel bottom and lower side. And, when drawing fuel from the barrel, the rotary hand pump could pick up and put water into the airplane's fuel tanks. Because water in avgas yields disappointing results, we employed a special funnel and filter between the hose nozzle and aircraft fuel tank opening when drawing from drums. The funnel contained a filter element that allowed gasoline to pass, but instantly blocked water and stopped particle contamination.

During our temporary operation from Tena, the Ecuadorian Army asked us to deliver fuel for them. One of their smaller turbine-powered helicopters ran low on fuel while deep in the Amazon. The pilot landed at a village strip and radioed for help. The good news was that we normally operated from the strip. The bad news was the pilot set down exactly in the middle and didn't have enough fuel to restart and hover-taxi to the cleared area off the runway. That meant we had to do a drop delivery.

A truck backed up to our temporary Tena ramp space and unloaded several five-gallon, plastic fuel containers of jet fuel. We removed the C-185 copilot door and seat, then loaded and secured the jugs in the airplane, leaving enough space for one seat directly behind the pilot. I flew while another pilot, John, rode behind me.

Flying with a door removed required extra considerations. We removed everything from our shirt pockets, turned collars completely inside our shirts, tucked pant cuffs inside our socks, and pushed exposed hair back under our helmets. Then we stowed all required loose cockpit items inside the survival kit and left non-essentials with Pancho. John put on a safety harness we fashioned from seat belts and cargo straps. Then he connected himself to a cabin cargo tie-down ring.

Our helmet's internal headphones and mic allowed us to talk above the engine roar and air blast. Finally, we lowered our helmet face shields to protect against flying grit and bugs as well as allow John to keep his glasses in place.

After a half-hour flight, we arrived over the strip. The helicopter sat in the exact center of the runway. Not enough room to land on either remaining end of the strip, nor sufficient space to roll by either side. The drop remained the only delivery option.

I switched the HF radio to the village frequency and spoke with the coordinator. He told us how to identify a known deep spot just upriver from the village site. Drop the jugs there, he said. The villagers would be waiting in a shallower spot down-river, safely away from 35-pound weights falling from the sky.

I surveyed the area, then planned a rectangular pattern that gave us a straight and level run over the drop zone as well as upriver, away from the waiting retrievers below. John checked his harness and its tethering strap then slid out of his seat and crawled to the open door frame on the right side of the cabin. I slowed the airplane to 80 knots and lowered the flaps to 20°.

We reviewed our procedures. My job: fly the airplane. John's job: make the drops. We rehearsed with a practice circuit, confirming an approach route, minimum descent height—about 50 feet—, drop point, and departure path.

Satisfied we could hit the target, I started the second circuit while John untied and drug the jet fuel filled jugs into position. On our first drop pass, he pushed out one jug, telling me over the intercom where it landed. I couldn't—and didn't try to—see it hit. I focused on staying over the center of the river, climbing and turning left at the chosen sandbar. I flew another low pass. John shoved out two more jugs.

On the downriver leg, at pattern altitude, when I could afford to look, I saw the red plastic jugs bobbing in the muddy brown current, drifting surely downstream into the arms of waiting villagers who caught and pulled them up onto the sandy bank.

After a half dozen more passes, all 12 jugs were delivered. As the helicopter pilot poured fuel into his machine, John and I headed back to Tena.

CHICHA

Three of the four Amazonian tribes we worked with shared a culinary staple called "chicha." Women grew yucca (aka manioc, or cassava) in their gardens surrounding the village clearing. After harvesting, they washed then mashed the bland, starchy white root into a paste. Next, they scooped the paste into their mouths, chewed it for a few minutes, then spit it into a container allowing it to ferment. The longer it sat, the higher the alcohol content. For children and general family meals, they waited a few hours, but for parties, days.

Every culture cherishes its own comfort foods. The Shuar, Atshuar, and Lowland Quichua craved chicha. If hungry, they hungered for chicha. If thirsty, they thirsted for chicha. The custom in Atshuar and Shuar villages dictated that while the men sat in a circle talking, their women stood just outside the circle. Upon request from a man, a woman dipped a half gourd bowl into the pot, filling it with the chicha mix. Raising it up, she ran her hand through the mix, pulling out a wad of yucca fibers. She squeezed the wad, wringing out the juice, threw the wad back into the large pot, then handed the bowl to the man.

One weekend early in our Ecuador time, Regina, the four kids, and I spent a weekend in Charapacocha (an Atshuar village on the Pastaza river). Our host invited me into the evening men's circle. His wife offered me a bowl which I accepted, neither wanting to offend nor to drink any. Under their expectant gaze, I finally sampled the dull white liquid. It tasted like cheap beer mixed with bad milk. I smiled, asked them questions about village life, their family history, hunting, fishing, the weather, anything I could think of to divert attention from the still full bowl I held on my lap. When we finally departed the circle, I set it next to the log I'd occupied. I sampled many unusual foods in the jungle, but never chicha a second time.

For them, however, chicha remained a necessity, similar to my culture's coffee. And, of course, when they traveled, they took chicha with them. We always put it in the pod, rather than the aircraft cabin.

Typically carried as a concentrated paste about the consistency of cooked oatmeal, they used one of two containers: the traditional method wrapped a mound of chicha paste with banana leaves then bound it with jungle vines to form a squishy, soccer ball-sized package. The modern method employed a plastic bowl and snap lid. Both enjoyed mixed success when traveling by air. The traditional bundle proved surprisingly durable if wrapped well. Not airtight, it allowed the fermentation process to continue unhindered. If poked too hard, or pierced, however, the package oozed a chicha puddle. The modern method, impervious to leakage, did not deal well with altitude changes or high temperature, responding by exploding and spraying the foul-smelling paste everywhere, drenching everything in the pod. It demonstrated once again new and modern was not automatically better.

Blowguns

Newly trusted with an airplane in the jungle, I wanted to fit in quickly. I already understood flight requests always exceed daylight hours. That, in turn, demanded focused hustle. So, I found the extra mud at Atshuar (the airstrip name is the same word as the tribal name) disappointing. Here it offered an odd blend of slippery and plastic. I slowed nearly to a stop but kept enough momentum at the end of my landing roll to turn and slide around to point back in the opposite direction. The main landing gear wheels plowed deep furrows, but I was stopped and positioned for takeoff.

I was moving mom, dad, four kids, two dogs and everything they owned to another village to care for an invalid grandma—a culturally unusual step. They struggled toward the plane through oatmeal like mud, balancing bags, baskets, and baby. We cut branches to form a mat and piled their belongings out of the mire—mostly. I estimated people weights, slung each package from a scale, and did the math while staring at the pile. I'd be within legal weight limits, but would it all fit inside? The mound contained neither furniture nor boxes, but only the bulky bundles that made their home.

The dogs (in burlap bags with heads out) and flatter bags fit into the pod beneath the airplane. I needed four seats for the family, so I filled the sixth seat area and rear cargo space— stacking, stuffing, shifting until all fit, barely leaving room for people.

Finally, I beckoned the passengers aboard, helped them with seat belts and harness, gave them the safety briefing (only dad spoke Spanish) and hopped into my seat. Fifteen minutes behind schedule, but I could make that up over the next few stops—maybe.

As I locked my harness, dad tapped my shoulder and asked, "What about that?" pointing to a man outside with a 12-foot blow-gun.

Blow-gun? A moment's disbelief, then flashback to the training: "Blow-guns just fit the length of the cabin," the instructor said. "Be sure to tie them to the floor between the seats before you load any cargo or passengers."

"Can't we bring it on another flight?" I asked.

"But Capitán," he responded, "how will I feed my family?"

The reloading went more quickly. I knew where everything fit.

CARGO - CRITTERS

BEEF

About the time I got proficient tying down cargo with bowlines, half hitches, clove hitches, and square knots, Gene added a new wrinkle—beef. The indigenous jungle folks did not eat beef but did raise it as a cash crop. To start a village herd, we flew live calves into the village. After some missteps using tranquilizers, we developed a reliable routine that brought them un-traumatized to their new homes.

First, we removed all seats except the pilot's seat. Then, we placed a cut-to-fit plywood sheet on the ground near the airplane and covered it with a large rubberized canvas tarp. Next, we led the calf alongside the tarp. Our rule of thumb said the calf's back had to be no higher than the pilot's belt which yielded a typical weight of 300 to 400 pounds.

We gently laid the calf down on the tarp, then "hog" tied its feet together like rodeo cowboys do. Once in position, we wrapped the tarp around the calf so all the edges converged just below its head forming a large bag that acted as a diaper. Four of us then lifted the wrapped calf and plywood into the aircraft. We secured the cargo net over the calf using the correct number of straps and tie down points for its weight. Finally, we restrained the entire package with the two large Herc straps.

In the C-185, the calf's head lay to my right in place of the copilot's seat, its big brown eyes staring up at me. Most remained calm during the 20-40-minute flight. But if they wiggled at all, they shook the whole plane. Amidst the racket, soft words produced minimal effects. But, after a few trips, I discovered laying a small cargo strap loosely across a calf's jaw and cheek dissuaded them from moving their head. And no head movement meant no body movement. Then the aircraft flew only where I directed it.

At the destination strip, I untied the net and straps but left the tarp wrapped in place. Then three village volunteers and I removed the plywood platform, set it on the ground, unwrapped the tarp, untied the calf's feet and helped it stand. Someone led the calf up and down the airstrip for three or four minutes and its wobbling settled into a normal gait. Finally, a gaggle of small boys vied for the honor of cleaning the tarp in the nearest stream. When they returned with the clean, mostly dry tarp, I folded it, stowed it in the pod, replaced the seats on their tracks and prepared for the next flight segment.

A village spent a year developing a small herd. Residents sometimes shared ownership of a cow. The more entrepreneurial might own several. Jungle humidity, mud, parasites, viruses, and predators didn't offer an ideal bovine environment, but the villagers persisted because beef provided one of the few means of acquiring cash.

When they decided to harvest the beef—either at the planned time or to meet an unexpected cash need—we followed a specific procedure to protect their investment.

First, the village radio operator requested a beef flight two to four days in advance. The flight coordinator notified a meat buyer in town and included the flight in requested day's schedule. On the designated morning, the flight coordinator confirmed the request again, verified the buyer ready to receive the beef, and let the village know the flight's approximate arrival time. Finally, about an hour before the plane's landing time, our dispatcher confirmed that the village still wanted the flight, the plane remained available, and the weather would likely continue operable long enough to retrieve the beef. If all those factors remained good, we authorized them to proceed.

After slaughtering and cleaning the cow, they removed the head, hooves, and skin and cut the carcass into four quarters—in half lengthwise then in half again crossways. Next, they hung the four quarters on a log frame that looked like a large doorway, 15 to 20 minutes prior to my landing.

When I arrived at the village airstrip, before I prepared the airplane, I inspected the hanging quarters and confirmed they had drained for at least 10 minutes. I met with the men who were to carry the beef and briefed them to start with the two rear quarters and insert the large end into the cabin first, concave side up. Then I asked them to wait for my signal. I returned to the airplane and removed the four rear seats, stowing them in the pod under the airplane or lashing them to aft cabin bulkhead. Then I connected one end of the cargo net and the long, not ratcheted end of each Herc strap to airframe tie-down points a foot behind the pilot's seat. I temporarily bundled and tied them to cargo rings on cabin ceiling. Finally, I unfolded and spread a rubberized tarp over the entire open cabin floor, extending it up each side, the aft end of the cabin, and up the pilot and copilot seat backs.

Satisfied the cabin was ready, I signaled the village men to bring the beef. If conducting the flight in a C-206 I stood outside the aft end of the main cargo doors. If using a C-185, I also removed and set aside the copilot's seat and door. I asked for a volunteer to climb into the cabin through the rear cargo door and crouch down between the tarp and aft bulkhead. I leaned into the cabin as far as possible through the pilot's door. The carriers pushed the large, rib end into the cabin towards the man crouched in back. I grabbed and pulled and helped pull it through the door while the aft helper pulled it back towards himself. When it completely inside the cabin we set it onto the tarp. The first quarter lay concave side up, leg pointing forward. They oriented the next quarter the same way and nestled it into the first. Then they brought the front two quarters also aligning them the same way, dish side up, leg forward.

The pieces in place, I backed out while the volunteer climbed out of the aft baggage door. I washed my hands and arms with gasoline from the airplane's fuel quick-drain if water wasn't available. Avgas evaporates quickly so my hands neither smelled nor presented a fire hazard.

Leaning in through each of the doors in turn, I spread the tarp across the entire load of meat. Then I untied the net and Herc strap bundle, ensured it wrapped around the front of the covered meat package, and tossed the loose ends aft. Returning to the aft door, I pulled the net tight, then tied its ends and sides tightly to airframe attach points. Finally, I attached the Herc straps and ratcheted them taut.

An average butchered beef weighed 800 pounds. Properly set up, the cargo net, its attach straps and large Herc straps working together held the covered meat bundle in place for even a sudden 10G stop—the equivalent of an 8,000-pound load. Any stop above 10Gs would likely destroy the airframe making higher rated restraints moot.

If using the C-185, I replaced the copilot's seat and door. If the C-206, I proceeded directly to boarding a passenger, if any, and preparing for departure. Because microbes living in hot, humid jungle air attacked fresh beef immediately, we always flew a beef directly to Shell. We tried to get the meat to the buyer as rapidly as possible to get the seller the best price.

Back in Shell, our hangar helpers unloaded the beef onto a baggage cart. The term "cart" misrepresented the large, bright red, welded angle iron framed wagons. They featured stout plywood floors set upon 4 wheels shod with large bush aircraft tires removed because of smooth tread. Each easily supported 1,000 pounds. The helpers piled all four quarters onto a cart, rolled it over to the cargo scale, weighed each quarter and calculated the price. Nobody got free meat. The only perk granted fell to the pilot making the flight. He got first option to buy—at full price— the cut he wanted, usually the tenderloin known locally as the "lomo." We then sent income from the beef sale, minus the flight fee, back to the village. Since we were also the jungle post office, we guaranteed delivery.

The villagers gave us their best weight guess when scheduling the flight, but since I was responsible for clearing the trees at the end of the runway when hauling it out, I learned to make my own estimate. I watched every official weighing and developed my own system. First, I looked at the size of the hanging quarters, particularly the diameter of the legs just above where the hoof had been. Then, I watched the men carrying each quarter to the plane.

The more they bent under the load the heavier the piece. If it required two men, even more. Third, I looked at how high the pieces stacked inside the cabin. After a few months hauling a beef or two a week, I consistently guessed beef weights within 50 pounds.

Bagre (Giant Cat Fish)

Another kind of meat flight came with little or no warning— "bagre," Spanish for the giant catfish inhabiting Amazon jungle rivers.

A village like Mashient, laying close to the Pastaza river, radioed asking (pleading?) for a flight to take a bagre to market. Too large and too rare to catch at a planned time, the indigenous folks relied on sharp observation and quick action. The prime watching time came immediately after the river level rose and then dropped quickly. Sudden low water sometimes trapped the giant bagre behind a sand or gravel bar. When spotted, the call went out. Men attempted to net or rope the huge fish, drag it out of the water up onto the bank, then finish it off with machete or club. Landing a bagre posed a high risk to men and women in the water and on land. But the high price paid warranted the extra effort.

When the call came, we tried to pick them up. Wasn't always easy. Typical bagre weighed 150 to 200 pounds. The biggest one I hauled topped 300 pounds. When laid on to a pickup bed in Shell with its head at the front end, the tail dropped over the open tailgate and touched the ground. As with beef, the flight's pilot got first dibs on purchasing the cut he wanted.

Pigs

Pigs required a different procedure. Jungle people usually transported live pigs rather than butchered. And pigs, being tough, strong, and smart, needed stout trussing and reliable containment—front legs bound together, rear legs tied as well and then the whole animal inserted into a quintal bag (very strong nylon woven bag similar to a burlap bag. The name comes from

its nominal 50 kilo capacity). Some, however, were too big to fit
into a hundred-pound sack so after front and back legs were tied,
both sets were also secured together, and the snout muzzled. Then
the entire animal except for the head was wrapped in a net or
material from cut up quintal bags.

Actually getting a 300 pound, bound, snorting, bucking hog
into a C-185 pod required a committed team. Their squeals
surpassed aircraft engine noise even in flight. And when they
thrashed despite containment, the whole airplane shook.
Unloading an angrier swine after landing proved more
challenging. Even the cute little ones created unique problems.

One afternoon, Job hopped from village to village picking up
school teachers at the end of their academic year. At his last
stop—Arajuno, only 15 minutes from Shell—waiting for the last
passenger delayed him as the afternoon wore on. Both MAF and
Ecuadorian civil aviation regulations required us to be on the
ground no later than official sunset. Violating the rule required
completing and presenting unpleasant paperwork to both
authorities. And on the equator day changed to night in minutes.

Job loaded the cargo, strapped the other passengers into the
airplane and sat in his seat, prepared to start the engine at the exact
minute that allowed him to reach Shell before sunset. Suddenly
the errant, gasping teacher ran up to the airplane with a backpack
in his left hand. Job jumped down from his perch, tossed the pack
into the pod, and directed the late arrival to climb into the
remaining seat. Then Job realized the teacher carried a small,
wiggling pig in his right hand. He checked his watch. One minute
until he had to start the engine or spend the night. He reopened
the pod door, set the pig into the only open space among the cargo
and quickly shut and secured the door. He belted the passenger
in, jumped back into his seat, completed the checklists and took
off at the last possible moment.

Arajuno sits in a river canyon just below the plateau that hosted
Shell. Job rose up over the canyon lip and leveled off en route to
home base. Five minutes after takeoff a boom rocked the airplane

and the entire airframe shook. Job followed the emergency procedures, scanned both engine and performance instruments looking for the problem. All read normal—airspeed, altitude, engine power, fuel flow. The airplane continued to function correctly, other than noise and shaking.

During his initial troubleshooting, the vibrating plane passed the halfway point to Shell, so Job elected to continue rather than turn back. He radioed our dispatcher, talked briefly with the maintenance director, then entered Shell's traffic pattern and landed normally.

In the hangar, we heard the radio conversation so gathered on the ramp when he taxied up. As he shut the engine down and opened his door we said, "Job, there's no pod door!"

He hopped to the ground, stooped down, peered into the pod and said, "No pig!"

Apparently, the piglet wiggled hard enough to push the leading edge of the pod door slightly open. The nearly 140 mile-per-hour slipstream grabbed and ripped it off the pod. Either the sudden air pressure change sucked the pig out, or else he tried to escape towards daylight. In either case, he was gone.

I conjectured what happened after the fall. An indigenous jungle man knelt in his thatched roof house, praying for help feeding his family. He told the Lord the hunting had been sparse and the yucca crop grew poorly. Suddenly, the pig crashed through the roof, hit and split the table. Astounded, he thanked God for the fast response and assembled the family for a feast.

On the aviation side, we modified the pod door design. Originally, the door was a separate piece of thick aluminum sheet. Its lower edge inserted into a track and then slid forward nesting into another track along its front edge. Finally, the upper, rear corner fastened to the pod with a wing-nut cam lock. The new design featured a piano-style hinge along the front edge and two cam locks at the aft end. After that, we lost neither doors nor pigs.

CHICKENS

We carried smaller animals in the pod so if they escaped containment, passengers remained safe from immediate injury and pilots could fly without distraction. Dogs, for example, traveled in sacks like pigs, but normally didn't need to be tied. Usually, they displayed more curiosity than fear. Cats always flew in cages, boxes or baskets

Chickens sometimes traveled in large, woven baskets. But villagers normally wrapped live chickens in large banana leaf diapers, leaving only the head exposed. They held each bird on the leaf, wrapping it around them, tying each one with jungle twine (lengths of vine ripped lengthwise yielding anything from thread to rope depending on the number of times torn). The swaddled chickens could then be bundled into two, four, or six packs complete with handle for easy carrying. My record was 43, bundled chickens all carried in the C-180 cabin.

SNAKES

Transporting snakes posed special problems. Typically captured for medical or biological research, most were poisonous. The trick was to contain, but not injure them, ensure they could not escape, and protect handlers from bites. Stout, lidded, wooden boxes with handles on the ends, a tight mesh air screen on top, and heavy hinges and padlock hasps provided the safest vessel. But sometimes the collector had to improvise.

Researchers visiting Zapallo Grande—a coastal jungle village in northwestern Ecuador—captured a six-foot pit viper and asked me to fly it to Quito for researchers trying to develop a better antivenom. They made a cage of woven bamboo to contain it. But even from a distance, the cage radiated a tangible presence, an evil that mere fauna ferocity did not explain. A continuous low-level buzz punctuated by an undulating hiss grew louder when anyone approached or handled the assembly.

To protect handlers, they enclosed the cage inside a wooden frame that extended six inches beyond all sides. They covered that with a layer of chicken fencing making it impossible for snake fang and human skin to connect. That, however, created a problem. It was too big to fit into a C-206 pod. The only option was to tie it down in the rear baggage area behind the seats. I understood how their request could help jungle people but having such a beast in the cabin did not thrill me—at all.

Fielding unusual flight and cargo requests formed a common thread through most of our work, but hauling that creature gave me more pause than any other petition. I asked for a moment alone, walked away from the airplane and prayed. It wasn't just my life and MAF's quarter million-dollar airplane at risk. I had to consider four passengers as well. Yes, the cage was strong. No, I did not see any way the viper could escape. Yes, I could tie it down so it wouldn't move, even if the plane were in the proverbial 'upside down and backward in a ditch position'. No, I did not see any unreasonable safety threat. But, still my "what if ..." training ran in high gear, producing several unpleasant scenarios. After a few moments, I felt peace—the kind that doesn't make any sense—and returned to the airplane. We loaded and secured the cage and took off. Forty-five minutes later a hospital vehicle and handlers met us on our Quito airport ramp to retrieve my special passenger.

PICTURE LINK INFORMATION

To see illustrations from this book, go to my website: www.JRManley.com. Click on the "Pictures" tab and look the title, *Mile-High Missionary*

Pilot Jargon Explained

This glossary unpacks some of aviation's secret language. The definitions pertain to how the term is used in this book and sometimes have more complex meanings than shown. If you have a question, go to the Contact tab on my website www.JRManley.com

100-hour Inspection Maintenance done every 100 flight hours.

10Gs, "G" "1G" means the normal force of gravity we experience every day on Earth. "10Gs" is the equivalent of ten times the force of gravity. Our cargo restraining system had to withstand a 10,000-pound shock to secure a 1,000-pound load.

A&P Aircraft mechanics earn two licenses. "A" is the airframe license. "P" is the power plant or engine license. A fully certified mechanic is often called an "A & P."

Abort, Abort Point Stopping a maneuver; the point where a maneuver is stopped.

Aft Toward the rear of the aircraft.

AGL Above Ground Level.

Aileron A small flap on the trailing edge of each wing used to bank or tilt the airplane.

Airframe The body of an airplane.

Airspeed How fast the airplane is moving through the air.

Airspeed Indicator A cockpit instrument that displays airspeed. A pilot flies the aircraft at predetermined airspeeds to achieve specific types of performance. Accurate airspeed control is a crucial, fundamental skill required of all pilots

Airstrips Another name for the runway. Usually used for shorter, less improved landing surfaces. Most airstrips in the jungle have either a bare dirt, or else a grass surface. A few are covered in gravel.

Airway A formally designated and named electronic highway in the sky.

Alas, "Alas Zero-Four", etc. Mission Aviation Fellowship is known as Alas de Socorro in Spanish speaking Central and South America. The literal translation is "Wings of Mercy." In Ecuador each aircraft is known by a radio call sign consisting of a shortened form of the organization's name followed by a number indicating the order it was added to the fleet. For example, the radio call sign for the fourth aircraft added to our fleet would be "Alas Zero-Four" The fifth "Alas Zero-Five", the sixth "Alas Zero-Six" and so on.

Altimeter A cockpit instrument that tells the pilot the airplanes altitude above Mean Sea Level.

Approach A segment of flight where an aircraft maneuvers around an airport and prepares to land. **Instrument approach** When an aircraft flies a predetermined procedure to land in bad weather. **Low approach** Where an aircraft flies level but at a low altitude over the runway area without attempting to land. **Approach Control** An Air Traffic Control (see ATC) sector that authorizes an aircraft traffic to leave cruise flight, begin an approach procedure and then talk to the airport control tower. **Missed approach** A procedure an aircraft flies after aborting an instrument approach.

Aravas The Spanish name for a 15,000 pound, twin-engine turboprop cargo aircraft manufactured in Israel.

ATC Air Traffic Control. A general name for an agency that controls air traffic within specified airspace such as, enroute, approach, tower, or ground control.

Attitude Indicator, gyro A cockpit instrument that tells the pilot where the horizon is. Using it he or she can position the aircraft nose vertically above or below the horizon as well as bank the wings at a specific angle to the horizon.

Avgas Gasoline blended for aircraft engines.

Avionics Communication, navigation and control electronics installed onboard an aircraft. **Avionics Master** A single switch controlling electrical power to all the aircraft's radios.

Bank Tilting the airplane's wings away from level. In straight and level flight the wings are parallel to the horizon. To turn left the pilot tilts (banks) the wings to the left, to turn right, he or she banks right.

Base (leg) Where the aircraft completes the downwind leg and turns to fly perpendicular to the runway while continuously descending.

Boeing B-727 An airliner with 3 engines mounted on its tail.

Boost Pump An electric pump the forces fuel into the engine either to prepare for starting or when the normal, engine-driven pump is not providing enough fuel.

Brake, A device on each wheel that allows the pilot to slow or stop an aircraft as it rolls on the ground. Left and right brakes are activated separately by tilting the left and right rudder pedals forward. **Rake Brake** A two-pronged fork mounted just ahead of the tail wheel. When deployed, the front, pointed end, dropped down. It immediately dug into the dirt and pivoted back. The tail wheel rode up onto it as the fork drug through the dirt stopping the plane in half the normal distance.

Brownline A type of rail installed on an aircraft floor that accommodates passenger seats, cargo tie-down rings, or both.

Ceiling The bottom of the clouds seen when looking up from the ground. **Clear** = no clouds. **Few** = ⅛ to 2/8 sky coverage. **Scattered** = ⅜ to 4/8 coverage. **Broken** = ⅝ to ⅞ coverage. **Overcast** = 8/8 coverage

Center Line A painted or imaginary line down the center of a runway's useable landing or takeoff surface.

Cessna C-150 A high-wing, 2-place aircraft with a single 100 hp engine and tricycle landing gear.

Cessna C-172 A high-wing, 4-place aircraft with a single 160 hp engine and tricycle landing gear.

Cessna C-180 A high-wing, 4-6 place aircraft with a single 235 hp engine and conventional (tailwheel) landing gear.

Cessna C-185 high-wing, 6-place aircraft with a single 285 hp engine and conventional (tailwheel) landing gear.

Cessna C-206 A high-wing, 6-place aircraft with a single 285-310 hp engine and tricycle landing gear.

Cessna C-210 A high-wing, 6-place aircraft with a single 285-310 hp engines and retractable tricycle landing gear.

Cessna C-337 A high-wing, 6-place aircraft with 2, 210 hp engines and retractable tricycle landing gear. The military version was called a Cessna O2

Checklist An ordered enumeration of settings for various aircraft components, instruments, and adjustments that must be completed prior to an aircraft operation such as takeoff. The pilot uses the list to confirm that he or she has properly prepared the aircraft for the intended operation.

Clearance An authorization from Air Traffic Control for a pilot to conduct a certain operation such as landing.

Climb Moving the aircraft from a lower to a higher altitude. **Climb Setting** The aircraft and engine configurations necessary for an aircraft to climb.

Clouds Visible water vapor suspended in the air. **Cumulus clouds** develop vertically, often into rain showers or thunderstorms with turbulence around and inside. **Stratus clouds** develop horizontally, cover wide areas with little wind associated. **Fog** stratus clouds touching the ground

Coax Cable that carries signals between a radio and its antenna.

Cockpit A space inside an airplane where the pilot(s) sit in order to control the airplane.

Com Abbreviation for a communications radio.

Compass An instrument that displays the angle in degrees between where the aircraft's nose is pointed and the Earth's north magnetic pole.

Contactor An electrical relay that acts like a switch. It allows a lower power device such as an ignition switch to activate a high power circuit such as a starter motor.

Control Wheel, Yoke, column A control that allows the pilot to pitch the aircraft nose up and down as well as bank the wings left or right. It comes in three configurations: a stick or "joy stick" extending up from the aircraft floor; a steering wheel or "yoke" protruding from the aircraft panel; or a short side-stick mounted to one side of the pilot's position.

Controlled Field An airport with an operating control tower. Operators in the tower must grant permission for each takeoff and landing.

Cowl Flaps Small doors in the engine cowling the pilot can open to provide more cooling air for the engine.

Cowl, Cowling A portion of the airframe that covers the engine(s).

Cross-Control Where to pilot commands the aircraft to bank in one direction but moves the rudder in the opposite direction.

Crosswind A wind blowing in any direction other than parallel to the runway

Crosswind (leg) Where the plane flies perpendicular to the runway but does not descend. Usually flown just beyond the opposite end of the runway from where the pilot intends to land.

Cruise The longest portion of a flight between two locations. The aircraft normally maintains a constant altitude and speed, and only occasionally adjusts its heading. **Cruise climb** A faster, flatter climb used to reach a cruising altitude when no obstacles interfere. Generally yields a shorter total trip time. **Cruise descent** A faster, flatter descent used to reach an approach or traffic pattern altitude when no obstacles interfere. Generally yields a shorter total trip time.

DAC Dirrección de Aviación General de Ecuador. Ecuadorian agency overseeing civil aviation.

De Havilland Canada Buffalo A high-wing, 40-passenger aircraft with 2, 3,100hp turbo-prop engines and retractable tricycle landing gear.

De Havilland Canada Twin Otter A high-wing, 20-passenger aircraft with 2, 578-750 hp turbo-prop engines and fixed tricycle landing gear.

Dead Reckoning A navigation system that relies on holding a constant heading at a constant speed for a specified amount of time.

Descent Moving to a lower altitude. **Descent rate** How fast an aircraft changes altitude. For passenger safety and comfort, pilots of non-pressurized aircraft limit descent rates to 500 feet per minute or less.

Dispatcher A person who organizes or tracks the movement of aircraft operating away from home base.

DME Distance Measuring Equipment.

Dornier DO-27 A high-wing, 6-place aircraft with a single 270 hp engine and fixed conventional (tailwheel) landing gear.

Downwind (leg) Where the aircraft flies about ½ mile from and parallel to the runway in the opposite direction of intended landing. The first portion of this leg is flown level and then, when opposite the point of intended landing, begins its descent.

Drag Air resistance to an aircraft's forward motion. Form drag is produced by the airframe pushing against the air. Induced drag is produced as a byproduct of lift.

Edge, leading, trailing The front or rear edge, respectively, of the wing, stabilizers, or propeller blades.

EFS Emergency Fuel System. An MAF device that feeds fuel from the aircraft's fuel tank directly into the engine bypassing the carburetor or fuel injection system.

Elevator The large flap(s) on the trailing edge of the horizontal stabilizer ("back wing") used to point the nose of the airplane up or down.

ELT Emergency Locator Transmitter.

Engine A motor mounted on the airframe that produces thrust to move the aircraft forward. **Multi Engine** An aircraft with more than one engine. **Single Engine** An aircraft with one engine.

ETA Estimated Time of Arrival. **ETD** Estimated Time of Departure. **ETE** Estimated Time Enroute

Exhaust Stack The exhaust manifold and pipe of an aircraft engine.

FBO Fixed Base Operator. A business that provides aircraft services such as fuel, maintenance, aircraft rental, flight planning facilities, pilot and passenger lounge, snacks, restrooms, and pilot supplies.

Ferry Flight A special flight to reposition an aircraft for maintenance or transfer to a different area.

Final Approach Where the aircraft flies a descending path directly towards an intended touchdown point on the runway or airstrip. A normal final approach is a straight course along the runway's extended centerline. Some bush airstrips, however, require a maneuvering final.

Flaps Large control surfaces on the trailing edge of each wing. Extended for takeoff and landing, they allow flight at slower airspeeds.

Flight Plan A document filed with civil aviation authorities declaring details of a proposed flight.

FOM, Flight Operations Manual MAF's aviation standards and procedures.

Forced Landing An unplanned landing due to mechanical, weather, fuel exhaustion, or other factors.

Forward Toward the front of the aircraft.

Frequency A characteristic of a radio wave. To communicate, a radio transmitter and receiver must be tuned to the same frequency.

Fuel Selector A valve that allows the pilot to select which tank the aircraft engine draws fuel from.

Fuselage The main body of an aircraft.

Gear, Landing Gear Wheels that allow the aircraft to move easily on the ground. Two main gear legs on either side of the fuselage carry most of the aircraft's weight. A 3rd wheel on either the nose or tail enables ground steering.

Glare Shield The top of an aircraft control panel that extends out towards the pilot to shade the instruments in bright sunlight.

Glide Flight (usually descending) without engine power. **Glide Path** Another name for the descending portion of a final approach to landing. Also the name of an electronic signal on an ILS (see ILS) that guides the pilot along that path. **Glide Speed** Each aircraft has an optimum glide speed yielding the greatest distance forward for a given altitude loss.

Green (instrument markings) A colored area on a variety of aircraft instruments indicating their normal operating range.

Gross Weight An aircraft's maximum authorized operating weight. Also, the total weight of a loaded and fueled aircraft.

Ground Effect Extra lift generated when a wing flies within ½ wingspan of the ground.

Ground Roll The distance from when an aircraft's wheels first touch the runway until it comes to a complete stop. Or the distance from the start of a takeoff until the wheels leave the ground.

Grumman AA-1B A low-wing, 2-place aircraft with a single 108 hp engine and tricycle landing gear.

Grumman AA-5B A low-wing, 4-place aircraft with a single 180 hp engine and tricycle landing gear.

Grumman S2F A high-wing, non-pressurized, military aircraft with 2, 1,525 engines and retractable tricycle landing gear. Later converted to anti forest fire tankers.

Gyro Gyroscope. Used in aircraft instruments that indicate attitude, heading, and turn rate.

Hangar A building used to house one or more aircraft.

Heading The direction the aircraft nose is pointed (see compass). **Heading Indicator,** A gyro instrument that indicates the direction an aircraft nose is pointing. Provides a much more stable indication than the aircraft's magnetic compass.

Helmet When I flew in Ecuador, MAF required all pilots to wear an aviation rated helmet that also contained headphones and a microphone.

HF High Frequency (commonly called 'short wave') radio wave used to communicate with stations beyond the horizon.

Hold the spot…When landing the pilot picks a touchdown point on the runway, notes where it is in the windscreen, then adjusts power to keep that point in the same place on the windshield. "Holding the spot" means he or she is aiming correctly.

Ice When an aircraft flies inside a cloud and the air temperature is between 14 and 32°F ice can form on aircraft surfaces such as wings. Ice degrades aircraft performance by adding weight, by reducing lift as it changes the wings shape, reducing propeller performance.

IFR, IMC Instrument Flight Rules, Instrument Meteorological Conditions.

ILS Instrument Landing System—a high precision system installed at some airports for landing in bad weather.

Intersection A named point where two electronic airways cross.

Inverted Vee Antenna An HF antenna wire supported by a single mast in the center.

Jet Fuel, Jet A An aircraft fuel similar to diesel burned in turbo-prop and jet engines.

Knots, Kts Shorthand for a nautical miles per hour. 1 nautical mile per hour = 1.15 statute miles per hour. Abbreviated "Kts" or "kts." In commercial and military aviation nautical miles are the international standard for speed and distance measurements. See Nautical Mile.

Lift An upward force produced when air flows across a wing.

MAF Mission Aviation Fellowship. A non-profit mission organization formed in 1945 by 5 military pilots—4 men and 1 woman—to provide transportation for missionaries and national church organizations working in remote locations.

Manifold Pressure, Gauge An instrument that indicates how much power an aircraft engine is producing.

MDA Minimum Descent Altitude.

Mean Sea Level The calculated average level of the world's oceans. Aircraft altitudes are named as being a certain number of feet above mean sea level.

Microphone, Mic A device for detecting the pilot's voice and feeding it to a radio transmitter. **Mic Button, PTT** Push To Talk. When pushed, it activates the communication transmitter and allows the pilot to speak to another station.

Mixture, Mixture Control Adjusts the ratio of an aircraft engine's air to fuel mixture. Similar to a car's choke.

Nautical mile The distance covered by 1 second of arc at the equator. 1 nautical mile = 1.15 statute mile. See Knots.

Nose The front of the aircraft.

OAT Outside Air Temperature.

One-way airstrip An airstrip whose obstructions permit takeoffs and landing only over one end of the runway regardless of wind direction.

Oxygen, Mask, System A pressurized tank that delivers breathable oxygen via a mask worn by pilot and passengers. Reduces or eliminates the danger of hypoxia during flight at higher altitudes.

Part 135 US Federal Aviation Administration rules covering commercial air taxi operations.

Part 91 US Federal Aviation Administration rules covering private, non-commercial aviation operations.

Pilatus Porter A high-wing, 10-place aircraft with a single 550-680 hp turbo prop engine and fixed conventional (tailwheel) landing gear.

Piper Aztec A low wing 6 place aircraft with 2, 250 hp engines and retractable tricycle landing gear.

Pitch The position of an aircraft's nose relative to the horizon, as in above or below the horizon. Also, the angle of a propeller blade to the air flowing over it.

Pitot Tube, Heat An "L" shaped tube protruding from beneath the wind out into the slipstream during flight. Provides air pressure for measuring the aircraft's speed through the air. Pitot heat prevents moist air from freezing inside the pitot tube.

Pod, Cargo Pod A compartment attached to the belly of the aircraft used to carry cargo. Increases the pilot's flexibility for carrying cargo and passenger mixes but does not increase the total weight the aircraft is allowed to carry.

Port Left, left side. Nautical term also used in aviation.

Power Curve A graph that compares airspeed vs the engine power required to maintain that airspeed in level flight. Level flight on the front side of the curve means an aircraft will climb when more power is added. Adding power during level flight at the same airspeed on back side of the curve does not produce a climb. When high power is required to fly level at very slow airspeeds, the aircraft is said to be "behind the power curve."

Prop, Propeller A two or three bladed fan attached to the engine crankshaft that pushes enough air backwards to move the aircraft forward. **Prop Control** Adjusts the pitch of the propeller blades for different phases of flight such as takeoff, climb, cruise, descent, and landing. Similar to a car's transmission.

Quintal Bag A very strong nylon woven bag similar to a burlap bag. The name comes from its nominal 50 kilo (110 pound) capacity.

Radio Channel, Channel is a shorthand name for specific, commonly used radio frequencies. See Frequency.

Radio Signals An electromagnetic field that enables communications between two or more separate stations without wires connecting them.

Right Stuff A term made famous in Tom Wolfe's book of the same name. It said that every successful pilot had an internal supply of courage, command, and composure. Sometimes, though, it could leak out leaving the unfortunate victim a deflated husk of his or her former intrepid self. Other terms for such a person are non-pilot, and human. A pilot full of the "Right Stuff" displays an attitude that he or she is not only in complete control, but also almost, but not quite, bored—regardless of the situation. On the positive side, it radiated a confidence and command that reassured nervous passengers. On the negative side, pilots rarely shared doubts, worries, or concerns about their own ability to perform. We missionary pilots, out of necessity, spent thousands of hours immersed in that worldview to learn the profession. Old habits die hard, so our Chief Pilot, genuinely concerned about our internal status as well as our technical ability, faced the extra burden of carefully pealing back the armor after any sort of unplanned event.

Roll Sideways motion around the longitudinal (fore to aft) axis of the aircraft. Often called "bank."

RPM Engine revolutions Per Minute.

Rudder A large control surface on the trailing edge of the vertical stabilizer used to move the aircraft nose left or right.

Soup Pilot jargon for the inside of clouds as in, "I'm in the soup."

Speed of Light The speed that light and other electromagnetic waves such as radio signals travel—186,000 mph.

Spooling Some aircraft instruments use mechanical gyroscopes (devices that contain small wheels spinning at very high speeds). As the accelerate up to, decelerate down from normal operating speed, they produce a smooth, continually raising or lowering sound called spooling.

Stabilizer, Horizontal A horizontal "back wing" that balances the aircraft around its center of lift pushing the tail down and the nose up.

    Stabilizer, Vertical A large vertical fin on the tail that helps the aircraft fly straight.

Stall When the angle (called Angle of Attack) between the wing and the air flowing over it exceeds a certain limit, the wing stops producing lift.

    Stall Horn An audible warning that sounds when the wing's angle of attack gets close to the critical limit.

Throttle Adjust the amount of fuel flowing to an aircraft engine. Similar to a car's gas pedal.

Touch Down, Point, Zone The spot or area a landing aircraft first touches the ground.

Tower, Control Tower A tall structure topped by a windowed room giving a 360° view. Found at larger airports that require a pilot obtain permission before taxi, takeoff, or landing.

Traffic pattern A standard, rectangular traffic flow around a runway consisting of four distinct legs. Pilots use these legs for landing, taking off, and departing. All turns are normally made to the left. Airstrips located in remote or "bush" areas often require unique patterns due to obstructions or other factors.

Trim, Trim Tab A small control surface attached to the trailing edge of larger control surfaces such as the elevator, rudder, or aileron. Used to reduce or eliminate the amount of control pressure a pilot must hold for a desired flight attitude.

Turbo, Turbo charging, Turbocharged A device that compresses an engine's incoming air allowing it to produce full power at a higher altitude.

Turn Coordinator A gyro instrument that indicates how rapidly the aircraft is changing direction (not how fast it is flying). It also shows if the aircraft is slipping or skidding around a turn (similar to a car's tires sliding rather than rolling through a turn).

Upwind (leg) Part of the traffic pattern around a runway. Flown at a constant altitude (normally a specified traffic pattern altitude) parallel to the runway in the same direction as an intended landing. Followed after a 90° turn by crosswind, then downwind. See crosswind, downwind, base, and final.

V Speeds Shorthand for airspeeds that yield specific performance. For example:

> **Va** = Maneuvering Speed. Slower than cruise. Used when flying in turbulence.
>
> **Vs** = Stalling Speed. The speed at which an aircraft's wing (in a defined configuration)
>
> **Vx** = Airspeed that yields the steepest angle of climb
>
> **Vy** = Airspeed that yields the highest rate of climb.

Vectors For aviation use, a specific direction of flight given by ATC to achieve a certain purpose such as traffic avoidance or positioning for landing. See ATC.

VFR Visual Flight Rules governing flight when the visibility is 3 miles or more.

VHF Very High Frequency radio waves. The communicating stations must be within line-of-sight (not over the horizon or with intervening terrain).

VHF Repeater A device that receives a VHF signal on one frequency and retransmits it on another frequency. Allows the use of VHF channels between stations beyond line-of-sight distances.

VOR A VHF radio beacon for aircraft navigation.

VSI Vertical Speed Indicator. Tells the pilot how fast (in feet-per-minute) the aircraft is climbing or descending.

WAC World Aeronautical Chart. Aeronautical charts rendered at a 1:1,000,000 scale.

Windshield brace, crossbar Airframe strengthening tubes that cross between the pilot and the windshield.

Wing The long, wide horizontal surfaces of the airframe that produce lift when the aircraft's engine(s) move it forward at a high enough speed.

Yaw Motion around an aircraft's vertical axis, left right motion.

Acknowledgements

On the surface, producing a book-length manuscript appears to be a solo endeavor. Such a project does, in fact, demand many hours sequestered away from the rest of life.

However, that separation from everything and everyone represents but a part of the process. Actually, every book—especially this one—appears only after a long team effort. The trick, of course, is wanting to name everyone. Obviously, I can't. A few are named in this book. Most are not. The book length would exceed your reading patience. However, that does not diminish the value of their contribution or my gratitude. I could not have ministered as I did or written this book without them.

First, Mission Aviation Fellowship's people accepted us (Regina, our four kids, and me) despite my being an old (comparatively speaking) dog with a checkered past. I fit neither their standard background nor training templates but they took a chance on me anyway. They invested hundreds of hours and thousands of dollars training us to serve Christ among cultures we'd never heard of in ways we never imagined.

Some risked their lives training me to fly like they flew, then they turned me loose in one of the nastiest operational environments on the planet. In a remarkably humbling way, they trusted me with their reputation, multi-thousand dollar airplanes, and passengers' lives. I am forever amazed, honored, and indebted.

Second, Regina & I also learned that God works through His Body, the Church. Hundreds of people joined us to become a ministry team. Without their sacrificial generosity, prayers, and friendship none of this book's events would have happened, let alone been recorded—no wounded bodies healed, no broken hearts mended, no shattered lives restored. There will be long lines in heaven waiting to thank them for their openhanded kindness.

Third, many friends, beta-readers, reviewers, writing mentors, and editors provided indispensable input and feedback. Their discernment, judgement, and skill made this book far better than my original efforts.

Finally, no quantity or quality of words would be sufficient to thank my wife, Regina, and my children, Obadiah, Lisa, Heather, and Christine for their patient endurance, consistent encouragement, and steadfast love while I dragged them to the middle of the Amazon Jungle so I could fly airplanes for Jesus. It's fearfully wonderful how God's love works.

About the Author

"I rarely experienced fear while flying. But my strongest memory, while hanging by one propeller and four wing attach-bolts over that vast jungle, was that Jesus was always very, very close. That's where my running conversation with Him grew from trickle to torrent."

Former MAF jungle pilot, Jim Manley, swims in a continual downpour of blessing and favor. His compilation of columns inviting contributions to the MAF newsletter, Around the World, will inspire you to see your life as an adventure, as well. Explore over a hundred examples of the Lord revealing Himself in life situations that change the Bible from printed page to living water.

Jim started following Jesus after a chance encounter while hitchhiking. A few years later he had secured an ideal middle class life—wife and children, a house in a mountain town, aviation business and a vibrant church. Life was good, life was understood. But he felt called to the ministry—not as a preacher or evangelist, but as a pilot. Mission Aviation Fellowship (MAF) sent Jim and family to Ecuador, South America. For 17 years he supported the work of several mission, translation, and humanitarian organizations. During his final six years there he also served as MAF's Ecuador program manager

After transferring to MAF's home staff in the USA he wrote print and web copy along with technical manuals. He served as editor for MAF's in-house newsletter, Around the World, and wrote a weekly column, Call For News. Additionally, Jim filled the role of webmaster for MAF's Learning Technologies division.

In 2015 he left MAF to pursue writing full-time. He now focuses on aviation and space commentary as well as science fiction novels that reach out to non-believers. Jim continues to serve as a volunteer ferry pilot and writer for MAF Blog Spot.

He and his wife live in Idaho. See his website, www.JRManley.com, for current posts and projects.

Printed in Great Britain
by Amazon